Amazon.com® For Dummies®

Cheat Sheet

What they sell

There are 19 stores in all, and you can access all of them from the Store Directory. To get to the Store Directory, click the See More Stores link at the top of each page to the right of the tabs.

Those 19 stores are as follows: Apparel & Accessories, Sporting Goods, Books, Computers, DVD, Magazine Subscriptions, Music, Video, Toys & Games, Baby, Camera & Photo, Computer & Video Games, Electronics, Office Products, Software, Home & Garden, Kitchen & Housewares, Outdoor Living, and Tools & Hardware.

Passwords, privacy, and security

✔ **Pick a password that's easy for you to remember and hard for someone else to guess.** Nonsense passwords are the best, but if that doesn't work for you, just make sure you don't pick something straight from your driver's license.

✔ **Amazon does not sell information to tele-marketers.** Your info is safe with them, but when you shop with one of their "Merchants" (companies like Toys 'R' Us or Target, who use Amazon to sell their own wares) you're subject to their privacy policies. You can check out those policies in the Help Department.

✔ **Your credit-card information is safe.** Amazon uses the industry standard, Secure Sockets Layers, to encrypt your credit card info when you send it.

Ways to make money

There are lots of money-making opportunities on Amazon.com. Here's a quick overview:

✔ **Marketplace.** Use it to sell items you own that are already listed in the Amazon catalog. Your items appear as "used" on the detail page of the same item that Amazon is selling "new."

✔ **Auctions.** A lot like eBay. You can auction off your goods – items that Amazon may not have in their catalog – to the highest bidder.

✔ **zShops.** This program allows you to sell merchandise that Amazon doesn't have in their catalog – in bigger quantities, and at a fixed price. You even get your own storefront on Amazon.com.

✔ **Associates.** This is the Web's largest online referral program! Put links on your Web site to Amazon.com and if your visitors use them and then buy, you earn referral fees.

✔ **Advantage.** This program helps independent publishers, studios, and labels get their titles on Amazon.com. You supply the titles and Amazon handles the inventory, distribution, selling – and takes a cut of the profits.

✔ **Honor System.** Use Amazon's payment system to request donations or charge your Web site visitors for digital content.

Amazon.com® For Dummies®

Cheat Sheet

Tips and tricks for better shopping

✔ **Customer Reviews.** Read them to get the nitty-gritty, but remember to consider them as a whole – you may not share the opinion of just one reviewer, but group consensus is useful!

✔ **Your Store.** Don't forsake Your Store! It's the tab right next to the Welcome tab and it's where you'll find goodies like Your Recommendations, your Wish List, and your Friends & Favorites area.

✔ **Listmania.** Put your two cents in by creating a themed list of products – best CDs for a romantic evening, or 10 things to have on a deserted island.

✔ **Wish List.** Hallelujah! Create a Wish List on Amazon and then tell your friends and family about it. No more appliquéd sweaters or ceramic figurines for you.

✔ **Digital Downloads.** Free music, Napster-style (minus the whole lawsuit thing). Download thousands of tracks for free in the Music store.

✔ **The Outlet.** Get there from the Store Directory. It's chock-full of clearance-priced goodies from all the stores.

A few terms you'll need to know

✔ **Tabs:** Remember your high school notebook's tabbed dividers? Same deal. You use these to get around the site; they're at the top of the page.

✔ **Subnav:** This is the strip of links just below the tabs. Again, you use these as you navigate the site.

✔ **Below the fold:** This expression is a newspaper term to refer to anything on the bottom half of the front page (below the fold). In the Web world, it means anything that's not visible when you first come to a page – things below the fold require you to scroll.

✔ **Cookies:** Little files that live on the hard drive of your computer. Web sites, like Amazon, use these to recognize you when you come to their site.

Copyright © 2004 Wiley Publishing, Inc.
All rights reserved.

Item 5840-4.

For more information about Wiley Publishing, call 1-800-762-2974.

For Dummies: Bestselling Book Series for Beginners

by Mara Friedman

WILEY

Wiley Publishing, Inc.

Amazon.com® For Dummies®

Published by
Wiley Publishing, Inc.
111 River Street
Hoboken, NJ 07030-5774

Copyright © 2004 by Wiley Publishing, Inc., Indianapolis, Indiana

Published by Wiley Publishing, Inc., Indianapolis, Indiana

Published simultaneously in Canada

For general information on our other products and services or to obtain technical support, please contact our Customer Care Department within the U.S. at 800-762-2974, outside the U.S. at 317-572-3993, or fax 317-572-4002.

Wiley also publishes its books in a variety of electronic formats. Some content that appears in print may not be available in electronic books.

Library of Congress Control Number is available from the publisher.

ISBN: 0-7645-5840-4

Manufactured in the United States of America

10 9 8 7 6 5 4 3 2 1

1B/RS/QR/QU/IN

WILEY

About the Author

In February 1998, **Mara Friedman** was hired to be the Amazon.com in-house copywriter. In the two-and-a-half years that followed, she was the marketing communications manager, the e-cards associate editor, and the senior editor of Outdoor Living. She watched the company grow from a start-up online bookstore to the world's largest online destination with more than 30 million customers.

Today, Mara is a partner at Smartypants Communications, a graphic design and marketing firm based in Seattle. She continues to work with Amazon.com and her writing has appeared in Marlo Thomas's *The Right Words at the Right Time, The Oprah Magazine,* and on Amazon.com itself.

Author's Acknowledgments

Thank you so much to Bill for his kindness and support, to Katie for her endless patience, to Steve, Paul, and Barry at Wiley for being nice to a newbie, to David for being an awesome tech editor, and to KC for putting up with me on a daily basis.

Publisher's Acknowledgments

We're proud of this book; please send us your comments through our online registration form located at www.dummies.com/register/.

Some of the people who helped bring this book to market include the following:

Acquisitions, Editorial, and Media Development

Project Editor: Paul Levesque

Acquisitions Editor: Steven Hayes

Copy Editor: Barry Childs-Helton

Technical Editor: David Risher

Editorial Manager: Kevin Kirschner

Permissions Editor: Carmen Krikorian

Media Development Manager: Laura Van Winkle

Media Development Supervisor: Richard Graves

Editorial Assistant: Amanda Foxworth

Cartoons: Rich Tennant, www.the5thwave.com

Production

Project Coordinator: Courtney MacIntyre

Layout and Graphics: Seth Conley, Andrea Dahl, Lauren Goddard, Joyce Haughey, Kristin McMullan, Jacque Schneider, Melanee Wolven

Proofreaders: Andy Hollandbeck, Carl William Pierce; TECHBOOKS Production Services

Indexer: TECHBOOKS Production Services

Publishing and Editorial for Technology Dummies

    Richard Swadley, Vice President and Executive Group Publisher

    Andy Cummings, Vice President and Publisher

    Mary C. Corder, Editorial Director

Publishing for Consumer Dummies

    Diane Graves Steele, Vice President and Publisher

    Joyce Pepple, Acquisitions Director

Composition Services

    Gerry Fahey, Vice President of Production Services

    Debbie Stailey, Director of Composition Services

Contents at a Glance

Table of Contents

Introduction

Welcome to *Amazon.com For Dummies* — the ultimate Amazon.com reference tool! "Wait," you say, "Amazon.com is so easy to use, it already *is* for dummies." And in some ways you're right. On the most basic level, Amazon.com is very easy to use. They do that on purpose so the 30 million people who already shop there will continue to buy things. But of those 30 million people, just a fraction are using Amazon.com to it's fullest potential. *Amazon.com For Dummies* is for everyone else — the millions of people who aren't yet Amazon.com customers, and the millions who are but so far just skate lightly across the store's surface.

Amazon.com isn't an ordinary store. It isn't even an ordinary online store. In fact, in many ways, it isn't a store at all. It's an internet-based cornucopia of shopping and selling delights! At Amazon, you can buy just about any book in the Library of Congress. You can get movie showtimes for your local theater. You can list your independently produced CD. You can auction off a vintage rocking chair. You can research, find, discover, buy, or sell just about anything. It's truly an amazing place (and I'm not just saying that just because I once worked there). But to make the most of what Amazon has to offer, you have to know how to use the site and, perhaps more important, you actually have to know what Amazon has to offer. That's where this book comes in.

Amazon.com For Dummies is both a starter's guide and a reference tool. If you've never been to Amazon.com before, you could pick this book up and use it to find your way around the store, set up your account, and make your first purchase. If you're already an Amazon customer, you might use it to get more from Amazon's personalization features or as a guide to help you start selling on the site. The book is a comprehensive map of the store with descriptions of and instructions on how to buy, sell, and do just about anything at Amazon.com.

About This Book

Even if you've already shopped there, and especially if you haven't, you should think of Amazon.com as an exciting destination and this book as your travel guide. You don't need to read every page and you don't need to read it chronologically. (But if you want to, feel free. You'll be an absolute shopping sage.) You should use the book to navigate your trip. In it, I tell you where to go, what to do when you get there, and what to bring along (if you're shopping, that'd be your adventurous spirit and your credit card).

More specifically, you get the word on how to

- ✔ Get to Amazon.com and set up your account.
- ✔ Find your way around the site.
- ✔ Make your first purchase (for those of you who are newbies).
- ✔ Use the Amazon.com personalization features to make your shopping experience richer.
- ✔ Create your own zShop or use Marketplace so you can sell things at Amazon.
- ✔ Participate in an Amazon.com Auction.
- ✔ Join the Amazon.com community.
- ✔ Take advantage of partnership opportunities with Amazon.com.

Foolish Assumptions

I hate to assume anything. But I have to believe that if you're reading this book, you already know a few things about Amazon.com and a few things about the Internet. I'm also hoping you're ready to use the site, and by *ready* I mean

- ✔ You have access to a computer that has access to the Internet.
- ✔ You are interested in buying the products that Amazon sells. And/or . . .
- ✔ You are interested in selling the products that Amazon allows its users to sell.
- ✔ You have a credit card. (It's not essential to shopping at Amazon.com, but it makes things a whole lot easier.)
- ✔ You are comfortable with the idea of using that credit card online. (Again, not absolutely essential, but extremely helpful.)

It's not hard to fall in love with Amazon.com. Once you've experienced the breadth of selection, the depth of information, and the wonders of no-hassle shopping, you'll be head over heels. But you do need a computer and it helps to know a little bit about the Internet. As for the credit-card issue, we talk more about that in Chapter 3, but for now, let's just say that shopping at Amazon without a credit card is like going for a swim in a down-filled snowsuit — it can be done, but it won't be very much fun.

How This Book Is Organized

Like all good reference tools, this book is set up to be read "as needed." It's divided into five parts: the basics, shopping and buying, using community features, selling, and the Part of Tens. So if you just want to know how to become an Amazon Associate, read Chapter 18. If you want to find out how to write a product review, read Chapter 12. If you're a complete novice and you want to be walked through the basics of the store, Chapters 1 and 2 do the trick.

That said, one of the most incredible things about Amazon is the sheer quantity of good stuff they have on their site. You may be someone who's been shopping at Amazon since the days of yore back in 1996, but I'll bet you're only aware of about one third of what there is at Amazon. So you may want to leaf through the whole book, or at least the Table of Contents. You'll be amazed.

Part 1: Testing the Waters: Finding Your Way Around the Store

This is where you cut your teeth on the Amazon basics. I walk you through the essentials of the site — what it is, what you can and can't do there, and so on — and give you a bird's eye view of what Amazon has to offer. I show you an account setup, cover site nomenclature, and help you discover what you need to know about the Help department so you can get answers to any questions you may still have down the line.

Part II: You Want It? They Got It: Shopping & Buying at Amazon.com

The question isn't, "What do they sell?" It's "What *don't* they sell?" In this part, I cover the items for sale in detail including gifts, services, and some of the wackier things you probably don't know about. I show you how to search for the things you want and then how to find out whether they're worth buying. I also walk you through the basic buying process (or the "order pipeline" as they say at Amazon) so you'll be ready to roll.

Part III: The More the Merrier: The Amazon.com Community

You may think you're a good shopper. You may even think of yourself as a shopping diva. But let me assure you, you haven't shopped until you've shopped at Amazon.com. They've turned the experience into an art form and it's truly a thing of beauty.

In this part, I show you how to use the cool personalization features that Amazon has created and explain how the combination of technology and a community of 30 million make for simply blissful buying.

Part IV: Making Money at Amazon.com

There are several ways to (believe it or not) make money at Amazon.com. There are straight selling opportunities, straight partnership opportunities, and a few opportunities that are a little bit of both. In this part, I cover them all.

You find out how to sell using Marketplace, how to post your own auction, and how to build your own storefront using zShops. I also show you how you can earn money on your own Web site by joining the Associates program and how you can "level the playing field" with Advantage — Amazon's distribution system for independent labels and publishers.

Part V: The Part of Tens

It wouldn't be a Dummies book without The Part of Tens. In this section, you find ten different e-mails that you might get from Amazon, ten ways to get great deals, and the ten strangest things you can find on the site.

You also find an appendix that covers Honor System and Amazon Anywhere — two of Amazon's lesser known (and slightly esoteric) programs.

Icons Used in This Book

Think of this as the Dummies version of a New York City cabby. You want a good shortcut? Need a hint on how to get where you want to go? The Tip icon will show you the way.

In the Internet age, it just isn't okay to tie little strings around your fingers. Instead, use these Remember icons. They point out things you may (or may not) already know that are worth keeping in mind.

There's no need to be afraid here. This isn't the skull and crossbones of Internet shopping — more like a "No lifeguard on duty" kind of warning. These friendly warnings can help you avoid potential pitfalls.

Part I

Testing the Waters: Finding Your Way Around the Store

The 5th Wave   By Rich Tennant

Online Shopping 50¢/Min.

In this part . . .

Amazon isn't called "Amazon" for nothing. It was named for the world's largest river (the Amazon holds more water than any other river), and it's a place that proudly boasts of having "Earth's Biggest Selection." In other words, Amazon is big. Really, really big. But it doesn't have to be scary.

In Part I, I give you the tools you need to navigate Amazon.com comfortably. You get a detailed overview of the site, see the different kinds of pages you may encounter while shopping, and learn how to make a purchase — from setting up your account to completing checkout. You also get a grasp on basic site nomenclature (what things are, where things are, and how to get there), and you get a quick briefing on the Help department so you can find answers to questions after you've put the book away.

Chapter 1

Amazon.com 101

· ·

In This Chapter

▶ Getting the basics of Amazon.com

▶ Finding out about the products they sell

▶ Discovering all the cool things you can do there besides shop

· ·

*N*o one (except maybe Amazon.com founder Jeff Bezos) ever imagined that one day there would be a way that you could buy everything from books to barbecues to baby blankets without ever leaving your house or speaking to another soul. And what seemed like an unlikely gamble more than eight years ago is now the world's most popular online shopping destination. But Amazon.com is more than just a great place to shop.

So what is it? You could say it's a shopping mall combined with a home improvement store, plus an outdoor bazaar and a travel agency. And don't forget the department store, the newsstand, and the car lot. It's a place to sell things and to buy things — to spend money and to make it. A place where you can get expert opinions and put your own two cents in. It's a community of other shoppers and sellers like you. And to get there, all you have to do is get online.

In this chapter, I give you a comprehensive overview of what Amazon.com is, what they sell, what they don't sell, and the myriad other ways you can interact with the site and the community outside of simply shopping. Soon enough you'll understand why Amazon has so many passionate devotees — you may even join their ranks.

But first, you have to get online and to get online, you need to have a computer with Internet access. After you've got that squared away, you're ready to go. If you're a true technological neophyte, you might consider reading *The Internet For Dummies*, 9th Edition, by John R. Levine, Carol Baroudi, and Margaret Levine Young (Wiley Publishing, Inc.). It'll give you the background you need to get yourself to Amazon.com comfortably. Otherwise, sit down at your computer, open the book, and prepare to start paddling!

What Is Amazon.com and Why Is It Unlike Any Other Store?

Good question. The best way to really understand Amazon is to stop thinking of it in brick-and-mortar terms and to start thinking of it in Internet terms. Amazon *is not* a place, and it doesn't have any of the restrictions that a physical place has. Amazon *is* a digital venue, and because it's a digital venue it can make use of all the benefits of the digital world.

Here are four concrete examples of how using Amazon is different than brick-and-mortar shopping:

- **Amazon has limitless shelf space.** Because they're more of an online catalog than a retail store, Amazon doesn't have to stock the entire inventory they offer. The downside to this (and to all online shopping) is that you don't get to leave the store with your purchase in hand. In fact, depending on the availability of the item you order, you may have to wait a few weeks! (Though that's rare.) The upshot is that they can offer anything and everything — so you get an infinitely larger selection of goods.

- **Customers are an integral part of Amazon's sales force.** Because Amazon is web based, they automatically have a place to post extensive product information, including customer reviews. So when you're looking to buy, you get the benefit of reading the unbiased opinions of other users like you — the most honest product information you can come by. You also get to write your own reviews.

- **You can sell things at Amazon.** I think that says it all. Let's face it, if you walked into a department store tomorrow and tried to sell their customers the same products — just slightly used and cheaper — you might find yourself spending the afternoon in the slammer. But not at Amazon. Instead of calling the cops, they help you peddle your wares and then they take a cut.

- **Amazon really knows you.** Sad though it may be, I can safely say that Amazon knows me better than several of my ex-boyfriends. That's because every time I shop, Amazon remembers what I bought and stores that information. It also gathers and stores information on you and on its 37 million other customers every time any of you shop. Then it combines all that information and uses it to determine what we like, what we *might* like, and what we *don't* like, so our shopping experience is better. Now don't be alarmed. They don't use this information to invade your privacy in any way. In fact, Amazon has one of the best privacy policies in the online world. If you're concerned, you can find out more about it in Chapter 4.

What's in a name?

In May of 1994, Amazon.com was just an idea in Amazon.com founder Jeff Bezos' head. He wanted to use the Internet as a platform to sell products. Simple, but smart. The first thing he did, after writing a business plan, was come up with the name. "We'll call it 'Cadabra,'" he said to a friend. "Cadaver?" the friend replied. Maybe not. Choice number two had two bits of criteria to live up to: It had to communicate depth and breadth and it had to start with an "A" so it would show up first in search results. Jeff got out the dictionary and started looking. On page 20, just after "amaze" but before "ambassador," Amazon.com was born. The name met both bits of criteria. It starts with an "A" and it metaphorically communicates both depth and breadth (the Amazon is the world's largest river in terms of water volume). In keeping with the spirit, Amazon's URLs are sprinkled with Portuguese — the language of Brazil, home to the watery Amazon. You may notice "obidos" in several of the URLs. That word refers to the part of the Amazon where the river's tributaries come together. Keep looking and you'll find others. It helps, of course, to speak Portuguese.

What Do They Sell There?

Amazon offers an amazing selection of goods and services from books to airline tickets to hardware. You can buy almost anything *at* Amazon. But you're not always buying *from* Amazon. One of the ways that Amazon can offer such an extensive selection is by allowing other people — whether large companies like Target™ or individuals like you and me — to sell on its site.

Amazon's product offering is made up of several elements:

- **Stuff they sell.** Like books or CDs or DVDs. These are the items that Amazon brings to you straight from the companies that produce them. In other words, when you buy these items, you're not buying through a "middleman" partner, but from Amazon directly — the same way you buy from any retail store.

- **Stuff that large partners are selling.** You can buy clothes from The Gap™ or placemats from Target™ at Amazon, but you're actually buying from the partner with Amazon providing the buying venue (and in some cases, not even that!).

- **Services.** The bulk of the services that Amazon has to offer are free, so you're not so much buying them as you are using them. You'll find everything from e-mail notification services to free e-cards.

- **Stuff that small partners are selling.** A small partner (including you!) can sell something as small and simple as a single book or set up an entire mini store on Amazon's site.

The stores

There are 19 different Amazon.com stores — not including certain partner stores, which I'll get to later. I'm defining a *store* here as a self-contained set of pages on Amazon's site, set up to sell a collection of like products — books, music, DVDs, and so on. I'm also excluding Auctions, zShops, and the Outlet (more on those later).

Those 19 stores are as follows: Apparel & Accessories, Sporting Goods, Books, Computers, DVD, Magazine Subscriptions, Music, Video, Toys & Games, Baby, Camera & Photo, Computer & Video Games, Electronics, Office Products, Software, Home & Garden, Kitchen & Housewares, Outdoor Living, and Tools & Hardware. That's today's list, but Amazon is always adding more stores.

Each one of these stores has its own home page, such as the one for music that you see in Figure 1-1. You could go to any one of these store home pages and find similar content options, features, and selection. They are "freestanding" in many ways (they have their own categories and subcategories, special features, and subnavigation options) though they often introduce merchandise from other stores when relevant.

Figure 1-1:
The music
home page
is "home
base" within
the music
store.

Partners

Amazon.com has three kinds of partners. Let's call the first kind "large partners." Large partners are companies like Target or Toys 'R' Us, who are selling their own merchandise in a buying and selling interface that Amazon provides. In other words, Amazon creates the actual pages on *their* site that allow you to make purchases from these other companies, but they don't determine the products that will be offered and they don't stock any of the inventory. You'll notice that when you go to these stores, they bear the partner's name along with (and even more prominently than) Amazon's name.

Let's refer to the second kind of partner as a "small partner." That's not necessarily a reflection of the size of the company, but rather their presence on Amazon's site. Small partners are companies that offer *some* of their products in existing Amazon stores. (In other words, they are not stores unto themselves.) Those products appear side by side with products from other similar partners and even products from Amazon itself. Small partners include companies like Circuit City in Electronics or The Gap in Apparel & Accessories.

Amazon calls the third partner type "trusted partners." Trusted partners are companies that offer products and/or services that Amazon doesn't — products like cars or medications and services like booking travel and photo development, and so on. Amazon checks these partners out, makes sure they're good to do business with, and then includes what are essentially links to these partners on their site. But when you interact with a trusted partner, you are typically using *the trusted partner* Web site, not Amazon.com. There will be a link to Amazon at the top of the page, but you're no longer actually there. And if you were to go to, say, Hotwire directly (by typing in the URL as opposed to clicking there from Amazon), there'd be no Amazon logo at the top of the page. Amazon's other trusted partners include: audible.com, CarsDirect.com, Ofoto.com, and The Vacation Store.

There is a significant difference between buying from partners and buying from Amazon itself. When you buy from a partner — whether it's large, small, or trusted — you are dealing with that company, even if you're doing it through Amazon's site. So make sure you're familiar with their rules and policies — especially returns policies.

Services

On their Web site, Amazon identifies the following long list of items as "services:" Amazon.com Visa Card, Associates Program, Cars, Chat, Corporate Accounts, Friends & Favorites, Movie Showtimes, Restaurants, Travel, Web

Services, Your Recommendations, and Your Store. It's true that everything on that list might serve you in some way as you use the site, but for the purposes of this book (and for the purposes of using the site effectively) I'm going to define "services" as something helpful, free, and voluntary. With that as the definition, I'd edit Amazon's list and add a few items.

Of the 12 items Amazon lists, only chat, corporate accounts, movie show-times, and restaurants are truly services by my definition. The others are cool personalization features (and we'll talk about those in Chapter 11), Amazon partnership opportunities, or stuff to buy. To our new list of four, I'd add special occasion reminders, e-mail notifications, and free e-cards. Figure 1-2 is the e-cards home page. E-cards is set up like its own little store and it's especially dear to me as I wrote a lot of them (only the good ones, of course).

Figure 1-2:
E-cards are
free *and* fun.

Table 1-1 has a quick overview of Amazon's free services:

Table 1-1	Amazon.com's Free Services
Service	**Description**
Chat	Your basic chat room. You can use this to get the scoop on products from other Amazon shoppers in real time.
Corporate accounts	This is for big, corporate buyers. You can set up a line of credit, authorize employees to use it, and track your spending.

Service	Description
Movie Showtimes	You can get showtimes for your area by entering your zip code.
Restaurants	You can view menus online, read and write restaurant reviews, and even upload a menu to the site. The bad news is that it only covers Chicago, Seattle, New York, Boston, Washington D.C., and San Francisco.
e-cards	You'll find free e-cards for any and every occasion. You can add music and/or attach gift certificates to any e-card.
Special occasion reminders	This free service ensures that you will never miss your mother's birthday again! Just enter in important dates and Amazon will send you a reminder e-mail. Technically, this is an e-mail notification, but I'm giving it it's own props because I think it's the handiest of the bunch.
E-mail notifications	Amazon offers seven different e-mail notifications that you can subscribe to for free. Most of them inform you of products you might want — things like new releases, CDs from your favorite artists, and so on.

Marketplace, Auctions, and zShops

Marketplace, Auctions, and zShops feature items being sold by other Amazon users — anything from a used copy of the book you're looking for to an antique lunch box. Marketplace, Auctions, and zShops are not one and the same. Here's a quick overview of each:

- **Marketplace.** This is the program that Amazon has developed to allow users like you and me to sell used versions of the items they already have for sale on the site. You can buy or sell items in the following categories: books, music, DVDs, videos, video games, PC games, camera and photo, electronics, kitchen tools, and hardware and outdoor living. But only items that are already in Amazon's catalog are eligible for Marketplace.

- **Auctions.** Amazon.com Auctions are like a mini eBay. People list their items and they go to the highest bidder. It's a good place to get rare or unusual finds. Figure 1-3 shows the Auctions home page.

- **zShops.** Think of these as Web boutiques. Most zShops are small retailers who want to have a Web presence and want to make use of Amazon's huge customer base. Sometimes zShops will offer the same items that you can find in the Amazon catalog, but more often than not, they offer specialty merchandise.

Figure 1-3: You can buy and sell strange and wonderful things at Amazon.com Auctions.

When you buy something from one of these three venues, you're not actually buying from Amazon, you're buying from a person like you through the Amazon Web site. That's not to say that it's a selling free-for-all. In fact, Amazon has very clear and defined rules about how sellers can sell and protection for buyers as well. It just means you may need to put in a little bit of due diligence before you buy.

What Don't They Sell There?

There are actually lots and lots of things that Amazon doesn't sell. (Though it doesn't often seem like it when you're trying to wade through search results.) The list is long and ever changing, and I won't bore you with it. Instead, I'll give you the basic what-they-won't-sell guidelines:

✔ No live animals.

✔ No firearms.

✔ Nothing immediately perishable. (You can buy a frozen T-bone or sub-scribe to a fruit-of-the-month club, but you can't exactly buy groceries.)

✔ No hard-core pornography.

That's about it. That's not to say that you can find anything else at Amazon. Just that it's a possibility.

What Can (and Can't) You Sell?

You can sell anything from a used dictionary to you grandmother's flowered tablecloth on Amazon.com. Among Marketplace, Auctions, and zShops, you'll find a venue for just about any item.

What's more important is what you *can't* sell at Amazon. Start with their list of no-nos — live animals, hard core porn, perishables and firearms — and add: offensive material, illegal items, stolen goods, items that infringe upon an individual's privacy, promotional media, copied video games, copied software, copies of movies or television programs, recopied or bootlegged music, devices that would allow unauthorized transmission of a satellite signal, replicas of trademarked items, items that use celebrity images or names to sell without the permission of said celebrities, domain names, advertisements, products that have been recalled by the Consumer Product Safety Commission (CPSC), real estate, and wine (or other alcoholic beverages).

Many of the things on the list inspire either a "huh?" or a "duh!" and we'll cover this list in more detail in Chapters 15 and 16. Suffice to say, though, that the main guideline you should rely on when selling is common sense. And remember, no decent person wants to buy a human heart or a hot car stereo online.

Partnership Opportunities

There are three other ways to use Amazon.com to make money outside of actually selling things. I like to call them "partnership opportunities" and Amazon calls them: Amazon Honor System, Associates Program, and Amazon.com Advantage.

Here's a brief overview of each:

- ✔ **Amazon Honor System.** The Honor System allows users who have their own Web sites to request voluntary donations from their visitors with payment running through Amazon.com. You can also use the Honor system to charge visitors to view or use the content on your site (a la online subscriptions). Amazon provides the graphics and software. You set it up.

- ✔ **Associates Program.** The Associates program is essentially an online referral arrangement. You put a link to Amazon on your site, and every time someone uses it and then buys something at Amazon, you get a referral fee. Again, they provide the materials; you provide the labor.

✔ **Amazon.com Advantage.** The Advantage program is part partnership opportunity and part selling opportunity. In a nutshell, it allows independent publishers, music labels, and movie studios to sell their work on Amazon.com. With the Advantage program, Amazon does more than just provide graphics. They help with marketing, inventory, distribution, and so on.

Ooh La La: International Stores

You may not know this, but Amazon is very international. No, I'm not talking about the global community and how the Web brings us all together. I'm talking actual international stores. Five of them to be exact: Amazon Canada, Amazon France, Amazon UK, Amazon Japan, and Amazon Germany.

Now you might ask, "Why does Amazon need international stores when anyone, anywhere can get online and buy stuff from Amazon?" And I would say, "That's true. But . . ." And then I'd explain that Amazon opened international stores for the following good reasons:

✔ **The Mother-Tongue Issue.** Despite the fact that every time I go to another country people automatically speak English to me even before I open my mouth (and, no, I'm not wearing a fanny pack and a Bears sweatshirt), not everyone on earth speaks English. So Amazon decided to create native-language stores in other countries that have high Internet penetration.

✔ **The Shipping Issue.** It's true that anyone anywhere can get online and buy from Amazon, even though it's an American company. But if they do, they're also paying shipping prices from America, even if they live halfway around the world. That'll put a kink in the whole good pricing thing. But when international shoppers buy from an international Amazon, their items are shipped from that country. Shipping problem solved!

✔ **The Currency Issue.** Remember, Amazon is all about convenience. I'm not that good at math, so if I were British, for example, I'd much rather buy items priced in pounds than try to figure out the whole conversion thing.

✔ **The Local Product Issue.** Local products are more readily available to . . . locals. So if you're looking for the newest PD James novel, check out Amazon.co.uk first; if you're looking for "Harry Potter et l'Ordre du Phénix," check out Amazon.fr.

✔ **The National Pride Issue.** Some people, though they may speak English (for example, Canadians, British folks, and bilingual Frenchmen), just want to buy from a local company. And local companies usually understand their own people better. So when Amazon opens these international stores, they work with a local team to make the store authentic and hip to all the appropriate cultural subtleties. (Well, okay, as an American, I don't know what those are, but I know they're very appropriate and very subtle.)

Though you can buy tons of foreign language titles at Amazon.com, you are often buying them as imports. That means they take much longer to arrive. That said, Amazon has a large selection of Spanish-language books and they are not all imports. Good news for the Spanish speakers out there as there are not yet any international Spanish-speaking Amazons.

What Amazon Knows about You That No One Else Knows

Amazon knows what you like. Okay, maybe there are other people who know what you like — your spouse, your mom, your best friend — but do they also know what you *will* like before you know it yourself? And do they know how often you spend money on what you like? And do they know what other things you should get to go with the stuff you like? And do they have your credit-card number?

One of the key things that makes Amazon different from any other "store" is its ability to collect and use information. They call it *aggregate customer data* — and they use it very wisely. Every time you shop at Amazon, the site remembers not only what you bought, but also the other items you looked at. Then the folks at Amazon use that information to find other things you *might* like.

They also consider all their customer data cumulatively. So if you liked *Star Wars* (and who didn't?) they'll find other people who liked it too and then look at the other items those people liked and see if the same items appeal to you. Smart.

Now don't get antsy. They're not going to sell your information to evil telemarketers. (Remember, Amazon is profitable these days.) They just want you to have a better shopping experience. But if you need reassurance, read Chapter 4 where I cover their privacy policy as well as credit-card safety issues.

Chapter 2

The Main Stops on the Shopping Circuit

- -

In This Chapter

▶ Getting a bird's-eye view of the site layout

▶ Familiarizing yourself with the home page

▶ Navigating your way through the stores

▶ Getting to know your shopping cart

- -

We all know how to shop. (I, for one, was born to do it.) You go to the store, you walk around, maybe you find what you're looking for, or maybe you need to ask a salesperson. Either way, there's certainly no challenge involved. In fact, for many of us, shopping is soothing (they don't call it "retail therapy" for nothing).

Throw a mouse, a computer, and the information superhighway into the mix and suddenly shopping becomes a little bit intimidating. But fear not, retail warrior! Internet shopping is just as easy as real-world shopping, and you can do it in your skivvies.

In this chapter, I walk you through the Amzon.com site level by level — from the home page to your shopping cart. Think of it as the mall equivalent of a directory. Once you take a good look, you'll know where things are and how to get there on your own.

Welcome Home: Amazon.com

There's no place like home! There's no place like home! Dorothy had it right. The home page is where the journey begins. You may not spend much of your time there, but it's definitely base camp 1 for all Amazon shoppers. Because of that, it's important for you to familiarize yourself with the turf.

Anatomy of the home page

At the simplest level, two components make up the home page (and all Amazon pages for that matter): navigation elements and content. The former is what you use to get around the site; the latter is the kind of information you find there. As a (somewhat flexible) rule, navigation elements live on the borders of the page, and content makes up the middle.

Figure 2-1 shows the Amazon.com home page and the following key navigational elements:

- **Top, or main, navigation:** These are the tabs that sit on top of the colored bar and offers choices like Books, Music, and so on.

- **Subnavigation:** This is the colored bar below the tabs. It's unusual on the home page, as it will take you to a variety of select spots with no particular similarity or theme. Within the stores, though, the subnavigation (or subnav) will take you to top-level places of interest within that store.

- **Shopping tools:** These are the four links — View Cart, Wish List, Your Account, and Help — that *always* sit in the upper-right corner of the page.

- **Search boxes:** There are two search boxes at the top of the left-hand column: one for searches within Amazon and one for searching the Web as a whole (via Google).

- **Browse box:** This sits below the Web-search boxes and holds links to the various stores and services available at Amazon.com.

Figure 2-1:
Home at Amazon.com — base camp 1 for all shopping.

At Amazon, the key navigation elements are in the same place throughout the site. They may not always offer the same choices (and we get to that later) but they're located in the same spot and they serve the same purpose. That's one reason Amazon is easy to use.

Top o' the page to you! Tabs, subnav, and other good stuff

You can get just about anywhere in the Amazon.com site by using the navigation elements at the top of Amazon's home page. Here's a more detailed description of the key elements:

- ✔ **Amazon.com logo:** You don't need ruby slippers to get back home. If you ever get lost, just close your eyes, say, "there's no place like home," and click the Amazon logo. The Amazon.com logo is on just about every page of the site. It sits in the upper-left corner and it almost always takes you back to the home page. The only times it won't is when you're mid-transaction — in the process of placing an order or setting up some sort of Amazon account.

- ✔ **Shopping Tools:** The four links above the main and subnavs are your keys to the nitty-gritty of Amazon shopping. Your Cart shows you what you're getting ready to buy; your Wish List shows what you're hoping someone else will buy for you. Your Account is where you store and manage critical data — like your credit-card info, shipping address, order history, and so on. And Help is exactly that — the place to go when you need a question answered (if you don't find it in this book!).

- ✔ **Tabs:** In the days of yore, when Amazon was just an online bookstore, it was pretty easy to get around. But as they added products, they needed to add navigational elements to accommodate them. Thus tabs were born. The tabs at Amazon are a lot like the tabs in your high school notebook — they're subject or product specific. Clicking the different tabs will take you directly to the various stores within Amazon.

- ✔ **See more stores:** You'll notice this at the top of the page, to the right of the tabs (there's a little arrow pointing at it to help you along). This is your link to the directory — the master list of all Amazon stores and destinations. So if you don't see the store you want in the tabs, try this.

- ✔ **Subnav:** The colored bar below the tabs is for subnavigation, or *subnav*. When you click a tab to go to a specific store, that tab is highlighted and the subnav offers destination choices within that store. When you're at the home page, the Welcome tab is automatically highlighted and your subnav choices are as follows: International, Top sellers, Target, Today's Deals, and Sell Your Stuff. As you move through the site and visit the different stores, the subnav will change to offer choices appropriate to that store.

There are also two or three fun things at the top of Amazon's home page. Here's a quick overview:

- **The Greeting:** It's nice to be greeted when you walk into a store — Amazon knows that — so at the top of the home page, just below the subnav, a little line of text welcomes you to the store and invites you to sign in.

- **Your Gold Box:** Calling all bargain shoppers! Your gold box is a collection of ten screamin' deals that Amazon gathers for you, basing the list on your shopping history. You get one chance per day to open your gold box, and one chance per deal to buy or pass. The deals get refreshed every 24 hours; it's good to check back each day.

- **The Segway:** Some people think it's weird that there's an ad for the Segway Human Transporter on just about every page of Amazon.com. They're right. Why is it there? Are the Segway people hurting for cash? No. It's there simply because Jeff Bezos loves it. And you have to admit, it *is* kind of cool.

Left, right, and center — the meat of the page

And a very meaty page it is! Here's an easy-to-digest description of the goodies you'll find below the subnav on the *left* side of the page:

- **Search:** The main search box for the site sits atop the Web search box on the left-hand side of the page. You can enter keywords to search the whole site or use the drop-down menu to search within specific stores.

- **Web Search:** Use this search feature to search the entire Web without leaving Amazon.com.

- **Browse:** The browse box on the left side of the page is a complete listing of all stores at Amazon.com. It serves the same purpose as the See More Stores link — just another way to navigate the site. You'll notice that the first heading within the Browse box is called Featured Stores. This spot is typically reserved for new stores that Amazon is introducing.

- **Make Money:** This box features links to all the moneymaking opportunities at Amazon. Again, you can find the same information at the See More Stores page.

- **Special Features:** The last stop on the left side. This is the catchall box for "everything else." You'll find a range of links from e-mail notifications to free e-cards.

Here's what you find on the *right* side of the page:

- **Featured Product:** Amazon picks the item or service featured in the box at the top of the right column, basing its pick on your shopping history.

✔ **What's new:** This box, on the right side of the page, is a snippet of the personalization Amazon.com has to offer. You can see what's in your shopping cart, get some recommendations, and view other features (such as New Releases).

And now for the middle:

✔ **Editorial Content:** The content you see in the middle of the page — before you start scrolling — is an assortment of featured products and their corresponding editorial content. Again, Amazon picks them according to your history. If you're a new customer, you'll be looking at content chosen according to the cumulative buying patterns of all Amazon customers. So if you want to get more personal, get shopping!

✔ **Abridged Help:** Toward the bottom of the page, below the editorial content, there's an abridged version of the links you'll find in the Help section. You can track orders, get shipping info, and access the help desk from this box.

✔ **Search #2:** Below the abridged Help box there's another Amazon search box. It works the same way as the one at the top of the left column.

✔ **The Footer:** Below the search box you'll find a series of blue links, including a directory of the stores (takes you to the same place as the See More Stores link), links to the international stores, and a bunch of miscellaneous links. This is where you'll find corporate info like press releases, job listings, investor information, and so on.

✔ **Bottom of the Page Deals:** More screamin' deals that change daily.

The mystery of the missing tabs: How the home page changes

It's not you. It's them. Amazon is always changing the home page. So if you go to the home page on Monday and then go back on Tuesday, it won't look the same.

Here are the parts of the home page that will change each time you visit:

✔ **The Tabs:** The Welcome tab will always be there but the other tabs change to reflect the stores you most frequently visit.

✔ **The Editorial Content:** Again, Amazon refreshes the editorial content on the home page depending on how you shop and what you buy.

✔ **Your What's New Box:** This, too, will update itself to reflect any new purchases or shopping data.

✔ **Featured Product:** Something new each time you visit.

✔ **Bottom of the Page Deals:** These change daily.

Showing you new merchandise is one way Amazon makes your shopping experience engaging. (People like novelty — just imagine if every time you went by your favorite boutique, everything in the window was exactly the same!) But how do they know what to feature and change? You tell them. Again (and I may be sounding like a broken record here), it's all based on your shopping history and that of the Amazon customer population at large.

Hello, John Doe: What happens after you buy

I've mentioned the greeting at the top of Amazon's home page. When you set up an account at Amazon.com, you are officially part of the club, so your greeting changes. Figure 2-2 shows what the home page looks like for me each time I visit Amazon.

Figure 2-2: A personalized greeting from Amazon.com.

Amazon uses cookies (for more about cookies see Chapter 3) to remember you, greet you by name, and offer you personalized recommendations.

Books, Music, and More: Pages in the Store

Though it's important to know your way around the home page, the really good stuff lives in the stores themselves. Navigating those is as simple as navigating the home page — and many of the elements are the same.

The Store Directory: Master list at your fingertips

Imagine you've gone to Amazon to buy a toaster, but when you get to the home page, there's no tab for "kitchen." Remember, the tabs are always changing in response to what you buy, so the home page may not always have a specific tab you're looking for. Instead, try the Store Directory, conveniently displayed for you in Figure 2-3.

There are three ways to access the Amazon Store Directory:

- ✔ **The Browse Box:** It's always on the left side of the home page. So if you're at a loss, click that Amazon logo at the top left, go back to the home page, and voilà!

- ✔ **See More Stores:** It'll always be at the top of every page, to the right of the tabs (see the arrow in a circle right next to it?). Click it and you're taken to the store directory.

- ✔ **The Footer:** The footer is at the bottom of every page on the site. The second blue link is the one for Directory of All Stores. Just click and you're there.

Anatomy of a store home page

The *store home pages* are a lot like the main home page. They're set up the same way — navigation at the top and left, content in the middle — but a few important things are different.

Figure 2-3:
The Store Directory is the place to find any store any time.

Here's a list of elements you already know about that change from store to store:

✔ **Subnav:** The subnavs are store specific, so each one is different. As a rule, though, the subnav offers links to top-level destinations within a given store. For example, you won't find a link to "juicers" in the Kitchen store's subnav — but you *do* find a link to "small appliances" and other broad categories.

✔ **Browse Box:** Here's where you get full access to the subcategories in each store. Figure 2-4 shows the Browse box for the Kitchen store.

You can also access each store's directory (where you find the master list of subcategories) by clicking the Browse link in that store's subnav. Each store has one, though the link isn't always called "Browse." I'm confident that your powers of deduction can find it!

Editorial Content: The center of any store's home page is devoted to content from, you guessed it, that store. (Forgive me if I'm taking this whole Dummy thing too far.)

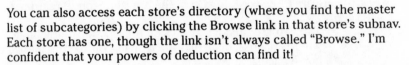

BROWSE

Your Favorites   [Edit]
Baking
Coffee, Tea & Espresso
Cook's Tools & Gadgets
Cookware
▸ **More Favorites**

Cook's Tools & Gadgets
Baking Tools
Bar & Wine Tools
Mandolines & Slicers
▸ All Cook's Tools & Gadgets

Cookware
Cookware Sets
Saucepans
Skillets
▸ All Cookware

Cutlery
Chef's Knives
Knife Sets
Steak Knives
▸ All Cutlery

Housewares
Heaters & Fans
Ironing
Vacuums & Floor Care
▸ All Housewares

Figure 2-4: Kitchen's Browse box includes links to all the subcategories.

The store home pages also offer some new elements:

✔ **Top Sellers:** Not every store has a Top Sellers box on the right side of the page, but most do. You'll also almost always find a Top Sellers link in the store subnavs.

✔ **Your Recent History:** Figure 2-5 shows an example of a Your Recent History box. This handy box of links lives at the bottom of the page below the editorial content. As you shop, Amazon keeps track of where you've been so that if you lose track of a specific store tab, you can still use these links to get back to the stores you've visited.

Figure 2-5:
Your Recent History helps you combat missing tabs!

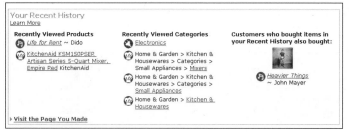

Your Recent History
Learn More

Recently Viewed Products
Life for Rent ~ Dido

KitchenAid KSM150PSER Artisan Series 5-Quart Mixer, Empire Red KitchenAid

Recently Viewed Categories
Electronics

Home & Garden > Kitchen & Housewares > Categories > Small Appliances > Mixers

Home & Garden > Kitchen & Housewares > Categories > Small Appliances

Home & Garden > Kitchen & Housewares

Customers who bought items in your Recent History also bought:

Heavier Things ~ John Mayer

▸ **Visit the Page You Made**

Drilling down to subcategories

If you know what you want, it's easy enough to go to Amazon, enter a keyword in the search box, and find it (and I show you exactly how to do that in Chapter 8). But if you're not that certain — say, you know you want a Latin CD, but you're not sure which one — *No hay ni una problema*. Each store at Amazon, including the Music store, is broken into several subcategories. Browsing is a snap.

There are two ways to access the subcategories within any Amazon store:

✔ **Use the Browse Box:** Ah the browse box. The source of so much shopping goodness. You'll find one in each store and it'll list subcategories galore. Just click to go straight to that subcategory page.

✔ **Click the Browse Link in the Subnav:** Clicking this link in a store's subnav will take you to that store's directory. Once there, you can click again to get to specific subcategory pages.

You should know that not all subcategory pages are created equal; they don't all work exactly the same way. They do, however, all serve the same purpose — and if you're comfortable with the way Amazon works as a site, you won't have any problem clicking your way around the subcategory pages.

Figure 2-6 shows the Latin subcategory in the Music store, broken down into even more specific genres. They've also thrown in a few featured items on the right side of the page.

Drill down one more level (to, say, Mambo) and the page changes again to reveal a list of products. This is the last stop until the detail page — the page that features an individual product (more on this later in the chapter).

Figure 2-6:
The Latin
music
subcategory
page.

Changing your view

You may have noticed that when you hit the subcategory pages a new navigation option shows up. Between the main and subnavs and the meat of the subcategory page there is a new set of tabs. These are the View tabs: Featured, Recommendations, New Releases, Top Sellers, and Used. Just as you can with the tabs on the main nav, you can click these tabs to change your view within a subcategory page.

Again, not every store has this View Change option in exactly the same place. Don't let this throw you off. Often (as with many Amazon navigational features) you can access the same information in a variety of ways — through the subnav, in the Browse box, on the right side of the page, and so on.

Where am I? Following the trail of breadcrumbs

It stinks to be lost. And when you're online, there's no kindly old man on the corner to ask for directions. Amazon has solved this problem with the Internet equivalent of a breadcrumb trail.

The breadcrumb trail is the simplest way to locate yourself when you're up to your ears in shopping. You'll find it at the top left of the page below the subnav, but you'll only find it on pages between the first subcategory level and the detail page (see the next section for more on the detail page). Happily, there's no hungry, evil witch waiting at the end of this trail to serve you as dinner.

Figure 2-7 shows the breadcrumb trail for the Comic page in the bookstore — the line going Books⇨Subjects⇨Literature & Fiction⇨General⇨Comic. Notice that you not only can use it to locate yourself, but you can also click the links in the trail to access the other parts of the store.

Figure 2-7:
A bread-crumb trail comes in handy when you're lost.

Getting the Most Out of the Detail Page

Every item sold at Amazon.com has its own *detail page* where you can (usually) see a picture of the product, get product information, read reviews, and actually add the product to your shopping cart. The detail page is the end of the "just looking" line — the last stop before you enter the order pipeline. It's also a wellspring of information — and if you're a serious shopper, it can help you make informed buying decisions.

Detail page basics

The detail page shares the same basic setup with both the home page and the store home pages: navigation on the top and left, content down the middle.

Here are some of the other new elements you'll find on the detail page (see Figure 2-8):

✔ **Product Image:** Most, but not all, of the items for sale at Amazon are accompanied by a product image. If you click the image, you can see a larger version of it.

✔ **Product Information:** You'll find the essential product information — price and availability — right next to the product image in the center of the page. There are links to more detailed buying information in the box in the left nav.

✔ **Ready to Buy? Box:** Here's where the magic happens. On the right side of the page, just below the nav, you'll find the Ready to Buy? box. If you're new to Amazon, it'll only offer you the option of adding the item to your cart. If you've already made a purchase, you'll also have the option to buy with 1-Click — the absolutely divine (and patented) technology that stores your credit card and shipping information and allows you to buy things by clicking just one button!

✔ **More Buying Choices:** This sits just below the Ready to Buy? box and offers you other options for the product you're looking at — usually used items, but sometimes the exact same product you're already looking at, offered at a better price from some other merchant. It pays to check this out!

Figure 2-8:
The detail page for *eBay For Dummies.*

More product information

You can actually find out a lot about a product on the detail page — more than just how much it costs and when it will ship. To get detailed product information, just scroll. Below the product image, but above the editorial reviews, you'll find a heading called Product Details, or maybe Features; it varies from store to store. Figure 2-9, for example, shows that "Features" is the term of choice for an item in the Electronics store. This is where you'll find more specific information about your product. If you're looking at an item in the Electronics store, you'll likely find technical data here. If you're browsing the Books store, you'll see stuff like the number of pages for a title and publisher info. You'll also discover the item's Amazon.com sales ranking — not essential, but kind of fun.

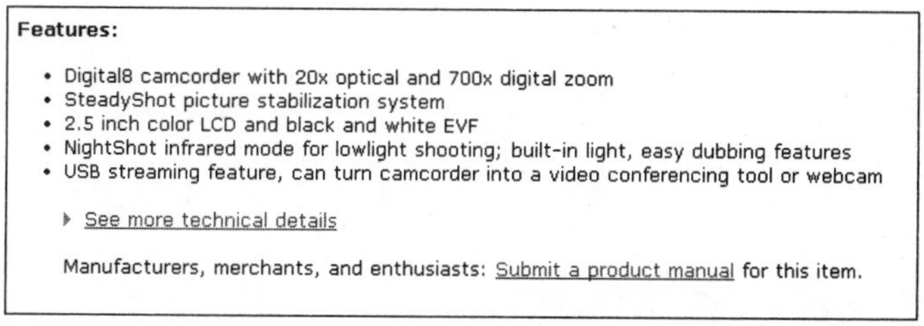

Figure 2-9:
Electronics
offers more
detailed
product
descriptions
than other
stores.

Features:

- Digital8 camcorder with 20x optical and 700x digital zoom
- SteadyShot picture stabilization system
- 2.5 inch color LCD and black and white EVF
- NightShot infrared mode for lowlight shooting; built-in light, easy dubbing features
- USB streaming feature, can turn camcorder into a video conferencing tool or webcam

▶ See more technical details

Manufacturers, merchants, and enthusiasts: Submit a product manual for this item.

Sooner or later, you come across some items where the product information is downright lame. Apparel, Home and Garden, Tools and Hardware, and certain other stores have the occasional dead end when it comes to information. That's when it's not a bad idea to visit that manufacturer's Web site to find out more about the product.

"Customers who bought this..." and other nifty tricks

Amazon's nothing if not an amazing discovery machine — and they know how to make online shopping fun. The detail page is a shining example of their genius at work — chock-full of clever, fun "discovery" mechanisms. Remember, they are always collecting data about their customers and then putting it to good use.

The Customers Who Bought This Also Bought This feature is one fun way of finding other products you might like. But it's not exactly the same store to store — it doesn't always have the same name and it isn't always in the exact same place and some items don't have it at all. Scroll below the product image and detailed information to check.

Editorial reviews

Editorial reviews are one of the things that put Amazon on the map. They are expert opinions — not entirely unbiased (because what opinions are?) — of people who are industry experts who've sampled the products, regular people who've sampled the products, or Amazon editors who've sampled the products. Either way, the reviews are legitimate, not a bunch of sales-ey schlock.

Not all products have editorial reviews, but if they do, you'll find them somewhere between the detailed product info and the footer. You might find just an Amazon.com review, or a review from another industry source, or a combination of both.

Customer reviews

What a novel (and risky) idea — let customers review the products they buy and post their reviews on the site. Customer reviews are one of the things that keep Amazon on the map. They're an essential and excellent part of shopping at Amazon.com.

Customer reviews always live beneath editorial reviews on the detail page. Some are positive. Some are negative. You'll often find both positive and negative reviews for the same product (as my mother would say, "that's what makes the world go 'round."). The key thing about customer reviews is that they're honest.

Figure 2-10 shows a customer review for *eBay For Dummies*. Every customer review is made up of five components: the star rating, a review title, the date it was written, the reviewer's information, and the review itself.

For more about customer reviews, see Chapter 8 — and get a head start on writing one of your own in Chapter 12.

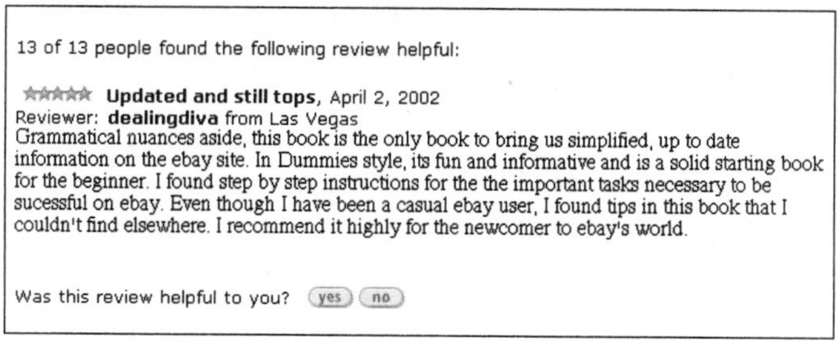

Figure 2-10:
A basic
customer
review.

13 of 13 people found the following review helpful:

⭐⭐⭐⭐⭐ **Updated and still tops**, April 2, 2002
Reviewer: **dealingdiva** from Las Vegas
Grammatical nuances aside, this book is the only book to bring us simplified, up to date
information on the ebay site. In Dummies style, its fun and informative and is a solid starting book
for the beginner. I found step by step instructions for the the important tasks necessary to be
sucessful on ebay. Even though I have been a casual ebay user, I found tips in this book that I
couldn't find elsewhere. I recommend it highly for the newcomer to ebay's world.

Was this review helpful to you? (yes) (no)

The Bottomless Shopping Cart

Is there anything more beautiful than a shopping cart that can never be too full? Mount Rainier on a clear summer day? The work of the Great Masters? The love between a boy and his dog? I don't know. My money's on the bottomless shopping cart. And the best thing is, no shopper's guilt. There are no hungry salespeople jonesing for a commission at Amazon.com. So you can pack that cart to the high heavens and never buy a single thing in it. I'm constantly putting outrageous items in my shopping cart, just because I can — plasma TVs, cashmere sweaters, the Segway Human Transporter. It's mine, it's private, it's impermanent, and, for crying out loud, it's bottomless!

How do you get there?

You can always access your shopping cart from the Shopping Tools at the top right of every page. Just click the link that says *view cart* (it's accompanied by a little picture of — you guessed it — a shopping cart).

Also, no matter what computer you use when you shop Amazon, you have the same shopping cart. So you can put stuff in there at home and buy it later when you're at work. (Shopping at work is fun.)

What's in it?

Even if you've never put anything in it, your shopping cart is full of possibility. There are three key components to your shopping cart:

✔ **Recently Viewed Items:** If nothing else, you'll have these in your cart. Amazon tracks your shopping — not just your buying — and offers up the other items you showed interest in right at the moment of truth.

✔ **Items to buy now:** These are the items you put in your cart very recently, like during the same visit. These will become saved items if you don't buy them in that visit.

✔ **Saved items:** There are actually two kinds of saved items in your shopping cart: the items that you've put in your cart within the last 90 days, but didn't buy, and the items you put in your cart and actively saved by clicking the Save for Later button to the right of the quantity field. (See Figure 2-11.) The former will disappear after 90 days. The latter won't. And here's the rub: If you unintentionally add something to your cart that's already in the saved section, it won't appear in the To Buy Now area. So don't be confused. Just go to your saved items and click the Move To Cart button. That'll take care of it.

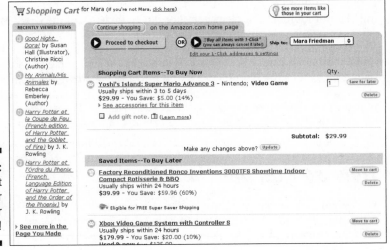

Figure 2-11:
Check out
the Save for
Later
button!

Chapter 3

You Are the Master
of Your Account

. . . .

In This Chapter

▶ Setting up your account

▶ Shipping, billing, and other important stuff

▶ Charging forward! (A crash course in credit-card info)

▶ Using the good stuff — recommendations, registries, and more

. . . .

*W*hat if you walked into your favorite department store and found a special place there with your name on it? And what if, in that special place, you found a wellspring of personal shopping data — a log of your shopping history, all your pertinent shopping information, lists of things you might like to buy in the future; you name it? And what if you could go to that special place without ever talking to a single salesperson? "Ah, to dream . . . " you might say. And to that I'd respond, "Today is your lucky day!" Because at Amazon.com, that special place is called "Your Account."

Your Account may very well be the most important area at Amazon.com. It's where you store and manage critical data like your order history, your credit-card information, your name and address, and your password. It's also the place where you'll shape your Amazon shopping experience with tools like 1-Click settings, your Address Book, and the Recommendation Wizard. But before you can reap the benefits of Your Account, you have to set up Your Account.

In this chapter, I walk you through an account set up, show you how to edit your existing account, and give you tips on how to get the most out of the features your account has to offer. By the time you're through, you will be truly the Master of Your Account.

Who Are You? Setting Up a New Account

Setting up a new account is a snap. It's a three-step process and won't take more than a minute or two. In fact, registering at Amazon is a commitment-phobe's delight. All they want from you is your name, your e-mail address, and a password. You don't give up the real goods — credit-card info, shipping addresses, and so on — until you buy.

Actually, you can browse the site and even add items to the shopping cart *before* you set up an account. When you're ready to buy, Amazon will walk you through the account setup as part of the buying process. But if you want to make use of Amazon's cool recommendation and personalization features, and you're not yet ready to buy, you'll need an account. Here's how to set one up:

1. **Fire up your favorite Web browser and point it to** www.amazon.com.

   The home page of the Amazon.com site duly appears.

2. **Click the Start Here link in the home page greeting. You'll find the Start Here link at the top right of the page, right underneath the navigation bars. (See Figure 3-1.)**

   You'll be taken to the Amazon Sign In screen that looks like Figure 3-2. You'll use this page to sign in every time you want to make a purchase, access Your Account, or do anything on the site that may be considered private or involve your personal information.

3. **Choose the No, I'm a New Customer option.**

   If you're new (and I'm guessing you are, or you wouldn't be reading this), you don't need to enter your e-mail yet. You'll enter it on the next screen.

4. **Click the Sign-In Using Our Secure Server button.**

   You'll come to a screen that looks like Figure 3-3. This is where you'll enter the information that will make up Your Account (initially, that is).

5. **Enter your name and e-mail address (twice) in the fields provided.**

   They want your name so that they can greet you by name when you come to the site and so there's no confusion if and when you do decide to buy (that is, your name matches the name on your credit card). They need your e-mail address because that's how they recognize you when you sign in for shopping adventures down the road. It's essentially your user ID. They also use it to contact you about the status of your orders. They ask for it twice to make sure you didn't mistype the first time.

   You'll notice that they also provide drop-down menus to enter your birthday. This is totally optional. They want it so they can send you a birthday e-mail with a little marketing sprinkled on top. You can also choose to have it show up as a part of your Wish List so that others can buy you nifty birthday presents! (More on Wish Lists in Chapter 13.)

6. **Enter your password (twice) in the fields provided.**

   They want you to have a password so your account is protected. They want you to enter it twice so that they're sure you didn't mistype. Choosing a good password is an important part of online shopping, not just at Amazon.com, but anywhere. Check out the Passwords section later in the chapter for some good tips on how to create yours.

The Start Here link

Figure 3-1:
Click this
link to get to
the sign-in
page.

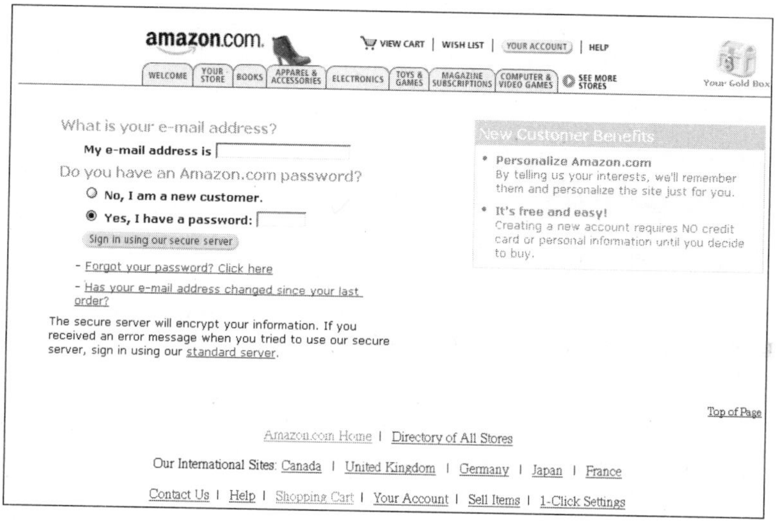

Figure 3-2:
This is the
Amazon.com
sign-in
screen.
You'll be
seeing this a
lot as you
use the site.

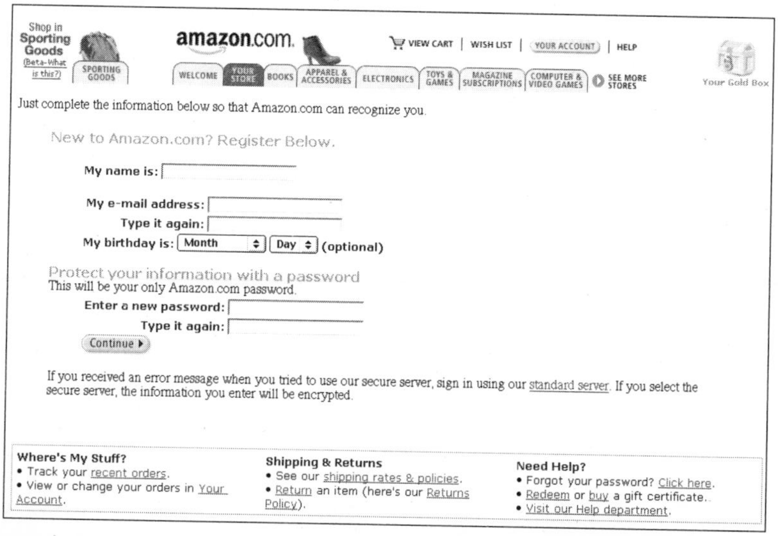

Figure 3-3:
The
Account
Registration
page is
where you'll
enter your
name,
e-mail
address,
and
password.

7. Click the Continue button.

You're done! You'll be offered the choice to start building your recommendations — giving Amazon.com some information about what you like and don't like so they can suggest products — or to continue shopping. Either way, you're armed to shop! The next time you visit the site, they'll recognize you (assuming your cookies are enabled); should you decide to buy, they ask you to sign in with your e-mail address and your password.

Before you give out even the smallest bit of information, you should be aware of the privacy policies of the company you're dealing with. Amazon has a good history of protecting their customers' privacy. I cover their privacy policy in more detail in Chapter 4, but the nutshell version is that they don't sell information and only share it with affiliates and subsidiaries when necessary. You can access their privacy policy in full from any page on the site. Just scroll to the bottom of the page and click the Privacy Notice link in the footer.

Passwords

A good password is like a good car. It keeps you safe, it keeps you moving, and it makes for a good trip. That said, make sure you pick a good password — something you'll remember that's also very difficult for someone else to guess. Your birthdate, your middle name, your dog's name . . . *not* good choices. Think 007 here. When it comes to passwords, you want to be mysterious. Here are a few suggestions for better password picking:

- **Combine numbers and letters.** This is the easiest way to make your password mysterious.
- **Don't choose anything that can be pulled straight from your driver's license.**
- **Try nonsense.** Though it's more difficult for you to remember if it has no significance, a nonsensical password is virtually uncrackable! A good way to create a "nonsense" password is to think of a sentence you'll remember — like "I am a supermodel" — then use the first letter of each of the words: "iaas," in this case.

Cookies . . . No Milk

Some cookies are yummy. Web cookies are not, but they can provide some tasty perks when shopping at Amazon. A *cookie* is a small file that lives on your computer's hard drive. You don't put it there yourself. Web sites such as Amazon.com put cookies on your computer through your browser. Don't worry. There's nothing sinister about it. They just want to be able to recognize you and track your shopping history so they can make your customer experience better.

10-4, good buddy — signing out

Knowing how to sign out is equally as important (and not nearly as intuitive) as signing in. If you're shopping at Amazon from an Internet café, a university computer lab, a public library, or any other place where privacy isn't a guarantee, you need to sign out. Amazon will "time out" on any session after a few minutes of inactivity, but if you don't sign out yourself, you've just given the next lucky user a window of opportunity to access your account. For all you know they'll buy $1,500 worth of Barney videos and completely destroy your recommendations (those nifty product suggestions that Amazon makes based on what you like and don't like). So sign out!

1. **Point your Web browser to** www.amazon.com.

   The Amazon.com home page appears.

2. **Click the link at the top of the home page that reads, "If you're not so and so, click here."**

3. **Choose the No, I Am a New Customer option and click the Sign In button — no need to enter your e-mail address.**

   Voilà! The Amazon.com site is primed for a new customer — which means you're signed out! Your personal info is safe and your recommendations will remain Barney-free.

Where's My Stuff?

Imagine this: You've placed an order at Amazon.com and suddenly you realize that you're going to be visiting your sister in Texas the week your package is scheduled to arrive. Or how about this: Your friend has a birthday coming up and you decide to get him the latest Hootie CD but the birthday is right around the corner — and the CD isn't. What do you do? You go to Your Account (see Figure 3-4). Just click the Your Account button in the Shopping Tools menu to get there. Within Your Account there's a section called (fittingly enough) "Where's My Stuff?" and the answers to all your order-related questions are in there.

Here are some of the key things you can do in Where's My Stuff?:

✔ View your complete order history

✔ Track specific orders

✔ Cancel existing orders

✔ Change your shipping and billing information

✔ Combine orders

✔ Make returns

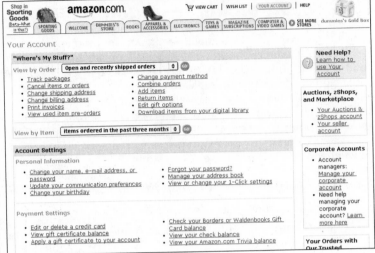

Figure 3-4:
The Your
Account
page.

Tracking packages

If you simply want to find your order and know where it is in the pipeline, all you have to do is click the Track Packages link in the Where's My Stuff? section of Your Account. When you do, you're taken to your Open and Recently Shipped Orders page, which will look something like Figure 3-5.

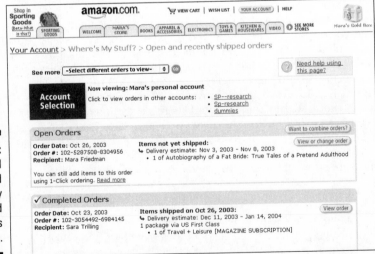

Figure 3-5:
A standard
Open and
Recently
Shipped
Orders
page.

At first glance you can tell whether the order is open or completed. You can also view the shipping status and estimated delivery date. If you want more specific shipping information, click the View or Change Order button by the item you're interested in and you'll be taken to that item's order summary page.

Ch-ch-ch-changes: Managing your order

Let's say you want to cancel an order, change the gift message, combine two orders, or change your shipping information. You can accomplish all those tasks and more by first going to your Open and Recently Shipped Order page.

Here's a little secret: Of the twelve links offered in the Where's My Stuff? section of Your Account, eight take you directly to the Open and Recently Shipped Orders page. The only thing that changes from link to link is the introductory paragraph. The content of the page stays the same (and so does what you can do there), regardless of how you get there.

Once you're there, you simply find the order you want to change and then click the View or Change Order button to go to that item's order summary. The Order summary page is where the real magic happens.

Figure 3-6 is a basic Order Summary page. If you click the appropriate button, you can do several handy tricks:

✔ Cancel an order or change quantities

✔ Change your shipping address

✔ Change your shipping speed

✔ Change your gift options

✔ Change your payment method

✔ Change your billing address

✔ Print an invoice

✔ Use a gift certificate or promotional code

All these activities are relatively self-explanatory, but there are two caveats:

✔ You can't make changes to an order that's already entered the shipping process.

✔ When you buy from some of Amazon's smaller partners — like certain zShops and Marketplace sellers — you have fewer order-management options. Instead of changes being just a click or two away, you'll likely have to deal with that vendor directly. And here's the tricky part. It's not always obvious that you're buying from a partner. When Amazon culls search results for you or puts together a subcategory page, it pulls products from all parts of the store to offer the widest selection possible. So you have to pay attention to the Item Information in the left column of the item's detail page to find out whether you're dealing with a small partner or with Amazon directly.

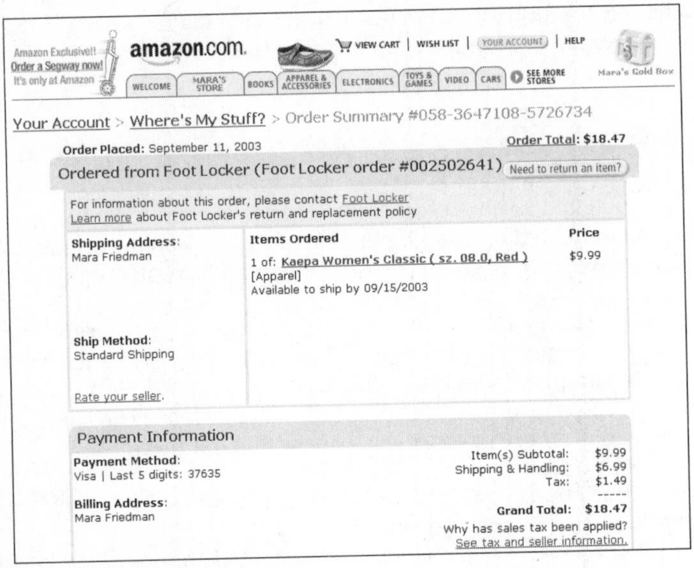

Figure 3-6:
You can make changes to existing orders from the Order Summary page.

Getting Personal

Unlike its brick-and-mortar counterparts, Amazon.com offers special shopping perks to the masses. But instead of having a well-coifed aide to help you find the ideal item, Amazon makes you your own personal shopper.

Business or pleasure?

Do you make purchases for your job or business? Customizable 1-click is great for people who use a business credit card to make work purchases.

Remember, anyone in your address book will show up in your 1-Click® drop-down menu (unless you customize it to exclude them). Remember, too, that you can customize the 1-Click® settings for any entry in your address book — so you can assign specific credit cards to specific entries.

To use 1-Click® for business, simply create another entry for yourself in your address book, but enter your work address in the address

fields. (To get to the New Address Entry page, just click on the Manage Your Address Book link in Your Account and then click on the Enter a New Address button.) Don't worry, you're not changing your official account info. You're just creating another entry in your address book.

Once you've got your work self in your address book, you can customize the 1-Click® settings for that address. Decide how the entry will appear in the 1-Click® drop-down menu — I suggest naming it simply "work" — and customize it to use your business credit card. Now you can save time *and* separate your professional from your personal expenses.

The key to taking advantage of your personal shopping privileges is first, knowing what perks are to be had, and second, taking a little time up front to get yourself set up.

Address Books

When you sign up at Amazon.com, you automatically have an Address Book that lives in Your Account. Of course, it's empty until you make your first purchase. After that, it's just you in there — a lonely e-row to hoe. Want a little company? You have two ways to beef up your Address Book:

✔ **Get gifty:** Every time you buy a gift and have it sent to a new address, Amazon automatically puts that address in your Address Book.

✔ **Do it the old-fashioned way:** There's nothing stopping you from sitting down with your paper address book and entering some of your favorite people into your Amazon Address Book. First, click the Your Account button at the top of the Amazon home page to go to Your Account, then click the Manage Your Address Book link and there, right at the top of the page, you'll see an Enter a New Address button. From there it's as simple as click and type. (You can delete or edit addresses just as easily.)

1-Click® settings

1-Click® ordering is Amazon's patented technology that allows you to complete the buying process — from choosing to shipping to payment — with just one click of your mouse. It's delightful and potentially devilish.

You're automatically set up for 1-Click® ordering after you make your first purchase, assuming you pay with a credit card. Amazon stores your shipping and billing information as your default 1-Click® Ordering settings. As soon as you've made a purchase, the detail pages for all your items show blue Ready to Buy? boxes like the one in Figure 3-7. You'll notice that the box still includes the Add To Shopping Cart option. It also includes a gift-wrap check box and a drop-down menu that will allow you to ship your 1-Click® orders to anyone in your address book.

Figure 3-7:
A typical
1-click
ordering
box.

If you buy gifts at Amazon and have them sent directly to the recipients, those addresses are stored in both your Address Book and your 1-Click Ship To: drop-down menu. Then you can buy for those people again with just one click. Very handy during the holidays!

You can change your 1-Click® settings easily. You manage your 1-Click® settings and your address book on the same page. (See Figure 3-8.) Here's how to turn your 1-Click® settings on or off:

1. **Click the Your Account button at the top of the Amazon home page to go to Your Account.**

2. **Click the View or Change Your 1-Click Settings link.**

   You'll find this link in the Account Settings section under Personal Information. (Refer to Figure 3-4 if you need some guidance here.)

3. **Turn 1-click on or off.**

   The box in the upper-right corner, below the nav bar, tells you the status of your 1-Click® ordering and offers a yellow button to change the status from "on" to "off" (or vice versa).

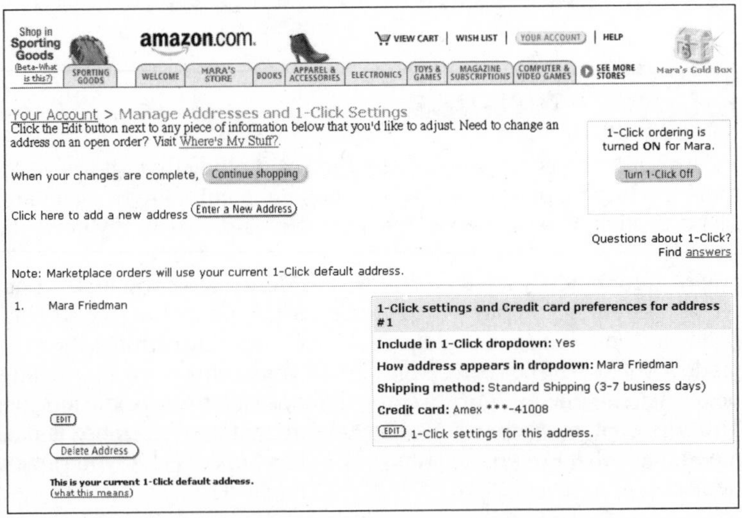

Figure 3-8:
You manage both your 1-Click® settings and your address book from this page.

You can also customize your 1-click settings according to the addresses in your Address Book. You can choose:

✔ Whether to put a particular person in your 1-Click Ship To: drop-down menu

✔ How you'd like the entry to appear in the drop-down menu

✔ What shipping method you'd like to use for that person

✔ What credit card you'd like to use for that person

To make any of these changes, simply click the Edit button in the 1-Click® settings box to the right of the address you want to customize. You'll come to a page that looks like Figure 3-9. Check the appropriate boxes and enter information in the fields provided. (If you scroll down, you'll find the credit-card information section.) When you're finished, click the Continue button. Your changes will be reflected in your 1-Click® drop-down immediately.

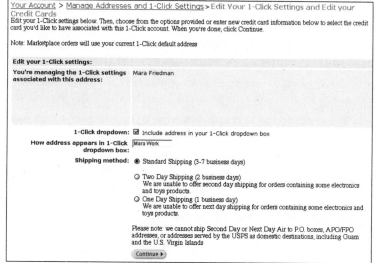

Your Account > Manage Addresses and 1-Click Settings > Edit Your 1-Click Settings and Edit your Credit Cards
Edit your 1-Click settings below. Then, choose from the options provided or enter new credit card information below to select the credit card you'd like to have associated with this 1-Click account. When you're done, click Continue.

Note: Marketplace orders will use your current 1-Click default address

Edit your 1-Click settings:

You're managing the 1-Click settings   Mara Friedman
associated with this address:

1-Click dropdown: ☑ Include address in your 1-Click dropdown box

How address appears in 1-Click Mara Work
dropdown box:

Shipping method: ● Standard Shipping (3-7 business days)

○ Two Day Shipping (2 business days)
We are unable to offer second day shipping for orders containing some electronics and toys products.

○ One Day Shipping (1 business day)
We are unable to offer next day shipping for orders containing some electronics and toys products.

Please note: we cannot ship Second Day or Next Day Air to P.O. boxes, APO/FPO addresses, or addresses served by the USPS as domestic destinations, including Guam and the U.S. Virgin Islands.

[Continue ▶]

Figure 3-9:
The
1-Click®
customiza-
tion page.

Recommendations

Amazon is always building your recommendations — compiling information about you and using it to suggest things you'll like. Every time you buy something from the folks at Amazon, they store that information and use it to further refine your recommendations. Amazon has hundreds of nifty ways to connect you with your dream book, video, sweater, bird house, chain saw, juicer . . . They know just how to tickle your fancy (and I talk more about how they do it in Part III). But when you first sign up at Amazon, you have no purchase history for them to work with. That's why they created the Recommendation Wizard — it's expressly for new shoppers.

The Recommendation Wizard is an amazing tool. You'll find it at the end of the sign-up process, or, if you chose the Continue Shopping option when you signed up, you can access it in Your Store, under Your Recommendations.

REMEMBER

To get to Your Store simply click on the tab that has your name on it — literally. (Once you sign up, Your Store changes to bear your name — for example, mine is Mara's Store.) You'll find that tab right next to the Welcome tab on just about every page of the site. You'll find Your Recommendations in the subnav.

Using the Recommendation Wizard is simple and fun. Here's how it works:

1. **Go to the Recommendations Wizard page.**

    You can do this by clicking on the Start Recommendations Wizard button either on the last page in the sign-up process or from Your Store. For the latter, click on the Your Store tab, then on Your Recommendations in the subnav. You'll see the Start Recommendations Wizard button in a blue box in the center of the page.

2. **Check the boxes next to the stores that interest you and then click the Continue button.**

    Check as many as you like. As you move through the wizard, you'll be asked to give more information for each store that you picked.

3. **In the new page that appears, check the categories that interest you and then click the Continue button.**

    Figure 3-10 shows the category choice page for the Books store. For each store you chose in the previous step, you're offered a separate page of category choices. If you chose 3 stores in Step 2, you have 3 pages of category choices to work through. When you complete your last page and click Continue, you come to the Add Details page.

Figure 3-10:
Select your
favorite
categories
by checking
the
appropriate
boxes.

4. **In the Add Details page, enter the requested information in the fields provided and click Continue.**

   For each store you chose in Step 2, you're asked to enter one favorite or Soon To Be Purchased item. So if you chose 3 stores in Step 2, you have to fill in 2 fields — one for each store. Now it's time to ask yourself some serious questions: Who *is* my favorite author? Which movie in the *Star Wars* trilogy is the best? Do I want to buy a juicer or a Dirt Devil?

5. **Choose the appropriate number rating for each item, and check the box if you own the item.**

   Amazon displays items from each store you've chosen based on the information you give them in Steps 2 through 4. You can give items a rating from 1 to 5 with 5 as the best. If you're unfamiliar with an item, leave it as a question mark. If you own it, check the I Own It box. This will keep them from offering it to you as a recommendation.

6. **Click Rate More Items or Finish.**

   At the bottom of the page, you have the option to finish or rate more items. If you click Rate More Items, Amazon will simply offer up another list. You can rate as many items as you like. Feeling frisky? Rate some more. It only helps hone your recommendations. Otherwise you're through and ready to reap the rewards of your efforts! When you do hit Finish, you're taken back to the Your Store home page with your recommendation changes recorded. Amazon generates instant recommendations based on the information you just gave them.

E-mail notifications: get 'em or get rid of 'em

Spam, or unsolicited junk e-mail, stinks. No two ways about it. But getting informative, relevant e-mail that you *asked for* is kind of fun. Amazon stays away from the former and is pretty good at the latter. Table 3-1 lists the e-mail notifications you can get from Amazon.com and gives a quick look at what they're about.

Table 3-1	E-mail Notifications at Amazon.com
The E-mail	*The Scoop*
Alerts	Lets you know whether one of your favorite authors, artists, actors, or directors has put out a new release.
Available to Order Notifications	Lets you know whether a not-yet-released or out-of-stock item is ready to order.

(continued)

Table 3-1 *(continued)*	
The E-mail	*The Scoop*
Delivers	Features recommendations and editorial content based on categories that you choose.
New for You	Uses your shopping history to offer recommendations and notify you of relevant new releases.
Share the Love	Part of the Share the Love program. If you choose to participate, you'll receive e-mail notifying you of discount opportunities that friends can send your way (via Amazon).
Special Occasion Reminders	You tell Amazon about important dates in your life and they'll send you an e-mail so you don't forget.
Weekly Movie Showtimes	Listing of movies playing in your area.

To sign up, go to Your Account by clicking on the Your Account button in the Shopping Tools menu at the top of almost every age on the site. Then click any of the seven choices in the E-mail Notifications section. To unsubscribe, do the same.

Shopping lists and gift registries

Making use of Amazon's lists and registries is a great way to give and get good gifts. There are three kinds of shopping lists or registries that you can use — Wish Lists and Baby and Wedding registries — and you can access them (yours or someone else's) by clicking the links in the Shopping Lists & Gift Registries section in Your Account. (I explain how to find specific lists and registries — and how to set up your own — in Chapter 13.)

You don't get those good gifts if your shipping address is wrong. The links to change or edit your addresses are also in the Shopping Lists & Gift Registries section in Your Account.

Money Talk: Credit Cards and Payment Issues

If you make a purchase at Amazon.com, it's likely you'll give them your credit-card number. Most people who shop at Amazon pay with a credit or check card because it's easy and it's safe. (Check out the sidebar if you need convincing.)

Give 'em a little credit

Amazon's Safe Shopping Guarantee begins with, "The Amazon.com Safe Shopping Guarantee protects you while you shop at Amazon.com, so that you never have to worry about credit-card safety. Period." And they mean it. Not only do they use the industry-standard Secure Sockets Layer (SSL) software to encrypt all your information, they also cover the cost of any unauthorized charges made to your credit card at Amazon.com. There is one big BUT. The guarantee does NOT cover third-party merchants who process their own credit-card transactions.

After you've given them that first number, it's easy to change, add, or delete credit cards. There's an entire section in Your Account devoted to payment settings. When you go there, the first link invites you to `Edit or delete a credit card`. (See Figure 3-11.) Doing either is as simple as clicking the appropriate button and then either confirming your desire to delete or entering new credit-card information.

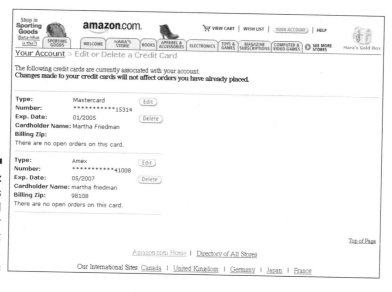

Figure 3-11: Here's where you'll edit, add, or delete credit cards.

For those of you who are squeamish about giving out your credit-card information, you should know that Amazon has a few other payment options. The first time you place an order, you can choose to enter only the last 5 digits of your credit card. Amazon.com will then give you a phone number to call to enter the rest of the credit card and complete the order. Amazon also accepts personal checks, money orders, and cashier's checks. The only hitch is that they don't place your order until they receive your personal check, money order, or cashier's check. So you end up waiting around for snail mail, which kind of defeats the purpose of shopping online. For a complete list of Amazon's payment options, first click the Help link at the top right of the Amazon.com home page and then click the Payment Methods We Accept link under the Ordering heading.

Chapter 4

Heeeeeeeeelp!

*W*hen you shop in the physical world, if you have a question, you find someone that works there and you get personalized answers in real time (unless you're me and then, inevitably, you find someone who is clueless and may as well be from outer space). Not so in the Internet world. With online shopping, you have to be resourceful and the key to being resourceful is being very familiar with the Help department.

Every good e-commerce Web site has a Help department; Amazon's is particularly good. Most of your questions already have an answer in Amazon's Help department. For the ones that don't, you can e-mail a customer service person and they'll help you directly.

In this chapter, I show you how to navigate Help to get answers to the questions you may have while shopping at Amazon.com.

A Quick Look at What's in Help

First things first. You can always get to Help from the Shopping Tools menu above the main nav bar in the upper-right corner of every page. Or you can go to the footer at the bottom of every page on the site and click the blue Help link.

Once you're there — there being a place that looks very much like Figure 4-1 — you'll find a menu of Help options broken out into the following main categories: Ordering, Gifts & Gift Certificates, Selling at Amazon.com, Digital Downloads, Using Your Account, Shipping, Returns, Amazon.com Services, and Privacy & Security.

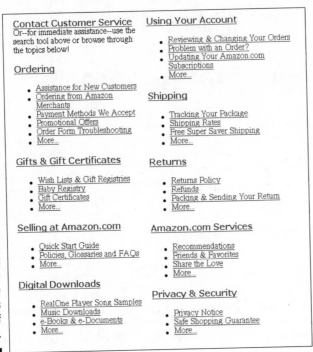

Contact Customer Service
Or--for immediate assistance--use the
search tool above or browse through
the topics below!

Ordering

- Assistance for New Customers
- Ordering from Amazon Merchants
- Payment Methods We Accept
- Promotional Offers
- Order Form Troubleshooting
- More...

Gifts & Gift Certificates

- Wish Lists & Gift Registries
- Baby Registry
- Gift Certificates
- More...

Selling at Amazon.com

- Quick Start Guide
- Policies, Glossaries and FAQs
- More...

Digital Downloads

- RealOne Player Song Samples
- Music Downloads
- e-Books & e-Documents
- More...

Using Your Account

- Reviewing & Changing Your Orders
- Problem with an Order?
- Updating Your Amazon.com Subscriptions
- More...

Shipping

- Tracking Your Package
- Shipping Rates
- Free Super Saver Shipping
- More...

Returns

- Returns Policy
- Refunds
- Packing & Sending Your Return
- More...

Amazon.com Services

- Recommendations
- Friends & Favorites
- Share the Love
- More...

Privacy & Security

- Privacy Notice
- Safe Shopping Guarantee
- More...

Figure 4-1:
Amazon's
Help
department
has
answers to
thousands
of
questions.

Within each one of these main sections you'll find several subsections and tons of subsubsections! In other words, the choices listed below the headings on the main Help page are just a smattering of the options (and answers) available within each section. In essence, the Help department is a massive collection of FAQs. If you browse around a little, you'll likely find the answers to any questions you may have.

Let's say you want to know about the return policies for Land's End, one of Amazon's apparel merchants. Here's how you can use the Help department to do that:

1. **Click on the Ordering from Amazon Merchants link under the Ordering main heading.**

   You'll bypass the general Ordering page and go straight to the page on ordering from merchants. There you'll find an assortment of links; among them links to the various product lines that include merchant merchandise.

2. **Click on Apparel & Accessories in the Browse box.**

   You'll come to a page that lists (as links) every apparel and accessory merchant.

3. **Click on Land's End.**

   Now you'll find yourself on Land's End's information page.

4. **Click on Returns and Exchanges.**

   Here's where you'll find the information you seek!

When browsing for your answer fails, you can use the Search function. And when all else fails, you can contact Customer Service. You'll notice a Contact Customer Service link and a Search box at the top of the page — the latter not visible in Figure 4-1, but trust me, it's there. It makes sense to try to find your answer among the existing information in Help before you contact Customer Service. You'll save them the time they might spend answering a question already answered on the site, and that's nice to do. But more important, you save yourself time and you get your answer faster.

Searching Help

Searching Help is actually very simple and effective. Here's how you do it:

1. **Enter your keyword in the Search box at the top of the Help page.**

   It's good to be specific, but not so specific that you're typing in an entire sentence. Just pick the one or two words that sum up your question.

2. **Click the "Go!" button.**

   You're transported to a Search Results page that looks like Figure 4-2.

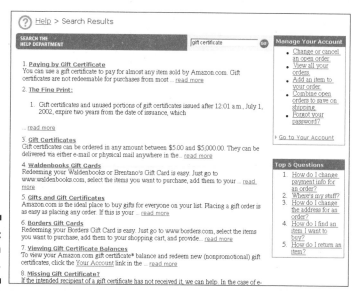

Figure 4-2:
Help search
results.

3. **Surf your search results.**

   Each entry has a title and then the beginning of an explanation. Skim the choices for the one that fits your question.

4. **Click a promising title from the Search Results list.**

   You're taken to a page that has a full and detailed answer to your question.

Contacting the Man behind the Curtain

So what happens if you do your homework — you check out the Help links and use the Search feature — but you don't find an answer to your question? That's when you contact the man behind the curtain. But before you do, there are few things you should know:

✔ **The folks at Amazon really don't want you to call them.** Amazon's customer service questions are asked and answered via e-mail.

✔ **The folks at Amazon can only read and respond to messages in English.** I'm guessing that if you're reading this book, that may not be an issue for you.

✔ **You need to allow at least 24 hours for them to reply.** Sometimes longer, so if it's urgent, call an Amazon-savvy pal.

Here's how to send e-mail to Amazon's customer service department:

1. **Click the Contact Customer Service link at the top left of the Help page.**

   You're taken to a page with a series of links to the following: Order & Refund Questions, Account Assistance, Typographical Errors, Web site and Product Suggestions, Gift Orders & Gift Certificates, Prices, Promotions, & Rebates, Selling Items, and Using Features & Services.

2. **Click the link in the menu that best describes what your question is about.** Don't be alarmed when you're taken to a page that *isn't* an e-mail question form. They want to make sure that you really checked to see whether your question has already been answered.

3. **Click the link in the bulleted list that begins, I have a question . . .**

   This will take you to the e-mail form that looks like Figure 4-3.

4. **Fill in the requested information and click Continue.**

   Actually, Amazon automatically fills in your name and e-mail address (assuming you're signed in). Just use the drop-down menu to choose a subject, enter your order number (if it's relevant), and type your question in the Comments field.

5. **Review your e-mail for spelling errors and other faux pas.**

   If you want to make changes, use the Edit button to send you back to Step 4.

6. **If your e-mail passes muster, click the Send E-Mail button.**

   Your question gets sent on its merry way to the Customer Service department.

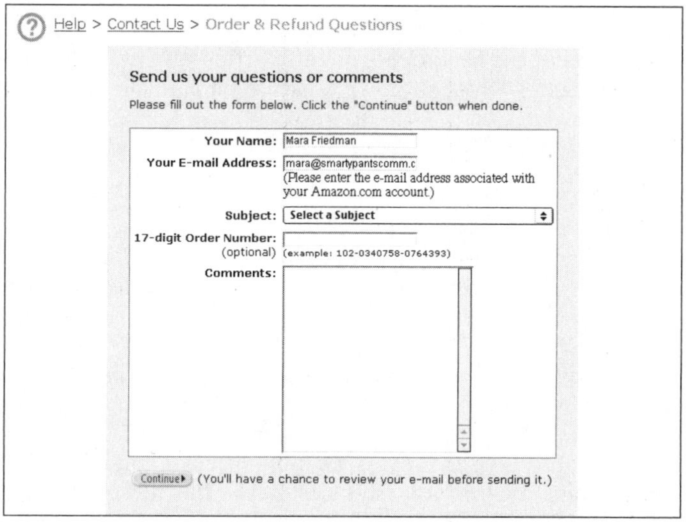

Figure 4-3:
The Customer Service E-Mail form.

Important Stuff You May Need Help With

There's actually lots of important information in Help, but certain topics — ordering, shipping, returns, and (not surprisingly) privacy — seem to be the real hot spots with most Amazon customers.

Amazon has done such a thorough job of putting together their Help department that I don't need to walk you through every possible question. I just help you get to the right information and point out any potholes along the way.

Ordering

Ordering itself is actually fairly simple (and I walk you through the process in Chapter 10). The reason I point out this section of the Help department is because there are some good answers here about what it means to order from an Amazon merchant or partner.

Go to the Ordering section of the Help page and then click the Ordering from Amazon Merchants link. The first eight choices in the Browse box will take you to pages that tell you not only who Amazon's merchants and partners are, but a little bit about them and what their policies are. This is stuff you need to know "just in case."

Shipping

You can find everything you might ever need to know about shipping in the Shipping section of the Help department. Particularly helpful are the items that demystify Super Saver shipping, In-store pickup, and shipping rates.

Returns

As far as I'm concerned, returns are the Achilles' heel of online shopping. That said, you *can* return Amazon purchases, but there are rules to this game — and you can find them all in the Returns section of the Help department.

Here's a quick overview of Amazon's return policy. The nutshell version goes like this: You can return items that you bought from Amazon (at Amazon is a different matter and I'll get to that in a moment) within 30 days of the delivery date *for a full refund,* as long as it's in its original condition with its original packaging and accessories, isn't flammable, has its serial or UPC code, and isn't a TV larger than 27 inches. You can get partial refunds for certain items that don't meet the above criteria. To find out more about such "partials," go to the Refunds section in the Help Department — you'll find it under the Returns heading.

And here are a few things to watch out for:

- ✔ **Most Merchants:** With the exception of Target and Marshall Field's, Amazon merchants have their own returns policies and if you buy from those merchants *at* Amazon, you have to abide by their policies. In other words, returns go to the merchant, not to Amazon.

- ✔ **Target and Marshall Field's:** If you buy something through Amazon from either of these partners, you can only return to Amazon.com. You can't take your item to a local Target or Marshall Field's and return it.

- ✔ **You won't get the shipping cost back.** Unless the return is the result of an Amazon error, you won't be reimbursed for shipping charges.

- ✔ **No exchanges.** If you want a different size or color, you'll have to reorder the item. Amazon can't process exchanges.

✔ **Big TVs.** If they're larger than 27 inches, you can't return them. What they advise you to do instead is to inspect the TV while the delivery person is still there — and if it doesn't work, refuse the delivery. That way you can get a refund. If you want to return it and the delivery person is gone, you have to contact the manufacturer directly. (Ick.)

To actually make a return, you go to the Returns Center. You can get there by clicking the yellow Visit Our Returns Center button on the main Returns page in Help.

Here's how to return an item that you bought from Amazon (I'll explain how to return something you received as a gift later in the chapter):

1. **At the Returns Center, click the circle next to I Ordered the Items and then click Continue.**

   The I Ordered the Items option will probably be selected already as it's the default. If you're not already signed in, you'll be taken to a Sign In screen.

2. **Enter your password in the field provided and click the Sign In Using Our Secure Server button.**

   You'll come to a page that lists all the orders eligible for return.

3. **Find the order for the item you want to return and click the Return an Item from This Order button.**

   You'll come to a page that looks something like Figure 4-4. (If there was more than one item in your order, they'll all be listed here.) Note that you can also return items that showed up in your shipment that you didn't order. (This is for those honest Abes out there.)

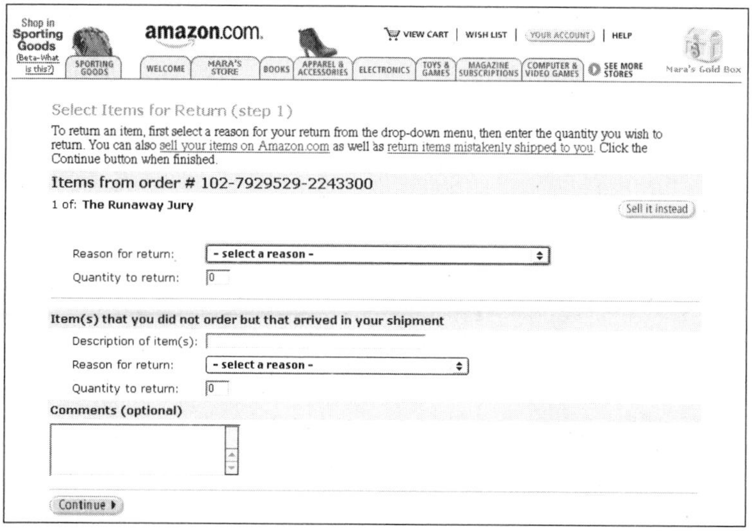

Figure 4-4:
Here's where you select the quantity of and reason for your return.

4. **Use the Reason drop-down menu to specify why you're returning the item. Use the Quantity drop-down menu to specify how many items you're returning, and then click the Continue button.**

Reasons include things like "I ordered the wrong item," "I found better prices elsewhere," and "Product was defective/damaged when it arrived." If the reason for return is not an Amazon error, the shipping costs are deducted from your refund amount, so make sure you choose the right option!

5. **In the new page that appears, choose your return shipping option and then click Continue.**

Of these four choices, pick the one that works best for you by clicking the circle next to it:

- You can use the U.S. Postal Service and print out a label on your printer (from a page that Amazon generates).

- You can take the package to the post office and write out the label yourself.

- You can take the package to UPS and use a label that Amazon generates.

- You can have UPS come to your house.

6. **In the new page that appears, follow the instructions for the shipping option you chose.**

The page you get varies according to the shipping option you chose. The first three choices generate either a shipping label that you can actually print out and use, or instructions that tell you what to put on a label you create yourself. Then you just pack up the item you're returning and send it off.

If you chose the fourth option (the UPS pickup), you're finished after you complete Step 5 in the steps given here; Amazon schedules the pickup for you. Make sure that this UPS option is really the one you want before you click; after you click it, it's a done deal.

Returning gifts is a different process. First of all, in order for *you* to receive the refund instead of the giver, the giver had to mark the item as a gift when they purchased it. If they did, here's what happens:

✔ For gifts purchased through your Wish List, they'll send you a check.

✔ Otherwise, they'll mail you an Amazon.com gift certificate.

Either way, they'll mail your refund to the same address where your order was shipped. And they won't notify the gift giver that you returned their present.

If the item wasn't marked as a gift when purchased or was not shipped directly to you, they'll send a refund to the gift giver. In other words, the giver will know and they'll get the cash. Darn.

To return a gift, you still have to go to the Returns Center (click the yellow Visit Our Returns Center button on the main Returns page in Help), but there the similarity ends. Here's how to return a gift you received from Amazon.com:

1. **At the Returns Center, click the circle next to I Received the Items as a Gift and then click Continue.**

   If you're not already signed in, you'll be taken to a Sign-In screen.

2. **Enter your password in the field provided and click the Sign In Using Our Secure Server button.**

   You'll come to a new page that asks you to enter your order number. To find your order number, get out the packing slip that arrived with your order. The order number is just below the bar code.

3. **Enter your order number and quantity in the fields provided and click the Continue button.**

   Note that multiple quantities of the same item count as one item here.

4. **Enter a description and quantity of the item you're returning in the fields provided. Use the drop-down menu to give a reason for your return and then click Continue.**

   Note that you can add optional comments here — a good thing to do if you have an unusual circumstance or a reason not listed in the drop-down.

5. **Enter your name, e-mail address, mailing address, and phone number in the fields provided and click Continue.**

6. **Choose your shipping label option and click Continue.**

   You'll be at a page that looks like Figure 4-5. If you have a printer, Amazon will generate a print-ready label that you can use. If not, you can write down the returns address and do it the old fashioned way.

MYOB! (privacy and security at Amazon.com)

Privacy and Security make up a category of their own within Help. If you go there, you'll find all the information you need to feel safe shopping at Amazon.

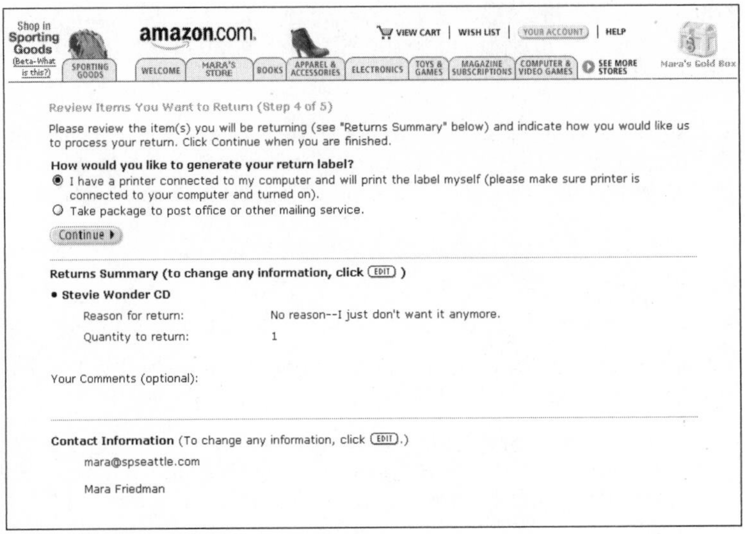

Figure 4-5:
The last page in the gift return process.

The Help department lists four key privacy and security policies:

- **Privacy Notice:** This is Amazon's privacy policy — the big daddy, chock-full of legalese. The nutshell version is that they don't sell information and only share it with trusted partners, but if you're concerned, you should read it in its entirety.

- **Safe Shopping Guarantee:** This is Amazon's promise to you that they've made it safe for you to give them your credit-card information online.

- **A-to-Z Guarantee Protection:** This guarantee protects you from fraud up to $2,500 when you shop with Marketplace, Auctions, or zShops sellers. You'll find much more on this in Amazon's Help Department. Click on Ordering from Amazon Merchants under the Ordering heading, and then click on A-to-Z Guarantee Protection.

- **Amazon.com Bill of Rights:** This is exactly what it sounds like: a list of your rights when you shop at Amazon.

Amazon.com will never ask you to give them your credit card number via e-mail. The only time you'll give them that information is on their Web site using their secure server.

Part II
You Want It? They Got It: Shopping and Buying at Amazon.com

The 5th Wave   By Rich Tennant

"He saw your laptop and wants to know how much Amazon.com charges for spears."

In this part . . .

Amazon is the kind of place you can go to look for one simple purchase, and end up spending half your day browsing around. There are so many good things to buy, so much good information, and a host of free features to take advantage of. The trick is finding your way around.

In this part, I walk you through the ins and outs of shopping at Amazon.com. I give you a better idea of what they actually sell there and show you how to use some of the free services on the site. I also give you a grand tour of some of the lesser-known parts of the store, including Auctions, zShops, and the Outlet. This isn't devoted solely to the "whats" of Amazon. You also get a look at the essential "hows" — how to search, how to browse, and how to buy anything on the site.

Chapter 5

A Closer Look at the Stores

There is no such thing as "one-stop shopping" in the physical world. I say this with regret in my heart because there's nothing I'd like more than to be able to buy designer jeans and mayonnaise in the same store and save myself a little time — so convenient! Alas, I can't. And I'm not fooled by these giant strip malls cropping up all over the place, either. They may sell clothes, toys, and electronics around the same parking lot, but that parking lot is the size of Delaware and you may as well be driving to another town to go from one end to the other.

Then there's Amazon.com. Do they sell everything there? Well, no. In fact, you won't find mayonnaise of any kind anywhere on their virtual shelves. But they do sell so many of the things most of us shop for — at different stores in different places — all on one convenient Web site.

In this chapter, I give you a more detailed picture of what you can buy at Amazon.com. I walk you through each store and cover some of the unique-to-Amazon things you can do there. I also show you how to make good use of the features that make Amazon the best place to do your gift shopping.

The Master List

Amazon.com is made up of a series of stores — mini destinations within the site that sell a collection of products. Some of these stores are actually partner stores — just online versions of brick-and-mortar destinations like Target or Marshall Fields. Some stores are thematic and are made up of a subset of products from one or several different categories. They're called Specialty

Stores and we'll get to them in a bit. But the stores that most people think of when they think of shopping at Amazon are what I'll call their *category stores*, of which there are currently 19: Apparel & Accessories, Sporting Goods, Books, DVD, Magazine Subscriptions, Music, Video, Camera & Photo, Computers, Computer & Video Games, Electronics, Office Products, Software, Home & Garden, Kitchen & Housewares, Outdoor Living, Toys, Babies, and Tools & Hardware.

Each store is somewhat unique, but here's what you find in every Amazon.com store:

- ✔ **Editorial Recommendations:** You'll find these in various incarnations sprinkled throughout the site — on store home pages, in feature "boxes" on the right side of the page, on subcategory pages, and so on.

- ✔ **Product Information:** The quality of product information varies from store to store (with newer stores often having a weaker offering), but it's there.

- ✔ **Editorial Reviews:** You won't find them for every item listed, but you will find hundreds (at the least) in every store.

- ✔ **Customer Reviews:** Again, not necessarily every product gets reviewed, but lots and lots of customers post reviews in every store.

Check out the next sections for overviews of each individual store.

Apparel & Accessories

The Apparel store is actually a huge collection of merchants selling their wares together in one place. In other words, Amazon never stocks apparel and when you buy from this store, you're buying directly from that apparel store (Nordstrom, Marshall Fields, and so on) or company (Eddie Bauer, Guess, and so on).

You can shop the Apparel store by category — Women, Men, Kids & Baby, Shoes, and Accessories — or by store, and there are more than 100 of those. One of the great things about the Apparel store is that it's a good place to find certain hard-to-find things. Very small sizes, very large sizes; they're all there.

Sporting Goods

This is Amazon's new baby. It's set up like the Apparel store — a collection of merchants selling products at Amazon — so remember, when you buy from Sporting Goods you need to be familiar with the policies of the company you're actually buying from.

You can shop Sporting Goods by store, just like in the Apparel store. They've got more than 100 sellers offering just about every sporting good you can envision. You can also shop Sporting Goods by, of course, sport. They've got everything from badminton to boxing, cheerleading to cricket. Alas, they've left out curling. How could they? I mean, how hard would it have been for them to just stick a few of the brooms from Tools & Hardware in the Sporting Goods store? What would our Canadian neighbors say?

Books

Books, as Jeff Bezos likes to say, were Amazon's first, best product. When Amazon started up, people were already used to buying books via mail order catalogs or book clubs, so the leap to online ordering wasn't too great. Moreover, books came in relatively predictable shapes — making them easy to ship — and one didn't necessarily need to try one on before buying. Today, books are still Amazon's best selling category and it's no wonder. Currently, Amazon offers countless titles in its catalog — every book listed in the Library of Congress even if it's no longer in print.

The Books store subcategories include: Arts & Photography, Books on Cassette and CD, Audio Downloads, Biographies & Memoirs, Business & Investing, Children's Books, Christian Books, Computers & Internet, Cooking, Food & Wine, e-Books, Entertainment, Español, Gay & Lesbian, Health, Mind & Body, History, Home & Garden, Horror, Literature & Fiction, Mystery & Thrillers, Nonfiction, Outdoors & Nature, Parenting & Families, Professional & Technical, Reference, Religion & Spirituality, Romance, Science, Science Fiction & Fantasy, Sports, Teens, Travel, Women's Fiction, Foreign Language Books, New & Used Textbooks, Large-Print Books, and Sheet Music & Scores. So, if you're a Francophile-scifi-freak-hockey-playing-aspiring-photographer-mystery buff, you're in luck. Also, each subcategory is broken down into even more specific genres.

The Books store, maybe because it's the oldest store at Amazon.com, is incredibly well stocked with hard-to-find goodies. You'll find tons of audio books, a decent selection of e-books, and book bargains coming out of your ears — way more than you'd find in a brick-and-mortar store.

Music

Amazon sells CDs in its music store. Lots of CDs. But it also sells cassettes, LPs, Super Audio CDs, and DVD-audio. It tips its hat to the past and to the future. In fact, you can actually download free MP3s from Amazon's Music store — but we'll get to that in the next section.

Amazon's music catalog is vast — far bigger than anything you'd find in the physical world. Subcategories include: Alternative Rock, Blues, Box Sets,

Broadway & Vocalists, Children's, Christian & Gospel, Classic Rock, Classical, Instrumental, Country, Dance & DJ, Folk, Free Downloads, Hard Rock & Metal, Imports, Indie Music, International, Jazz, Latin, Music Accessories, New Age, Opera & Vocal, Pop, R&B/Soul, Rap & Hip-Hop, Rock, and Soundtracks. The Music store also has 18 "label stores" that include everything from Blue Note Records to Disney.

Of course, there's no public listening station like in a neighborhood record store, so you can't put on the headphones and shimmy to the beat. But secretly, your friends think you look like you're having an allergic reaction when you do that, so it's just as well that you shimmy in the comfort of your own home.

Video & DVD

Forgive me, technophiles! I know they're not the same thing (and they're also not the same store), but the video and DVD stores have almost identical subcategories. And let's face it, they're both things you put in a player and watch on a screen, so . . .

These are the subcategories you'll find in both the video and DVD stores: Action & Adventure, African American Cinema, Animation, Anime & Manga, Art House & International, Boxed Sets, Christian Video, Classics, Comedy, Cult Movies, Disney Home Video, Documentary, Drama, Educational, Fitness & Yoga, Gay & Lesbian, Hong Kong Action, Horror, Independently Distributed, Kids & Family, Military & War, Music Video & Concerts, Musicals & Performing Arts, Mystery & Suspense, Romantic Comedies, Science Fiction & Fantasy, Special Interests, Sports, Television, and Westerns. And for those of you wondering what Manga is — no, it's not a tropical fruit or a friendly chimp who has a show on TV. It's a kind of Japanese comic (in this case animated) — very cool.

If you're a collector, you'll be happy to find out about Amazon Essentials. These are superlative lists — things like Essential Suspense Classics, or Essential Woody Allen. You'll also find lists of Academy Award winners and AFI best films.

Magazine Subscriptions

This is the biggest newsstand you've ever been to! You'll find everything from the gossip mags that overstuff the grocery checkout to obscure science journals. You can also subscribe to trade journals and newspapers at Amazon.

Subcategories in the Magazine subscriptions include: Arts & Crafts, Automotive, Bridal, Business & Finance, Children's, Computer & Internet, Electronics & Audio, Entertainment, Family & Parenting, Fashion & Style, Food & Gourmet, Games & Hobbies, Gay & Lesbian, Health & Fitness, History, Home & Garden, International, Lifestyle & Cultures, Literary, Men's Interest,

Music, News & Politics, Newspapers, Pets, Professional & Trade, Religion & Spirituality, Science & Nature, Spanish-Language, Sports & Leisure, Teens, Travel & Regional, and Women's Interest. Guess what the top seller is in Men's Interest? Yes. That's right. Playboy. Guess what it is in Women's Interest? Uh huh. You guessed it. Oprah's magazine. (Okay, fine. They're updated daily, but still . . .)

You don't just have to get new subscriptions here. You can renew your existing magazine subscription through Amazon.com. Just wait till your current subscription is coming to an end (two months or so), then place your new order through Amazon.com. The magazine publishers are smart enough to tack your new subscription on to your existing one, so it'll definitely be less expensive.

Camera and Photo

Amazon's goal is always to offer the widest, deepest selection possible. Camera and Photo is no exception. Amazon has also partnered with Ofoto (which is owned by Kodak) for film and digital photo processing.

Subcategories in Camera and Photo include: Accessories, Binoculars, Camcorders, Digital Cameras, Film Cameras, Frames & Albums, Microscopes, Printers & Scanners, Projectors, and Telescopes. Wait a minute! Binoculars? Telescopes? What kind of Camera and Photo store is this? We're talking Peeping Tom heaven here.

Computers

Guess what they sell here? But seriously, they sell a really expansive selection of computers, plus all the add-ons and peripherals you could ever want. And happily, they're not pc-biased. You'll find a healthy selection of Macs here too.

You can shop by brand — and there are tons of them, the ones you've heard of and maybe some you haven't — and by category. Those include: Accessories and Supplies, Computers (duh), Computer add-ons, Handhelds and PDAs, Office Electronics, Monitors, Printers and Software. It is a geek Valhalla.

Computer and Video Games

The Computer and video games store is organized by game system. You'll find the big three — Game Cube, PS2, and Xbox — plus a bunch of older systems. Subcategories are: Game Boy, Game Boy Advance, GameCube, Mac Games, Nintendo 64, PC Games, PlayStation, PlayStation2, Sega Dreamcast, Xbox, and Other Systems.

Electronics

The Electronics store is absolutely huge and even includes three of the other stores — Camera and Photo, Computer and Video Games, and Software — in its mix. You can buy everything from a TV to a PDA to a DVD player there. (High-tech alphabet soup, anyone?)

This Amazon store has excellent product information. So if you're in the market for something, I recommend using the site to do research, even if you aren't sure you want to buy there. You'll also find lots of downloadable product manuals in the Electronics store and some very helpful, customer-written So You'd Like To guides.

Also, Amazon has made a deal with Circuit City: Customers can buy things on the site and then opt for in-store pickup. It'll save you money on shipping and you'll get your new goody sooner.

The subcategories in the Electronics store are: Accessories & Supplies, Audio & Video, Camera & Photo, Cell Phones & Service, Computers, Computer & Video Games, Handhelds & PDAs, Office Electronics, Portable Electronics, and Software. Notice that Camera & Photo, Computers, Software, Computer & Video Games are all categories within the Electronics store. So you see, Electronics is the mother ship . . . the queen bee . . . the mama pajama.

Office Products

Office Products is an example of what I like to call Amazon's "team player" stores. They already offered several of the products in this store through their Electronics store and then made a deal with Office Depot to fill in the blanks.

What this arrangement means to you is that when you buy certain products from Amazon's Office Products store, you're actually dealing with Office Depot. So just make sure you're familiar with their rules and policies.

Office Depot is another of the stores with whom Amazon has an in-store pickup deal. You can order and pay online and then pick up the item around the corner.

Subcategories include: Business Presentation Supplies, Cleaning & Maintenance, Computers, Computer Add-Ons, Furniture & Accessories, Lighting, Lunchroom Supplies, Mailroom Supplies, Office Electronics, Office Supplies, Safety & First Aid, Software, and Teaching Materials (where, conveniently, you can buy both rulers and first aid supplies — yes sir . . . may I have another?).

Software

You'll find a little bit of overlap between Software and Computer and Video Games, but otherwise the Software store is a universe unto itself.

The subcategories are: Business & Office, Children's Software, Education & Reference, Graphics, Home & Hobbies, Language & Travel, Linux, Macintosh, Networking, Operating Systems, PC Games, Personal Finance, Programming, Software Downloads, Software for Handhelds, Utilities, Video & Music, Virus Protection, and Web Development. You'll even find software for your cat (check out the Part of Tens for more on this), but not enough of it to warrant its own category.

Those software downloads can be pretty handy. You'll find everything from children's software to applications for your PDA. Is it April 13? Are you still thinking you're doing your own taxes? Did you forget to buy the program? No sweat. You can download it here.

Tools & Hardware

The Tools & Hardware store came into being when a former bigwig at Black and Decker came to be a bigwig at Amazon and said, "Hey, why not sell tools online?" Why not, indeed? Amazon partnered with a strangely named but well-respected tool-catalog company — Tool Crib of the North — and the Amazon.com Tools & Hardware store was born. The selection is ten times what you'd find at a brick-and-mortar store, and now when you're shopping for your friend's baby shower you can also pick up some scaffolding and maybe a power paint sprayer. Hey, why not give that as a shower gift? They can use it to paint the nursery and when that's done they can hook it up to the garden hose for some great summertime fun! (That's not true. I made that up.)

Subcategories include: Hand Tools, Job Site Equipment, Lawn & Garden Tools, Power Tools, and Other Categories (like the Village People's Greatest Hits . . . okay, not really).

Home and Garden, Kitchen and Housewares, and Outdoor Living

These three stores have lots of overlap in their offerings (though the Kitchen store is the most "its own" of the three). You'll also see some overlap between Outdoor Living and Tools and Hardware. So why didn't they just make one big store and call it, "Inside/Outside Home"? Because one thing Amazon is really good at is offering up a huge selection of stuff in digestible chunks. They know that if you're looking for a shower curtain, you probably don't want to wade through a bunch of grills to get there.

The subcategories in Home & Garden are: Bed & Bath, Furniture & Décor, Kitchen, Housewares, Outdoor Living, Spa & Personal Care, Tools & Hardware, Vacuums & Floor Care.

The subcategories in Kitchen and Housewares run the gamut from practical to gracious: Baking, Bar Tools & Glasses, Coffee, Tea & Espresso, Cookbooks, Cook's Tools & Gadgets, Cookware, Cutlery, Grills & Fryers, Kitchen Furniture, Housewares, Small Appliances, Spa & Personal Care, and Tableware. As in the Electronics store, you'll find lots of downloadable product manuals here — good for research and if you lost yours!

The subcategories in Outdoor Living are a pretty civilized take on rough-and-ready pastimes: Backyard Birding, Camping, Gifts, Grills, Fryers & Outdoor Cooking, Heating & Lighting, Lawn & Garden Tools, Outdoor Décor, Patio Furniture, Pest Control, Plants, Seeds & Flowers, and Sports & Lawn Games.

Toys and Games and Baby

Both of these stores are partnerships with the 'R' Us stores (that'd be Toys 'R' Us and Babies 'R' Us). So, again, make sure that when you buy you're familiar with their way of doing things.

Subcategories in the toy store are guaranteed to make you feel, well, like a kid in a toy store: Action Figures, Activities & Learning, Arts & Crafts, Baby Toys, Bikes, Scooters & More, Building Sets, Blocks & Models, Characters and Interests, Collectors at Toysrus.com, Dolls, Electronics, Kids 'R' Us Room Décor Store, Games, Preschool, Pretend Play & Dress-Up, Puzzles, Science & Discovery, Sports & Outdoor Play, Stuffed, Vehicles & Die-Cast, Video Games, and Winners of Awards.

To make it appropriate for kids, only the more family-friendly games are offered in Toys & Games. You'll find the full selection in the Computer and Video Games store. You'll also find used games there, but not in the Toy store.

In the Baby store, play takes a backseat to the practical: Gear, Nursery, Feeding, Activity, Health & Safety, Bath & Potty, and Toys. I keep hoping they'll add a Pregnant Lady category where they'll sell things like gallon tubs of ice cream and husbands who do whatever you tell them to do.

Special Features

There are so many things you can do at Amazon that make shopping better. Some of them aren't even shopping! The trick is peeling the onion until you hit that special feature that'll make your shopping day.

These are a few of my favorites, but they aren't the only special features you'll find. There are enough cool things happening at Amazon to fill several tomes. As you explore the site, you'll discover your own favorites. In the meantime, give these a try.

Free Downloads

Downloading music from the Web has gotten some people into trouble. Not at Amazon.com. Here you can download the day away. Free Downloads is packed with electronic files (MP3 and Windows Media) that you can download to your computer's hard drive and play — either on a free player (that you can also download off the Internet) or on your own MP3 player (which you can buy at Amazon if need be).

Free Downloads is Amazon's way of letting you sample the merchandise. There are literally hundreds of songs just waiting for you to lay your ears on them, and don't worry, this isn't a mini-Napster here. Artists and labels voluntarily put their music up on Amazon's site to invite you to get hooked and buy the CD.

You'll find the Free Downloads section by clicking on it in the subnav of the Music store. It's set up like a mini-music store. You'll find a Browse box filled with genres, editorial content, Top Downloads — everything you'd expect to find in a music store. The big difference is that the music here is free!

Amazon's free downloads come in two file formats: MP3 and Windows Media. But there's one glitch: They used to come in Liquid Audio format too, but Liquid Audio is no longer creating free players. (This wouldn't be *much* of a glitch except for the links in the Free Downloads section that still encourage you to get a Liquid player — and take you to a very nice Dear John letter on Liquid's site. If you're not a fan of wild goose chases, avoid the Liquid Audio links and you should be fine.

If you can hear sound on your computer when you're using the Internet, then you shouldn't have any problem with MP3s or Windows Media. What you do need, though, is a player so you can listen to the music after you've downloaded it. Here's the good news: An entire page in Free Downloads is devoted to helping users get players. To get there, follow these steps:

1. **Go to the Free Downloads section of the Music store.**

   You'll find it by clicking Free Downloads in the Music store subnav.

2. **With the Free Downloads page loaded on your screen, scroll down until you see the Help with Downloads box on the left-hand side.**

3. Click on the Download a Free MP3 Player link.

You'll come to the Media Player Download Instructions page, where you'll find links for downloading the RealOne Player and the Windows Media player for both Macs and PCs. (You'll also find Liquid Audio players offered, but remember, these are no longer available.) Click on the link for the player that you want and you'll be walked through the download process. If you're uncertain about which one to download, take advantage of the information provided on this page (below the links to the players).

When you're set up with a player, you're ready to start trying out the music. To download tracks, do the following:

1. Sign in to access your Amazon.com account.

If you don't already have an Amazon.com account, now is the time to set one up; you can't download songs unless you're signed in to their site, and you can't sign in if you don't have an account. (Need help with signing in? See Chapter 4.)

2. Go to the Free Downloads section of the Music store.

Again, you'll find it by clicking the Free Downloads tab in the Music store subnav.

3. Find a song and go to its detail page.

This is the fun part. You can browse for free downloads just like you would for anything else at Amazon.com — poke around until you see something that tickles your fancy. Or, if you know the song's title, use the Free Downloads search box and see if it's available.

Keep in mind that you may not find it. Though it's a well-stocked part of the site, you won't find everything there. If you could, they'd have a hard time making people pay for those CDs. When you've found a song you want, go to that song's detail page. (All downloading happens from the detail page.)

4. Click the Download Song now button.

You'll find it next to the image of a CD.

Downloading music to your hard drive is just like saving anything else to your hard drive. You'll need to decide where to put it, what to call it, and so on. So create a music folder for yourself and prepare to rock!

Essentials

Finding new music can be scary. Have you ever thought to yourself, "I want to get into jazz; I'm going to go to the record store and buy a jazz CD!"? Did you then walk over to the record store and stand in front of *thousands* of jazz CDs, feeling totally overwhelmed? Scary.

You needed Essentials — another feature in the Music store. It's a compilation representing the work of Amazon's expert music editors who've put together hundreds of must-have lists for everything from rock to baroque music.

Like Free Downloads, you can get to Essentials by clicking on it in the Music subnav. Once you're there, you're on your way to new music heaven. You can browse Essentials by artist, composer, style — you'll even find Essentials by Year. Each Essentials list is accompanied by a brief history of that genre. (See Figure 5-1 for the Bebop Essentials page.) Clicking either the Classical or Jazz link under the Get Started In heading takes you to more detailed introductions to these two genres of music that include an "audio tour" — very cool.

Look Inside

For so long, customers said that the reason they'd choose a physical bookstore over Amazon is because they wanted to be able to leaf through the books before they bought. Look Inside eliminated the obstacle.

Look Inside allows you to view pages in the book you're considering. You won't find this feature on every book, but you will find it on many, and often on bestsellers. You'll know that a book has Look Inside if there's a little fellow peeking over the top edge of the book's image on the detail page. To use the feature, just click on the little fellow.

Figure 5-1: Essentials gives a brief history of the genre followed by a list of "must-have" CDs.

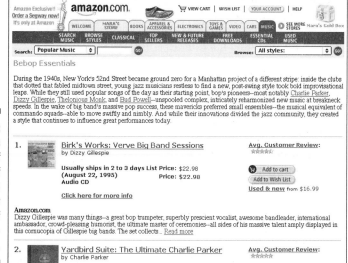

The Look Inside pages look like Figure 5-2. You'll usually be given access to an introduction, table of contents, excerpt, and index (if there is one). To get around, use the yellow arrows on either side of the book, or the Previous Page and Next Page links at the top of the page. To see thumbnails of all the available pages, click on the See All Sample Pages link at the top center of the page.

Search Inside the Book

This new feature is Look Inside's sassy little sister. It's a feature that let's you search the actual text of more than 120,000 books on Amazon's site. That's more than 33 million pages of text, thank you very much.

You don't have to do anything special to use Search Inside, just perform keyword searches like you always do. If there's a relevant match with Search Inside, a link to an excerpt will show up in your search results at the bottom of each entry.

A few things you should know:

- ✔ **You can't read the entire book online.** Sorry Charlie. First of all, Search Inside only shows the pages with your search term on them. Second of all, once you access a particular page, you can browse forward or back two pages. That's it.

- ✔ **You can perform a search solely on the text of that book.** Once you find a book that has Search Inside, you can go to its Search Inside area and do a search for a different term just within the book's text.

- ✔ **You have to have an Amazon account, including credit card, to use the feature.** When you click the excerpt link from your search results, you'll be asked to sign in. If you don't have an account, you'll be asked to set one up. Amazon, in their FAQ for the feature, explains this as a means of protecting the publishers who participate in the program.

Preordering new releases

No more standing in line waiting for store doors to open. No more clobbering fellow shoppers with your handbag to get the last of the latest Harry Potter books. (Oh wait, that wasn't you. It was me. Oops!) Amazon Preordering has civilized the shopping world.

Figure 5-2: Look Inside gives you a taste of the books you're considering.

There's no secret magic to preordering at Amazon — as a feature it blends right in. A few months before a book is due to release, it will show up on the site. If you go to its detail page, you'll notice that instead of it saying "buy now" in the buy box, it'll say, "preorder now" You put it in your shopping cart or use 1-Click as usual and when the book is released, they'll ship you one.

If you're one of those people who have to have it on the day it's released, don't use this feature. Remember, they have to get it from their warehouse and then ship it to you, which takes a few days.

Specialty Stores

Are you mad about Monty Python? Batty for Barbie? Gaga for George Foreman? Then Specialty Stores are for you.

Specialty Stores are smaller, thematic stores with merchandise culled from Amazon's existing catalog. Some are just subsets within a category store — like the Black and Decker store in Tools and Hardware — and some are cross product, like the Disney store. There are close to 200 Specialty Stores at Amazon — too many to list here — but there is surely one that matches your interests.

To get to the Specialty Store directory, go to the main store directory page (by clicking on the See More Stores link at the top of the page next to the tabs). Then click on the link in the box that looks like Figure 5-3.

Figure 5-3:
Click here to
get to the
Specialty
Stores
directory.

Got Gift? The Amazon Gifts Store

You don't need to go to the Gifts Store to give a gift from Amazon.com. There are no products there that you can't find in another part of the store. But if you need some help, you'll be glad the Gifts Store is there.

The main purpose of the Gifts Store is to help those people who *don't* always get just the right thing. Maybe you don't know much about the giftee except that he's two years old. Maybe you have no idea what to get someone as a housewarming gift. Maybe you're on a tight budget but don't want to look like a tightwad. The Gifts Store lets you browse for gifts by occasion, price, and recipient. You'll also find easy access to registries, wish lists, and other gift services there. For a more detailed look at gift giving Amazon style, check out Chapter 13.

How to send free e-cards

Amazon.com has a free e-card for every occasion. And I mean *every* occasion. I know, because for a few months, I wrote them.

You can get to the E-Cards page from the Gifts Store subnav — just click the Free E-Cards tab — or from the main store directory (and you can get there by clicking the See More Stores link at the top of the page next to the tabs). Once you're there, you'll find a feast of electronic greetings for everything from Wiccan holidays to new babies. Some are animated, some are click-through cards, and some are stills.

Here's how to send one:

1. **On the E-Cards page, browse the categories or use the search function to find an e-card you like.**

   You can click on the thumbnails to view the complete card

2. **Click the Send This Ecard button.**

   You'll be taken to that card's page, which features a bigger view of the card and the option to send with or without a gift certificate (more on the latter in the next section).

3. **Click the new Send this Ecard button.**

   That's right. You click this button on the card's main page too. The next page is a form where you'll "fill out" your card.

4. **Enter the information requested in the fields provided and then click Continue.**

   Enter all your message information, including the recipient's e-mail address; choose whether to add music and pick your appearance and delivery options. The next page is a preview of your card.

5. **Preview your e-card and click Send Now.**

   Make sure the card looks the way you want it to. If it doesn't, click the Edit button and make the necessary changes.

Gift certificates

For the longest time I thought that gift certificates were terrible. "They'll know how much I spent!" I thought. And then I got a gift certificate, and I was thrilled. "You mean I get to go out and buy my *own* birthday present . . . with *your* money?" Delightful!

Amazon has three kinds of gift certificates: paper, e-mail, and e-card. Sending them is a piece of cake (and they go well with birthday cake too).

Sending paper gift certificates

Paper gift certificates are not dead. Some people like to send tangible things — and other people like to get them. Here's how to send a paper gift certificate:

1. **Make your way to the Gift Certificates page by clicking the See More Stores link on the Amazon home page, clicking the Gift Certificates link under the Gifts & Registries heading, and then clicking the yellow Order Gift Certificates button under the Friends and Family option.**

   The Gift Certificates Samples page appears, showing samples of e-mail, e-card, and paper gift certificates.

2. **Click the yellow Order Paper Gift Certificates button.**

   A new page appears, outlining the Amazon.com Safe Shopping Guarantee and providing you with a link to Amazon's secure server.

3. **Click the Click Here to Continue Your Order on Our Secure Server link.**

   You'll come to a page that is both a Sign In screen and a gift certificate form.

4. **Enter your gift certificate information in the fields provided.**

   The "from," "to," and "message" are optional. The amount and the quantity are not. Note that you have to send an amount no less than $5 and no more than $5,000.

5. **Enter your e-mail address and password in the fields provided and click Continue.**

   You do this on the same screen, below the gift certificate info. The next page will ask you to either select a shipping address from the list of addresses associated with your account, or enter a new shipping address.

6. **Choose your shipping address by clicking the appropriate Use this Address button or click Enter a New Address.**

   If you choose the latter, you'll add one step to the process — that of entering the new address. Just enter the info in the fields provided and click Continue. You'll be taken to the credit-card info page.

7. **Enter your credit-card information in the fields provided and then click Continue.**

   You'll be taken to an order confirmation page.

8. **Confirm your order and then click the Place Your Order button.**

   Even though it's a paper gift certificate, you'll receive your confirmation via e-mail.

Sending e-mail gift certificates

Here's how to send an e-mail gift certificate:

1. **Make your way to the Gift Certificates page by clicking the See More Stores link on the Amazon home page, clicking the Gift Certificates link under the Gifts & Registries heading, and then clicking the yellow Order Gift Certificates button under the Friends and Family option.**

   The Gift Certificates Samples page appears, showing samples of e-mail, e-card, and paper gift certificates

2. **Click the yellow Order E-Mail Gift Certificates button.**

   A new page appears, outlining the Amazon.com Safe Shopping Guarantee and providing you with a link to Amazon's secure server.

3. Click the Click Here to Continue Your Order on Our Secure Server link.

You'll come to a page that looks like Figure 5-4.

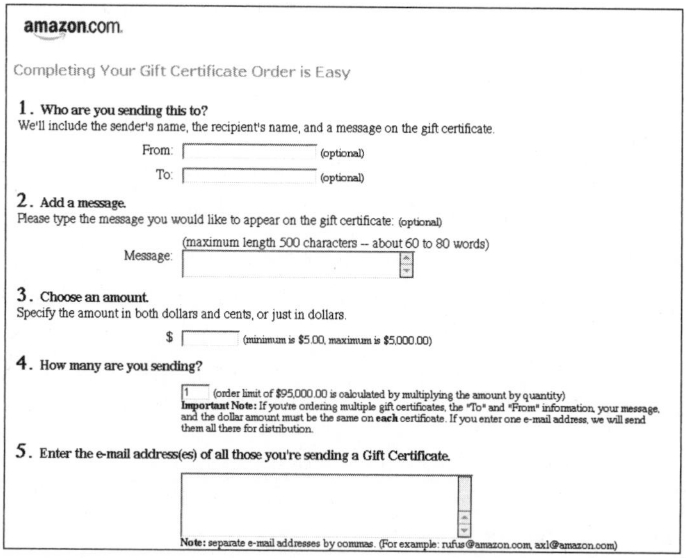

Figure 5-4:
To send a gift certificate, just enter your information in the fields provided.

4. Enter the critical information in the fields provided.

You don't have to enter anything in the To or From fields or even add a message, but you do have to tell them how much (minimum is $5, maximum is $5,000), how many certificates you want to send (because you can send more than one at a time as long as they're all for the same amount), and the e-mail address of the person or people you're sending it to.

5. Sign in by entering your e-mail address and your password in the spaces provided at the bottom of the page and then click the Continue button.

You'll come to a page that asks you to enter your credit-card information. Even if you've already bought with Amazon, you'll have to reenter your credit-card information here.

6. Enter your credit-card information in the fields provided and then click Continue.

You'll be taken to an order confirmation page. Check it carefully to make sure everything is as you want it.

7. Confirm your order and then click the Place Your Order button.

Sending e-cards with a gift certificate attached

This is a good way to make the gift certificate even more personal. Here's how to do it:

1. **On the E-Cards page, browse the categories or use the search function to find an e-card you like.**

   You can click on the thumbnails to view the complete card

2. **Click Send This Ecard.**

   You'll be taken to that card's page. (See Figure 5-5.)

3. **Click the Send with a Gift Certificate button.**

   The next page is a form where you'll "fill out" your card.

4. **Enter the information requested in the fields provided and then click Continue.**

   Enter all your message information, including the recipient's e-mail address; choose whether to add music, and pick your appearance and delivery options. For the gift certificate section, you must enter an amount between $5 and $5,000. When you click Continue, you'll be taken to a preview of your card.

   The gift certificate option will be checked "Yes" as a default, but if you change your mind, you can just check "No" and send the e-card sans cash.

Figure 5-5:
You can choose to send with or without gift certificate.

5. **Preview your e-card and click Continue.**

   Make sure the card looks the way you want it to. If it doesn't, click the Edit button and make the necessary changes. Next you'll come to a sign-in screen.

6. **Enter your e-mail address and your password in the spaces provided and then click the Continue button.**

   You'll come to a page that asks you to enter your credit-card information. Even if you've already bought with Amazon, you'll have to reenter your credit-card information here.

7. **Enter your credit-card information in the fields provided and then click Continue.**

   You'll be taken to an order confirmation page.

8. **Confirm your order and then click the Place Your Order button.**

   That's it!

It's a wrap!

Gifts are more fun when they're wrapped up in fancy paper. When you buy a gift at Amazon, you have the option to have it wrapped; just check the Add Gift Wrap box in the Ready to Buy? box. But it's not free. In fact, here's how much it costs:

- ✔ $2.99 per CD
- ✔ $3.49 per small item
- ✔ $4.49 per medium item
- ✔ $4.99 per large item

If you choose to have it wrapped, your gift will be swaddled up nicely in silver paper with white swirls, with a white grosgrain ribbon and a matching silver gift card (that bears your gift message) — very elegant. If you don't want wrapping, your gift will be, for all intents and purposes, nude — in the box, with a packing slip that bears your gift message. (There's nothing wrong with that, it's just not as festive.)

Chapter 6

Services at Amazon.com

I t's time to put on your Magellan hat, because there's an entire crop of good stuff to be discovered at Amazon that you probably don't know anything about. This *stuff* I speak of isn't really shopping and it isn't really selling. It's services, and they've got a whole slew of them. Most are free, some aren't — and they are, for the most part, undiscovered.

But I don't want to mislead you. We're not talking shoeshines or estate planning here. The services you'll find at Amazon are definitely shopping related. In fact, if you join the seven other people who know about them, I think you'll find that Amazon's services make your shopping even better.

In this chapter, I guide you through a generous handful of the services you can find at Amazon. I tell you what they are, what they're good for, and how to actually use them.

Get the 411 in Real Time: Amazon Chat

I love to chat. In grade school I got very good marks for school work and very bad marks for classroom behavior — too much talking in class (and also chewing the occasional forbidden chunk of Hubba Bubba). So it pleases me that I'm never more than three or four clicks away from a good discussion.

Amazon Chat could be a great service, and not just for chatty Cathys like me. It's easy to use, it's free, and it's a natural fit for getting feedback on products you're considering from people who've actually used them. The truth is, though, Amazon.com Chat is relatively unpopulated. So you won't find people in every chat room at any given time. Another good place to chat is at `groups.google.com`. (You don't have to type the "www" but if you do it's okay — it'll take you to the same place.)

That said, it's always worth a shot. Right now, Amazon has about 50 different chat rooms spread out over 7 categories: books, DVD, electronics, cameras, PC & video games, music, and toys. Chatting itself is actually pretty simple. You need to be the proud owner of an Amazon.com account — e-mail and password — and you need to be 13 years of age or older. If you're both, you can chat. Here's how:

1. **Click the See More Stores link at the top right of the page.**

   The link is right above the main nav; clicking it takes you straight to the store directory.

2. **Under the Services heading, click the Chat link.**

   You'll come to the main Amazon.com Chat page.

3. **From the Browse Amazon.com Chat box on the left, click the name of the chat room that interests you.**

   You've got nearly 50 to choose from! When you choose one, a dialog box will pop up and ask you to confirm that you've read the user agreement and that you're over the age of 13.

4. **Check the Terms and Conditions/Age Verification box and then click Continue.**

   You should actually read the agreement or at least scan it. To do that, click the Terms and Conditions link in the dialog box. After you click Continue, you'll come to a window that looks like Figure 6-1. The square at the top left is where you can view the chatting and read other people's comments. The square next to it on the right shows you who's in the room; the field just below those two squares is where you enter your comments.

5. **Type in your first bit of chat in the field provided and then click Send.**

   You'll see your text appear in the top left window along with other chatters. That's it! You're chatting.

You can use the Block and Whisper buttons to customize your chatting experience. If there's a nimrod in the chat room and you don't want to see their comments, you can block them by clicking on their name in the In the Room window and then clicking the Block button. If you change your mind about them, simply unblock. You can also whisper (that is, only talk to certain people in the chat room). To do that, click on the names of the people you *don't* want to talk to (in the In the Room window) and then click the Whisper button. Your chat will only show up in the windows of the people you didn't choose. The others won't see your input until you "unwhisper" them.

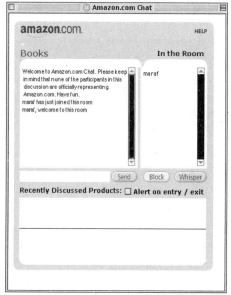

Figure 6-1:
Chat rooms
are a great
place to get
the goods
on the
goods you
want.

Chatting in a chat room is not exactly like chatting in your living room for two main reasons. One, you have to type. Two, you don't know these people. So here are a few good rough-and-ready rules to follow for any online chatting (and Amazon chat is no exception).

✔ **Never give out your personal information in a chat room!** You are chatting with strangers to get info and maybe pass a little time. Amazon does not closely monitor these chat rooms and there is no reason — ever — for you to have to give anyone your real name, credit-card info, e-mail address, and so on. So don't do it!

✔ **Be Polite.** Just because you're sitting in your jammies, eating chocolate chips straight from the bag, enjoying your relative anonymity, doesn't mean you should abuse it. No bad language. No rudeness. Be nice in the chat room. Even if someone else isn't.

✔ **Don't type in all caps.** BECAUSE THAT'S THE INTERNET EQUIVALENT OF SHOUTING. So check to make sure that your "caps lock" button isn't on. Otherwise people will think you're a newbie, or a jerk.

✔ **Don't lie.** Especially in an Amazon chat room, because people are genuinely there to get solid information. Electronic communication is often a breeding ground for little misrepresentations. (Hey! You said, "6'2" with rugged good looks . . . ") I am all for exploring your inner fantasy life, but not in the Amazon chat rooms. Keep it honest and keep your karma clean.

Setting Up Corporate Accounts

Hey big spenders! Spend a little time setting up a corporate account. Actually, corporate accounts at Amazon aren't necessarily for big spenders. They're for companies or organizations that buy from Amazon on a regular basis. So why would someone want a corporate account instead of just using a credit card? Here are the three reasons Amazon gives (and I think they're good ones):

✔ **You can pay by purchase order.** Or rather, your employees can pay by purchase order. This will spare them (and your accounting department) the hassle of using a personal credit card and getting reimbursed. It's also a good way for your company to keep track of purchases made by employees — it puts all the info in one central location.

✔ **You can get a line of credit.** That way you get a monthly bill from Amazon. Why is this good? Lots of reasons, I'm sure, but the one that comes to mind is that you get to hold on to your money longer.

✔ **You can add additional purchasers to your account.** So you're not always the one stuck doing the shopping, for crying out loud.

✔ **You can track purchase history across your organization.** Why is Frank in accounting spending hundreds of dollars a month on self-help books? Without a corporate account you would never have known.

Setting up a corporate account is easy. Here's how to do it:

1. **Under the Services heading, click the Corporate Accounts link from the store directory.**

    The Corporate Accounts at Amazon.com page appears, ready to do your bidding.

    You can get to the store directory by clicking the See More Stores link at the top right of the page, right above the main nav.

2. **Click the yellow Open a Corporate Account button in the box in the left column.**

    You'll come to a sign-in screen.

3. **Enter your email address and password in the fields provided and click Continue.**

   You'll come to the Account info page. Notice that at the top of the page there are four icons telling you where you are in the process.

4. **Enter your contact information, your company information, and a name for your account. Then click Continue.**

   The next page you come to will ask you to enter the shipping address associated with the account. You'll have the option to use the shipping address you entered on the last screen or enter a new address.

5. **Click the yellow Use This Shipping Address button or enter a new shipping address and click Continue.**

   You'll come to a review screen. Make sure that all your information is correct. If not, use the Edit buttons to go back to the previous screens to make changes.

6. **Click Continue.**

   You'll come to the Payment Method screen.

7. **Choose a payment method.**

   You have two choices here. You can apply for a line of credit — to do that you simply fill out a form that will look like Figure 6-2. Or you can enter a credit-card number. If you choose the credit-card option, you'll enter your credit-card information as if you were setting up a personal Amazon account.

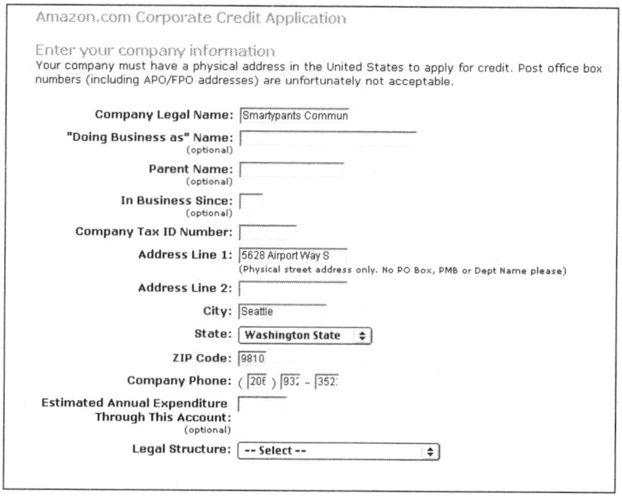

Figure 6-2: Enter your information to apply for a line of credit.

Amazon.com Corporate Credit Application

Enter your company information
Your company must have a physical address in the United States to apply for credit. Post office box numbers (including APO/FPO addresses) are unfortunately not acceptable.

Company Legal Name: Smartypants Commun
"Doing Business as" Name: (optional)
Parent Name: (optional)
In Business Since: (optional)
Company Tax ID Number:
Address Line 1: 5628 Airport Way S
(Physical street address only. No PO Box, PMB or Dept Name please)
Address Line 2:
City: Seattle
State: Washington State
ZIP Code: 9810
Company Phone: (20E) 93. – 352.
Estimated Annual Expenditure Through This Account: (optional)
Legal Structure: -- Select --

To qualify for a line of credit, you must have a tax identification number. Also, you don't have to apply for a line of credit immediately. You can set up your corporate account with a credit card and apply for the line of credit at any time.

At the Movies in Your Neck of the Woods

Movie Showtimes is a service so filled with goodness, I hardly know where to begin. First off, let me say that if you're a movie buff and you hold on to the Sunday paper in case you want to see a movie during the week . . . don't. You can get movie showtimes in a few seconds at Amazon — for free, of course. Here's how:

1. **Under the Services heading, click Movie Showtimes in the store directory.**

   The Movie Showtimes page appears in all its cinematic glory.

   You can get to the store directory, you know, by clicking the See More Stores link on any page of the site.

2. **Enter your zip code in the field provided and click Submit.**

   You'll see the Zip Code field at the top center of the Movie Showtimes home page.

That's it! You'll get a search-results-style list with theaters and showtimes in your area. It's so simple and so wonderful. But it's just the tip of the Movie Showtimes iceberg (*Titanic* reference! *Titanic* reference!). Here are some other things you can do from the Movie Showtimes home page:

✔ **Read Reviews.** Click the Now Playing link and you'll find your way to hundreds of both editor and customer reviews for movies that are in the theaters now.

✔ **Get a Sneak Preview.** A complete listing of soon-to-be-released movies is waiting in the Coming Soon box on the lower-right side of the screen.

✔ **Watch Trailers.** That's right. Movie trailers right on your computer. The selection of trailers you find in the Featured Trailers section isn't nearly as broad as the selection in Coming Soon or Now Playing, but it's still cool.

✔ **Sign up to get movie show times e-mailed to you.** Just sign in and enter your ZIP code in the box at the upper right of the Movie Showtimes home page and you get an e-mail each Friday with local show times.

And a Bite to Eat

The Restaurant section at Amazon is relatively new and growing. Right now, it covers Boston, New York, Chicago, San Francisco, Washington D.C., and Seattle.

What you find in the Restaurant section are restaurant vitals (address, phone number, and price range), menus, and customer reviews. What you don't find are editorial reviews. In other words, this section is entirely built by customers. It's not a mini-Frommers.

Finding restaurants

You find restaurants the same way you find anything else at Amazon.com. You search for them. Use the Restaurant Search box at the top-left column on the Restaurant home page to find the restaurant you're looking for. A few things to note:

- ✔ **You can use the drop-down menu to search specific cities.** The drop-down includes all six covered cities as well as an All Cities options and the ubiquitous All Products.

- ✔ **You can search by restaurant name or menu item.** So if you're craving Chicken Cordon Bleu and you're in Boston for the weekend, you can find the best pace to get it. One thing to note: Be as specific as you can when searching by dish. I entered "fried chicken" in Seattle and got more than 550 results. That's a lot of chicken.

- ✔ **You *can't* search for restaurants by type.** Per se. If you enter "Mexican" in a keyword search you'll get lots of Mexican restaurants, but you'll also get any restaurant that has a dish with the word "Mexican" in it.

How to submit a menu

When I said that customers built the Restaurant section, I meant it. You, too, can contribute to the site by submitting a menu. Here's how:

1. **Go to the Restaurants home page.**

   You'll come to the menu submission page.

2. **Enter the restaurant information in the fields provided and then click the yellow Submit Menu button.**

   You have to enter the name and choose a city. Optional information includes address, phone number, type of cuisine, and corporate/chain information.

3. **Mail Amazon a hard copy of the menu.**

   Amazon does not trust us to upload images to the restaurant section, and I think that's a good thing. So what you have to do is get a hard copy of the menu (in color and in good condition is a good idea) and send it to: Amazon.com Restaurant Service, 1200 12th Avenue South, Suite 1200, Seattle, WA 98144.

Travel Services

Amazon's Travel Services section is really a combination of partnerships and repurposed content. They've made it convenient for you to plan your trip from soup to nuts by offering up their own travel-related products along with the services of Hotwire and the Vacation store. So when I talk about services that aren't free, I need to offer a little clarification: The easy access to partners is the service Amazon is providing — and that's actually free. The travel you book with either Hotwire or The Vacation store, is, however, not free. But you knew that.

Cruising with the Vacation Store

The Vacation Store specializes in cruises, but it also offers vacation packages. You'll find everything there from a three-day jaunt to Mexico to a three-week cruise from Vancouver through the Panama Canal.

To access the Vacation Store, click on Travel in the store directory (you can get there by clicking the See More Stores link at the top of each page). Once at the Travel home page, you can either click on the Vacation Store link in the Browse box or click on the Vacation Store logo in the center of the page.

The Vacation Store is convenient and easy to use, but remember that it's not actually Amazon.com. It's what Amazon calls a "trusted partner," but it's still a separate company. So if you're going to buy a trip with them, make sure you clearly understand their rules, regulations, and policies.

What's Hotwire?

Hotwire is also one of Amazon's trusted partners. It's a full-service travel site where you can do everything from book hotels to buy plane tickets. Possibly the best thing about Hotwire is that it's focused on low prices.

You can access Hotwire by clicking on Travel in the store directory. Like the Vacation Store, Hotwire has a link in the Browse box and a logo in the center of the page.

Hotwire is both a broad and deep site. Using it comfortably may take some practice, but if you can navigate Amazon, you can get around Hotwire.

Here are a few things that you need to know:

- ✔ **You can't change your mind!** Hotwire offers discounted travel — rental cars, airline tickets, hotel rooms, and so on. Once you buy, however, it's yours. No returns, refunds, or changes are allowed.

- ✔ **Use the "Hot-Fare Finder."** This is the box that's front-and-center on the home page (refer to Figure 6-3). It allows you to search all the major categories, and even some combinations, directly from the home page.

- ✔ **Use Customer Care.** Like Amazon, Hotwire has a very thorough help section. You'll see the link to "Customer Care" at the top right of every page on the site. Use it when you need help.

Figure 6-3:
The Hotwire home page.

Shopping by Catalog Online

Shopping by catalog may seem a bit old fashioned, but Amazon gives you access to online catalogs — and this free service *isn't* listed under Services on their Web site. A few (somewhat obscure) product lines are among those that Amazon doesn't stock or ship themselves, but they wanted to offer those to their customers anyway. Their solution was to post popular catalogs for those products on their site and give consumers the information they'd need to order directly from those companies.

The areas in which Amazon offers catalogs are: Industrial Supplies, Medical Supplies, Scientific Supplies, Arts & Hobbies, Car Parts & Accessories, and Pet Toys & Supplies. Here's what you find in those areas of the store:

- ✔ **Lots of catalogs.** Each of the six sections offers a slew of catalogs. If you're not familiar with any of them, you might check out Most Popular in the subnav.

- ✔ **Complete digital versions.** You'll be able to go through each catalog page by page.

- ✔ **Customer reviews.** There are reviews of the catalogs themselves, not products within the catalogs.

- ✔ **Cataloger telephone numbers.** You'll find this in a box at the top right of the individual catalog page, below the subnav.

Here are a few things to keep in mind when using this service:

- ✔ **You're not ordering from Amazon.com.** You're ordering directly from that specific cataloger. So make sure you get to know their policies before you buy.

- ✔ **You won't be able to pay using your Amazon account.**

- ✔ **You won't be able to track your order status on Amazon's site.** Because you're placing an order with the cataloger directly, Amazon will have no record of your transaction.

Chapter 7

The Strange, the Special, and the Super Cheap

· ·

In This Chapter

▶ Exploring Auctions and zShops

▶ Getting the lowdown on Amazon Outlet

▶ Making the most of Specialty Stores

· ·

*E*verybody (even my mom) knows that Amazon sells books. Lots of people know that Amazon sells music and videos. Some people know they're selling things like toys and electronics. And these are just their big category stores! Hardly anyone knows that Amazon has Auctions or an Outlet. Ask some guy on the street what a zShop is and he'll likely mutter something about vintage Datsuns. And Specialty Stores — there are 205 of them. 205.

These are the best-kept secrets of Amazon.com, the unsung heroes of shopping. They're where you can find truly strange — and often very cheap — stuff. But these shops are also trickier waters to navigate, and they raise a bounty of good questions: Who owns zShops and how do I find what I want there? How do I choose between a factory-reconditioned blender and a used blender? Where is this "outlet" and will I be forced to eat a mammoth soft pretzel when I get there?

In this chapter, you will navigate your way around the wilds of Amazon. I'll give you a thorough walk-through of Auctions and zShops. I'll cover the different things you can find there and what you should know about buying them. I'll show you the Outlet (and, no, you won't have to eat any soft pretzels or any fudge) and show you how to figure out if you're getting a good deal. And last, but certainly not least, I'll take a close look at Specialty Stores and show you what it's like to boutique shop on the Web!

Auctions & zShops

This is where you'll find the truly unique products at Amazon, because both Auctions and zShops are "stocked" by users, not by Amazon. That also means you need to be diligent about staying informed when you buy.

You can access both Auctions and zShops from the store directory. To get there, simply click on the See More Stores link at the top of each page next to the tabs. Auctions and zShops are under the Bargains heading.

Going, going, gone!

Online auctions are a great idea . . . that eBay had first. Amazon came in a close second, but eBay has definitely cornered that market. (And if you want to get way into the online auction scene, check out Marsha Collier's book, *eBay For Dummies.*) A cornered market isn't such great news for Amazon — but it's actually good news for you. Here's why:

✔ **Amazon Auctions are easier to navigate.** If you've ever even done a search on eBay, you know that housing the world's largest online auctions community can be a little bit overwhelming. (You may want to bust out that book even before you look.) Amazon's auctions are not so overwhelming. Let me put it to you this way: when I search for "Christian Dior" on Amazon I get 519 search results. When I search on eBay, I get 4,025. Of course, the flip side to this is that there's less selection at Amazon, which is why I encourage you to shop both! (See the next bullet.)

✔ **You can use both sites.** That's right. Forget loyalty, my friends. Bargain shopping is a take-no-prisoners quest. Maybe Amazon can't shop at eBay, but you can. Amazon went into the auction biz a heartbeat too late, but you increased your chances of finding that strange and special something. Search both sites. If you find it at Amazon, start bidding there. (You'll probably get it cheaper.) If you don't find it, go to eBay. Of course, if you're selling and you only have one of the item you're going to list, you can only list it at one site. After all, if you put two listings up you'll likely have two winners. One item and two winners equal auction unhappiness.

✔ **You can find better deals on Amazon.** There are fewer people competing for the goods at Amazon. So things just don't get bid up the same way they do at eBay. You won't *always* get a better deal, but less competition is a good place to start.

✔ **You can pay with your Amazon account.** No dealing with PayPal or money orders, or check's in the mail stuff. Amazon has created an auctions payment system called Amazon.com Payments that's virtually seamless. No need to sign up for anything new. Just click away!

So what do you find at Amazon Auctions? Almost anything. Here are the categories on the Auctions directory page (which you can access by clicking Browse Categories in the Auctions subnav): Art & Antiques, Books, Cars & Transportation, Clothing & Accessories, Coins & Stamps, Collectibles, Comics, Cards & Sci-Fi, Computers & Software, Electronics & Photography, Family & Living, Food & Beverages, Home & Garden, Jewelry, Gems & Watches, Movies & Video, Music, Sports, Tools & Hardware, Toys & Games, Travel & Real Estate, and Other Goods & Services. So you might find a used juicer, a vintage Lone Ranger lunchbox, a diamond ring, or anything else you can think of that's legal. Who knows? That's what makes it fun.

Bidding

Bidding on an auction is somehow thrilling — even online. To bid at Amazon Auctions, you'll need to have an Amazon account in place and be signed in (if you're not, they'll ask you to do that en route). These instructions are for first time bidders. Once you join the ranks of Auctions buyers, you'll get to skip a few of the setup steps and bidding becomes even easier.

So here's how you do it:

1. **Find an item you want to bid on.**

   You can get to the Auctions home page by clicking on the See More Stores link (at the tops of each page to the right of the tabs) and then on Auctions (under Bargains). Browse the categories or do a search just the way you would for any other item at Amazon.

2. **Enter your maximum bid in the appropriately named Enter Your Maximum Bid text box.**

   Figure 7-1 shows an Auction detail page. The bidding box is on the right side of the page. Your maximum bid is the most you're willing to pay for the item, but not necessarily what you *will* pay for the item. Amazon's system pits bidders against each other automatically, upping the ante little by little, until there's a winner. So if you're bidding against other people whose maximum bids are significantly lower than yours, you may end up getting a real deal!

3. **Click the Bid Now! button.**

   You'll come to a Sign In screen.

4. **Enter your e-mail address and passwords in the fields provided and click the Sign In Using Our Secure Server button.**

   You'll come to the Billing Address page, which shows you every address ever associated with your account, including the addresses of people you've sent gifts to. You'll be asked to choose one as a billing address or enter a new address for billing.

5. **Choose your billing address from the list of possible addresses or enter a new billing address and click Continue.**

   Choose the address that goes with the credit card you'd like to pay with by clicking the Use This Address button next to it. Clicking that button has the same effect as clicking Continue — it takes you to the credit card/nickname/agreement page.

6. **Review your credit-card information and billing address and check the box that states that you've read and agree to the participation agreement.**

   Make sure they're showing the credit card that you want to use for your Amazon Payments. When you're asked to read and agree to the participation agreement, definitely read it. Auctions are not the same as regular purchases — and the agreement clearly outlines the differences.

7. **Give yourself a nickname and then click Continue.**

   Your nickname is how you show up as a buyer or seller on the Auctions site. Amazon will give you a default nickname — probably something close to your e-mail address — but you are free to change it. When you click Continue, you'll come to the confirmation page.

8. **In the new page that appears, confirm your bid.**

   This is your last chance — to review the details of your auction and to change your mind. Make sure you take more than a cursory glance at the details because once you click, you're committed. When you're sure, click the Confirm Your Bid button.

Amazon lets you know via e-mail if you've been outbid, and gives you an opportunity to raise your maximum bid. They're good about keeping you in the game. In fact, one difference between Amazon's auctions and auctions at eBay is that at Amazon, if a new bid is received with less than ten minutes to go in the auction, the auction is automatically extended for an additional ten minutes. So you don't have to worry about someone creeping in at the last second and snatching up your item. If you win your auction, they'll send you an e-mail notifying you — very exciting!

If you're desperate to have some cherished item and you don't want to risk losing the auction, you can use the Take-It Now option. This is a fixed price that the seller is willing to take for the item. It's higher than the minimum bid, but it's a sure thing. You can also use 1-Click to buy auction items with Take-It Now, but unlike usual Amazon 1-Click shopping, you can't cancel a 1-Click Auctions take-it now purchase.

Figure 7-1:
An Auction
detail page
and the Bid
Now box.

Everything from A to zShops

zShops is a collection of smaller merchants (we're not talking Macys here), selling just about everything at a fixed price. You'll find individuals like you and me running zShops and even small companies (such as the jewelrynetwork.com) selling through Amazon zShops.

As with auctions, zShops are run by people other than Amazon. What Amazon provides is (simply) the venue. Product selection within any given zShop can be very eclectic indeed. It's something of an online bazaar.

Each of the zShops merchants has a storefront in zShops. But you don't actually shop zShops by storefront. Instead, it's set up the way all Amazon stores are arranged — by category. You can access several of the categories in the Browse box on the left side of the page or, to access them all, click Browse Categories in the zShops subnav. You can also do a search for items within zShops. So how do you access these "storefronts" I've mentioned?

Let's say you're looking to buy a vintage lunchbox. You might browse the categories or do a search and make your way to a detail page for a vintage lunchbox. (See Figure 7-2 for a zShops detail page.) On that page, you'll see a link next to the bolded "merchant". Click on that and you'll find yourself at that merchant's storefront. That's an easy way to access storefronts — by first landing on the detail page of an item that interests you.

What you'll find at a zShops storefront varies from merchant to merchant. Some merchants do very little with their storefronts and some really dress theirs up. You may find a collection of similar products or a hodgepodge of stuff. Some people use zShops to list just one high-ticket item at a fixed price (because they can't sell it through Marketplace and they don't want to auction it off).

Here are two important things to look for when you visit a merchant's storefront:

✔ **Feedback Rating.** Actually, this is *the* most important thing. You'll find the Feedback — how customers would rate their experience with the merchant — just below the navigational boxes on the left side of the page. Remember, you're not buying from Amazon here, so it's essential that you do your homework. The highest rating is 5 stars and the lowest is 0. Make sure you consider not only the total score, but also how many people rated the seller.

✔ **Company Information.** In the upper-right corner of the storefront, below the subnav, is a spot for merchants to tell buyers about their company. Click on the link that begins "Learn more about" and you come to that merchant's information page. Here you can discover important things — like what payment methods they accept and what their shipping and returns policies are — and some more fluffy stuff — like what their company is all about.

Figure 7-2:
Get to
merchant
storefronts
from the
zShops
detail
pages.

Payment, shipping, and other important matters

Buying from Auctions and zShops is fun. It's also very different from buying directly from Amazon.com. Here's why:

- ✔ **You can't always cancel your order.** In fact, with Auctions, after you confirm your bid, you've committed to buying it. If you win, it's sold and it's yours. Period. Some zShops merchants will let you cancel an order, but you have to deal with them directly.

- ✔ **You can't always return things.** Again, Auctions sellers won't let you return (unless it's a very, very nice and patient person). zShops merchants are required to accept returns, but they have their own policies, so make sure you know what they are before you buy.

- ✔ **Amazon is not shipping your order.** The individual seller is, so shipping charges and times may vary.

- ✔ **You can't use gift certificates to buy from zShops or Auctions.** I'm guessing that this is something that will eventually change, but right now — because you're not really buying from Amazon — you can't put gift-certificate cash toward Auctions or zShops purchases.

The good news is you use Amazon.com Payments to pay. So the paying process is seamless. You pay Amazon and they pay the seller, which is easier for you and just like buying from Amazon directly. Some sellers also allow other forms of payment, but take my word for it, Amazon.com Payments is the way to go.

Outlet

I love outlet malls (despite my flippant comments about the soft pretzels and fudge factories). I love them because I love a good deal and I'm not ashamed to admit it. (I also love soft pretzels and fudge, but I am a little ashamed about that.)

To access the Amazon.com Outlet, just click on the See More Stores link at the top of the page to the right of the tabs. You'll find it in the store directory under the Bargains heading. And bargain-licious it is!

Amazon's Outlet is bigger and better than any outlet you'll find in the physical world. There are literally hundreds of "stores" in the Amazon.com Outlet with thousands of products on sale. Every Amazon category, most every Amazon partner, and many Amazon smaller partners are represented in the outlet. Hold on to your purse strings, people. It's a dangerous place for any crazed bargain hunter carrying money.

Bargains vs. Used vs. Factory Reconditioned

The Amazon.com Outlet is a little bit different than your average outlet mall because they don't just sell new products for less. They also sell used merchandise and factory-reconditioned merchandise. So what's the difference? Table 7-1 gives you a quick look at the three types of merchandise in the Amazon.com Outlet.

Table 7-1	"Bargain," "Used," and "Factory Reconditioned"
Type of Product	**Description**
Bargain	These are your basic sale and clearance items. They're new, in perfect condition, and haven't been owned before.
	In books, they'll probably be "remainders" — publishers' overstocks that just didn't sell as well as the publisher predicted. You can often find hardback books for about $5. In the Music world the extras are called "cut-outs" and you'll find lots of those in the Music outletIn the other products lines, they're likely to be items that an Amazon.com buyer just bought too many off. Lucky for you!
Used	These are Marketplace items that are being repurposed and offered in the Outlet. In other words, these are items being sold by individuals, not by Amazon — so all the usual rules of buying from a non-Amazon entity apply. You'll only find used items in the following categories: Books, Camera & Photo, DVD, Electronics, Music, Video, and Video Games.
Factory Reconditioned	These are items that were returned to the manufacturer for one reason or another (sometimes because they were broken but often "just because"). The manufacturer thoroughly cleans, inspects, and, if necessary, repairs the item, and then sells it again at a dramatically reduced cost. The upshot: great prices and more often than not, it works perfectly because it's actually been tested. The downside: It may not come in its original packaging so it won't make a great gift.

How good are the deals?

Sometimes they are outstanding (I just bought a pair of red leather Kaepa tennies for $9.99, down from $49.99) and sometimes not so great (like two dollars off a $25 book). How do you know you're getting a good deal? The obvious answer is to look at the list price versus the sale price. When you see a 75 percent discount, you know that's got to be good. But there is another good way to check. Do a Web search before you buy.

You can use Google to search from the Amazon site. On most store home pages at Amazon.com, there's a Web-search box just beneath the Amazon site-search box. Use it to find out what your item is selling for on other sites. If you're getting ready to buy a pair of red leather Kaepa tennies, search for "red leather Kaepa shoes" and see what you come up with. (For the record, no one could touch my $9.99 deal!) I also use this little technique when I'm getting ready to bid on an auction, just to make sure I'm not being snowed.

Specialty Stores

Specialty Stores are the online boutiques of Amazon shopping. There are more than 200 of them (that's a lot of boutiques!) and what makes them fun (and different from the rest of Amazon.com) is that they're thematic: All the products in a given specialty store relate to its theme. But none of the products that you can find in a Specialty Store are unique to that store. They all live somewhere else on Amazon as well.

You can access the Specialty Stores directory from the main store directory. (Just click the See More Stores link and then the Specialty Stores link in the box on the right side of the page.) So why would you shop in a Specialty Store? You'd shop there because you're passionately interested in (say) Lego, Jazz, cult movies, or power tools. This isn't utilitarian shopping where you go to the site and quickly get what you want. Specialty Stores are good for browsing and for satisfying your personal interests. They're also another great way to find gifts, assuming you know what the recipient is into.

There are a few different kinds of Specialty Stores at Amazon. Table 7-2 outlines the various types and gives a few examples of each.

Table 7-2	Specialty Stores at Amazon.com	
Type of Store	*Description*	*Examples*
Brand	Brand stores feature all the products at Amazon from one company (or brand).	KitchenAid, Lego, Sony, Black & Decker
Genre	These stores lives primarily in books, music, and video/DVD.	Westerns, Anime, Cult Movies
Celebrity/ Character	Ah, celebrities and the products associated with them. There are so many celebrity or character-based stores at Amazon, you won't know where to begin.	Emeril Lagasse, James Bond™, Rick Steves, Harry Potter™
Interest/ Activity	These stores pull in all the relevant products that relate to a particular hobby or interest.	Early Adopters, Cooking with Kids, Summer Entertaining, The Router Workshop

Okay, I admit it. Some specialties are lame — just category pages from one of the bigger stores stuck in the Specialty Store lineup. But lots of them are great. My personal favorites are Early Adopters (because those gadgets are amazing) and Cooking with Kids (because they have a great Essentials section).

Where are they?

You'll find Specialty Stores sprinkled throughout the site. You can access them from relevant "big store" category pages or from the Specialty Store directory page. Getting there is easy. Here's how:

1. **Click on the See More Stores link.**

   You'll find it to the right of the main nav on any page of the site.

2. **Click on the Specialty Stores link.**

   This link lives at the top of the Specialty Stores box at the lower-right corner of the page.

Once you're there, you'll find 205 Specialty Stores to choose from. Figure 7-3 is the Specialty Stores directory. Shopping Nirvana!

Figure 7-3:
The
Specialty
Stores
directory is
a complete
roster of
every
"boutique"
at Amazon.

Store Directory > Specialty Stores

Seasonal Stores
Birthday Store
Early Adopters
University Store

Apparel & Accessories
Women
Men
Kids & Baby
Shoes
Maternity
Petites
Women's Plus-Size & Tall
Big & Tall
Dress Shirts Store

Books
Anne Rice
Clifford
Dear America Store
Dino Store
Dr. Seuss
Dungeons & Dragons
e-Books
Emeril Lagasse
Garden Patch
Harry Potter
HOWdesign Studio
I Can Read
IVP Bible Study Store
James Patterson

Electronics
Early Adopters
Gift Ideas
Outlet, Used & Refurbished
Segway Human Transporter
Sony
Today's Deals

Camera & Photo
Canon
Fujifilm
Gift Ideas
Olympus
Outlet, Used & Refurbished
Prints, Sharing & More
Sony
Today's Deals

Toys & Games
Action Man Store
Barbie
Between the Lions
Collectors@toysrus.com
Fisher-Price
Gundam Wing
Imaginarium
Leapfrog
LEGO
Madeline
Pokémon
"R" Zone

Health & Beauty
Baby Bloom
Gifts
GNC Live Well Store
Home Spa
Natural & Organic Store
Pet Store
Salon Hair Care
Weight Management

Music
Beatles Store
Blue Note Records
Box Sets
Children's Music
Free Downloads
Ken Burns Jazz Store
Label Stores
Motown Records
Music Accessories
Music Outlet
Red Hot Organization
Used Music
Verve Music Group

Baby & Baby Registry
Avent
Baby Björn
Baby Outlet
Baby Registry
Books, Music & More

What's with the Segway?

Many an Amazon shopper (and employee) has asked this question. What *is* with the Segway and why does it get its own Specialty Store? (Strictly speaking, the Segway Human Transporter isn't a Specialty Store. It's actually just a detail page — an extremely *detailed* detail page. Figure 7-4 shows just a little bit of what you'll find on the Segway page.) The answer is simple: Jeff loves the Segway. That said, it is an amazing invention, and it's also a unique spot on the Amazon Web site.

First off, for those of you who don't know, the Segway is the "World's first dynamically stabilized Human Transporter." In other words, it's a two-wheeled scooter that's steadied by automatic gyroscopes, sturdy enough to hold an adult, and (so far) legal for traveling on (many, but not all) city sidewalks. Here are a few other interesting bits about the Segway:

✔ **Amazon is the only place to buy it online.** You can also buy it by calling Segway directly or in person at one of the ten dealerships around the country.

✔ **It sells for $4,950 plus shipping and taxes.** This is no run-of-the-mill scooter.

✔ **It can go up to 12 miles per hour.** That may not sound fast, but most people walk around 3 mph.

✔ **It's electric.** That's right. No gas.

✔ **You can rent one for the day.** There are eight rentals shops in the United States. To check out the nearest rental location near you, visit the Segway Web site at

```
www.segway.com/connect/locator/rentals.html
```

There are actually two Segways out there, as the new Segway HT p Series was released in 2003. The HT p Series is lighter, smaller, and about $1,000 cheaper than its predecessor, the HT i Series.

Figure 7-4: Get a lesson in physics on the Segway detail page.

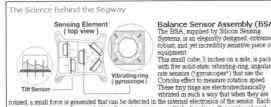

The Science Behind the Segway

Sensing Element (top view)

Tilt Sensor

Vibrating ring (gyroscope)

Balance Sensor Assembly (BSA)
The BSA, supplied by Silicon Sensing Systems, is an elegantly designed, extremely robust, and yet incredibly sensitive piece of equipment.
This small cube, 3 inches on a side, is packed with five solid-state, vibrating-ring, angular-rate sensors ("gyroscopes") that use the Coriolis effect to measure rotation speed. These tiny rings are electromechanically vibrated in such a way that when they are rotated, a small force is generated that can be detected in the internal electronics of the sensor. Each "gyro" is placed at a unique angle that allows it to measure multiple directions. Segway's onboard computers constantly compare the data from all five gyros to determine if any of the five is supplying faulty data--in this condition, it can compensate and use data from the remaining sensors to continue balancing through a controlled safety shutdown. Two tilt sensors filled with an electrolyte fluid provide a gravity reference in the same way your inner ear does for your own sense of balance. The BSA is monitored by two independent microprocessors and is split into two independent halves for redundancy. Even the communication between sides is performed optically to avoid electrical faults on one side propagating to the other.

B side windings

A

B

A side windings

Magnets

Motor
The Segway HT's motors are unique in a number of respects. Produced by Pacific Scientific, a division of Danaher, they are the highest-power motors for their size and weight ever put into mass production.
The motors use brushless servo technology, meaning there are no contacts to wear, arc, and reduce performance. The magnets are constructed of an incredibly powerful rare-earth material: neodymium-iron-boron. Each motor is constructed with two independent sets of windings, each driven by a separate board and motor. Under normal conditions, both sets of windings work in parallel, sharing the load. In the

Chapter 8

Get What You Want: Find It and Suss It Out

*T*here's nothing more frustrating than knowing what you want and not being able to find it. Truth. Everlasting love. A decent pair of black boots. Where are they? You could spend your whole life searching. But not at Amazon.com. Search for "truth" or "love" at Amazon and you'll find thousands of products that offer to fit the bill. Searching is miraculously simple and remarkably fruitful.

Search results, on the other hand, can be something to contend with. So many products, in so many categories! How do you know where to begin? And what do you do when you've finally found that Italian espresso maker? That item you've been hunting for. How do you know if it's really what you wanted after all? Getting the right information is key to successful shopping — especially online when you can't hold the merchandise in your hand — and Amazon is rife with good information. You just have to know where to find it.

In this chapter, I'll show you how to search for the items you want using Amazon's search functions. I'll help you sort through your search results to find what you're really looking for, and I'll show you where you can get the best information on the products you're considering. By chapter's end, you'll be a searching sage. An e-shopping bloodhound!

Search Box: All Products or the Stores

The search box (shown in Figure 8-1) is on every "shopping" page of the Amazon.com site. You won't find it in places like the order pipeline and it occasionally moves to be centered on the page, but otherwise it's there, gracing the top of the left side of the page, just below the navigation bar.

Get to know the search box. Make it your friend, because more often than not, it's where your directed shopping begins.

Figure 8-1:
The search
box, where
shopping
magic
begins.

You'll notice that there are really only three important elements that make up the search box: the search field, the drop-down menu, and the Go button. These are the only elements you need to know to do a basic search at Amazon. Here's how it works:

1. **Enter your keyword/s in the Search field.**

   Keywords can sometimes cause problems, so check out the sidebar entitled The key to keywords" for some good keyword advice.

2. **Choose an option from the drop-down menu.**

   This is what you'll use to decide which part of the site to search. You can choose All Products, or, if you know you're looking for something that is likely to be in a specific store, choose that store for a much narrower search result.

3. **Click the Go button.**

   This is how to get the search going!

The default for the drop-down menu is All Products. If you search without changing it, you'll likely get results from every store at Amazon. That can be a *lot* of results to sift through. If you know what kind of product you're looking for, use the drop-down menu and search a specific store.

The key to keywords

When Amazon adds an item to their store, they aren't just putting it on a shelf somewhere. There's a technical process involved, which includes entering information about the product into their database. They enter all the basic information — title, author, label, manufacturer — and then they enter descriptive information about the product. The idea is to help out when you're searching for something: If you don't know the exact title or name of what you're looking for, you can use keywords like "pleated khakis" or "green sweater" that describe the product. You can also use ISBN numbers or UPC codes as keywords. These numbers identify specific products (ISBNs identify books and UPCs identify just about everything else) and when you use them as keywords, Amazon.com will take you right to that product's detail page.

AAAGHH! Search Results Demystified

Scenario 1: you've just gotten a new puppy and you know you need stuff, but you're not sure what stuff, so you go to Amazon and do an All Products search on "puppy." You are faced with search results that look remarkably like Figure 8-2. What does it mean?!

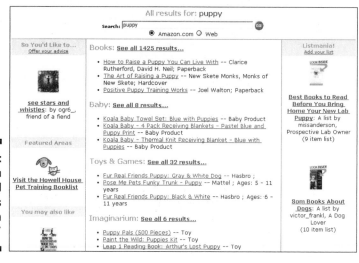

Figure 8-2: Results from an All Products search on "puppy."

Here's a quick anatomy of an All Products search-results page:

- ✔ **If at all possible, the search engine offers you search results from every store.** And for the matches that are sort of miscellaneous, there's the Everything Else category.

- ✔ **You'll find cool extras on the sides of the page.** Notice that the right and left columns feature some interesting Amazon extras — most notably Listmania lists and So You'd Like To guides. Other Amazon customers create these lists and guides. Amazon surfaces them in your search results based on their relevant content. You can find out more about these (and how to create your own) in Chapter 12.

- ✔ **Amazon anticipates possible spelling errors.** At the bottom of the page, you'll see a line that reads (in the case of the "puppy" search) `No matches for 'puppy'. Below are matches for 'poppy'.` That's how they manage to offer restaurant-menu matches on my search for "puppy."

How about Scenario 2? This time, you've already got a new puppy, but you know that what you need is a book on how to train a puppy. So you go to Amazon, type **puppy** in the search field, and use the drop-down menu to select Books. Conveniently, three popular books on raising puppies are listed first. But you still get 1,427 results! What if you don't want one of the three most popular? Are you going to go through 1,427 detail pages? Mais non! Remember, search results are more specific when you enter a more specific set of keywords. To come up with search results that look like Figure 8-3 — a much more manageable 86 — you enter **puppy training**; then select Books from the drop-down menu.

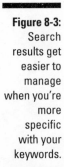

Figure 8-3:
Search results get easier to manage when you're more specific with your keywords.

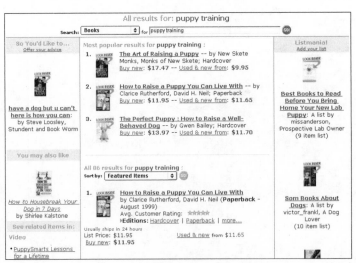

Picky, Picky: Refining Your Search Results

The easiest way to narrow down your search results is to add more specific keywords. Once you've done that, you can then use the drop-down menu that sits at the top of the "All results" list to sort them.

The drop-down menu varies some from store to store, but it usually offers some or all the following choices: Bestselling, Featured Items, Average Customer Rating, Price: Low to High, Price: High to Low, Alphabetical: A to Z, and Alphabetical: Z to A. When you select one of the choices from the drop-down menu, Amazon sorts it accordingly, making it easier to find what you're looking.

In certain stores, like Apparel and Sporting Goods, you can actually refine your search results using the left nav — the links running down the left side of the page. Figure 8-4 shows the results for a search on "puppy" in the apparel store. The left nav lets you refine your search by category, brand, or price by simply clicking on the link that interests you. You'll also notice that each link in the left nav tells you how many results are in each location (in parentheses at the end of each link).

Figure 8-4:
You can refine search results in the apparel store by using the left nav.

Advanced Search

Several stores at Amazon have an Advanced Search function — a search tool specific to the store that'll help you pinpoint exactly what you're hunting for. Table 8-1 outlines which stores have this additional search function, and offers a few tips on how to best use it.

Table 8-1	Advanced Searching
Store	*Tips*
Books	To access Books advanced search, click on Search in the Books subnav. Enter information for author, title, subject, ISBN, and publisher. Use the drop-down menus to further refine your results and to sort — by reader age, by format, by publication date, and so on. Use Power Search, a more technical tool, to enter search terms (according to Amazon's syntax) and qualifiers like "and," "or," and "not."
Music	To access Music advanced search, click on Search Music in the Music subnav. Search music by artist, title, label, and/or (a hidden gem) song title. Want to hear Boom Boom (Let's Go Back To My Room), but don't know which Paul Lekakis album contains the song? You're in luck! You can also choose your format — CD, cassette, DVD audio, and vinyl. This page also offers a link to the classical and opera advanced search page.
Video	To access Video advanced search, click on Advanced Search in the Video subnav. Search by title, actor, and director. Refine your search using the drop-down menus for format, price, release date, rating, genre, and languages. You can also search for used items and subtitled items.
DVD	To access DVD advanced search, click on Advanced Search in the DVD subnav. DVD offers the same search functions as Video plus a few more: picture format, audio type, region code, and a long checklist of special features.
Auctions	To access Auctions advanced search, click on Advanced Search in the Auctions subnav. Search Auctions by keyword, member nickname, or auction ID. Refine your search according to category, zip codes, auction status, and auction location.
Outlet	To access the Outlet's advanced search, click on Advanced Search in the Outlet subnav. Outlet Advanced Search is not so advanced. Search by keyword and refine according to outlet store.

Store	Tips
zShops	To access zShops advanced search, click on Advanced Search in the zShops subnav. Search by keyword, store, and listing ID. Refine your search by category, zip code, status, and location.
Toys & Games	To access the Toys & Games advanced search (which is actually called the "Toy Finder"), click on Toy Finder in the Toys & Games subnav. Search by keyword and use the drop-down menus to further refine your results by age, category, price, or video game system.

Product Information

There's something to be said for being able to handle a product before buying it. That's why so many people were skeptical about online shopping — how an item *feels* is part of the decision-making process. But with the right information, the need to feel diminishes, and the urge for convenience takes over.

You can find all different kinds of product information at Amazon. In fact, certain stores give you access to far more information than you'd find at a comparable brick-and mortar-retailer. So how do you access it? In most of the stores, the left nav on the detail page has a Product Information (or Item Information, or Toy Information, and so on) box like the one in Figure 8-5. This is the master list of the kinds of information Amazon offers for that product. If you don't see that box, then you know that item has limited information on the site; you can find whatever information there is by scrolling below the product image.

Here are the different kinds of product information offered at Amazon.com:

- ✔ **Buying Info:** This is the basic information — price, shipping information, and so on — that you'll find for every product at Amazon. It lives right next to the item's image on the detail page. Occasionally, you'll have to click a link to see complete buying info — especially if there's a lot of info associated with the item you're looking at.

- ✔ **Big Pictures:** Click on images for a bigger view of the goodies you've been ogling from afar.

- ✔ **Product Features or Details:** Many products also have feature information. This is usually a bulleted list of the most prominent characteristics of that item. You'll find this information farther down the detail page, above the reviews.

- ✔ **Technical Specs:** Many items (typically electronic or mechanical things) offer more details in the form of technical specifications. You can access them from the left nav Item Information box on the detail page.

✔ **Product Manuals:** Some products on the site (again, usually electronic or mechanical) have PDF files you can download that contain electronic versions of their manuals. You'll find these in the left nav information box or below the product details on the detail page. If you need some help downloading and viewing PDFs, check out the "Kiss your paper-weight goodbye" sidebar.

✔ **Editorial Reviews:** Amazon hires pros to review their products, so you can be assured that anything they tell you is worth knowing. You'll find these on the detail page, above customer reviews and below product details.

✔ **Customer Reviews:** This is the cornerstone of Amazon's success as a source of information about various products. Customers review the products, giving you the lowdown on what real people think of them. That can be a great help when you're trying to decide what you should and shouldn't buy.

But wait! There's more. When it comes to product information, Amazon is king. Explore the detail pages of the different stores as you visit them. They vary from store to store and each one offers its own informational gems. You'll find things like a link to all the books written by the author whose book you're looking at. You'll see entire segments of the page devoted to showing you like products based on other customers' purchases. On many detail pages, you'll even find customer suggestions on what to buy *instead of* the item you're looking at.

Kiss your paperweight goodbye

PDF, or *portable document format*, is a universal file format created by Adobe. It's used to convert other types of online documents — complete with graphics, images, and text — into files that anyone can read with Adobe's free reader software. You can download this free software from the Adobe site; go to `www.` `adobe.com/products/acrobat/read step2.html` and follow the download instructions. When you've got Adobe Reader installed, you can download all kinds of great stuff (not just technical manuals from Amazon.com).

Striking Infogold: Expert Advice

Sprinkled throughout Amazon.com are little informational gems — checklists, buying guides, articles, and so on — that'll help you make smart buying decisions. These gems are extremely helpful and, unfortunately, a little bit hard to find. In some stores, they're on the subcategory pages under the heading Expert Advice. Other stores put them all together in information centers. But right now, there is no centralized directory, though there are hundreds of guides, articles, and other helpful bits living on the site.

To find these informational gems, you have to happen upon them in the various stores. For example, the digital camera buying guide is on the digital camera page in the Camera and Photo section of the electronics store. But if you want information on buying a car seat for your child, all you have to do is go the resource center (Figure 8-6) in the Baby store — it's a choice in the subnav.

Figure 8-6:
The Resource Center is an excellent place to get information on baby products.

Here's a quick list of the kinds of expert advice you'll find at Amazon:

- **Buying Guides:** Buying guides give you all the basic information you need if you're going to buy a specific type of product (say, a digital camera).

- **Articles:** These are often taken from magazines or other expert sources, and can be anything from a lifestyle piece to a step-by-step how-to project.

- **Checklists/Essentials:** These quick lists show you everything-you-need-to-have or the-basics-you-need-to-have to tackle complicated undertakings. You'll find lots of these in (for example) the Baby store.

- **Tips:** Typically these take the form of a top-ten list of helpful hints.

- **Introduction to:** These are exactly what they sound like — the shopping equivalent of a 101 class. Unlike buying guides, these aren't product-driven. They're hobby-driven!

- **Glossary of terms:** Here's your basic list of important terms and their definitions — handy for talking to salespeople or asking questions of the experts.

Table 8-2 gives you a quick look at which stores have these informational gems and where you'll find them within the stores.

Table 8-2	Expert Advice at Amazon.com	
Store	**Type of Info**	**Where You'll Find It**
Baby	Buying Guides, Checklists, Articles	In the Baby Resource Center. It's a choice in the subnav in the Baby store.
Electronics: Camera & Photo	Buying Guides, Tips, Articles, Introduction To, Glossaries	There is actually a camera-and-photo info center that is home to smaller info centers for digital cameras, film cameras, and camcorders, but you can't get there from the subnav. To access it, go to the category pages for digital cameras, film cameras, or camcorders and scroll down to the Expert Advice header — it should be on the right side of the page.
Kitchen & Housewares	Buying Guides Galore!	In the Kitchen & Housewares info center. Again, not in the subnav, but you can access it from most of the top-level category pages in Kitchen under the Expert Advice header.

Store	Type of Info	Where You'll Find It
Outdoor Living	Buying Guides, Essentials, Articles	Again, not in the subnav, but you can access it from some of the top-level category pages under the Expert Advice header (for example, try Backyard Birding). You can also access it from the Kitchen info center.
Tools & Hardware	Buying Guides Galore!	Again, not in the subnav, but you can access it from some of the top-level category pages under the Expert Advice header. You can also access it from the Kitchen info center.
Electronics	Buying Guides, Tips, Articles, Introduction To, Glossary	There isn't a single, centrally located electronics info center, but you'll find a lot of information sprinkled throughout the Electronics store. Keep your eye out for that Expert Advice header.
Music, Video, DVD	Essentials	Essentials is a choice in the subnav for all three stores. For these particular stores, Essentials are the "must-haves" for specific genres or artists.

Some of these info centers are hard to find, and you can't dig them up by using any of Amazon's search tools. Amazon is always changing, and while the info centers aren't going anywhere, there's no guarantee that the path you took to get there the first time will be the same the next time. One way to find your way back is to bookmark any info center you visit.

Reviews

Reviews are one of the things that make Amazon Amazon. Without them, it'd be tough to buy online. You'll find product reviews for many, but not all, products at Amazon.com. They live on the detail page, usually below the fold (that's the newspaper throwback term for content that you have to scroll to see) under the product information and other marketing stuff. There are a few different kinds of reviews at Amazon:

✔ **Amazon.com Review:** This is written by an Amazon editor who has sampled the product (read the book, used the camera, listened to the CD, whatever). The significant difference between a review and a product description is that a review puts forth an opinion of a product. The description only describes its features or how it works. You'll find reviews all over the store — they're not product specific.

✔ **Amazon.com Product Description:** Product descriptions are detailed accounts of the product's features, but no opinion. You'll find descriptions all over Amazon.com, but particularly in the stores that sell products that can be described objectively — Electronics, Kitchen, Tools, and so on (but not so much in books, music, and DVD/video).

✔ **Customer Reviews:** This is where you'll get the account of any product that's most free of manufacturer's hype. Customers, of course, write customer reviews. Sometime they're insightful and helpful and other times they aren't. It's a good idea to consider an item's customer reviews as a whole. Because, let's face it, not everyone is playing with a full deck, but just about anyone can write a customer review.

✔ **Industry Reviews:** Occasionally, you'll find an editorial snippet from a relevant publication or source (such as *The New York Times* in the Books store). There doesn't appear to be any rhyme or reason as to when these industry reviews show up, but they're a good added voice when you're making a buying decision — and, as you can imagine, they're typically positive reviews.

✔ **Information from the source:** Amazon often includes information that the manufacturer, publisher, label, or studio has provided. This is usually factual stuff — not just a professional opinion — but keep in mind that whoever made the item is in business to *sell* it, so you may not find out much about its shortcomings here. In fact, sometimes this information is a bit fluffy.

It's in the Stars: Customer Reviews

Customer reviews live just below the editorial reviews on the detail page and they are an essential part of any Amazon shopping experience. I think that the best way to find out if a product is worth buying is to check out the customer reviews — carefully. Like I mentioned, customer reviews are almost always unbiased. These people aren't trying to sell. They're just putting their two cents in (and if you want to put in your own two cents, Chapter 12 tells you how); by and large, you can trust them. The key is knowing how to look at each individual review and how to consider the reviews as a whole.

Your standard customer review

Here's a quick anatomy of the customer review (Figure 8-7):

✔ **Stars:** Customers rate reviews on a five-star system, with zero as the worst and five as the best.

✔ **Title:** This is the title given to the review by the reviewer. Often it's a bite-sized version of what they thought of the product (but not always).

✔ **Date:** Lets you know when the review was written. This is more important for products that may go out of date as new versions come on the market — electronics, computers, and so on.

✔ **Top Reviewer Icon:** Occasionally, you'll see an icon next to the reviewer information that says "Top (*insert number here*) Reviewer." It means that this person has written lots of helpful reviews. You'll notice that you have the option to vote on a review. Top Reviewers are chosen because their reviews are voted "most helpful most often."

✔ **Reviewer Info:** A name or an online alias, and where they're from.

✔ **Review Helpfulness:** You may see a statement just above the review that tells you how many people found it to be helpful. This is a part of the review voting system.

✔ **Review:** This is the actual review — what they thought of the product.

✔ **Voting Option:** Below the review is the question, "Was this review helpful to you?" followed by a Yes button and a No button. If you want, you can choose one of the two and click. Your vote will be tabulated with the other votes for that review to contribute to the Review Helpfulness line and, maybe, that person's Top Reviewer status.

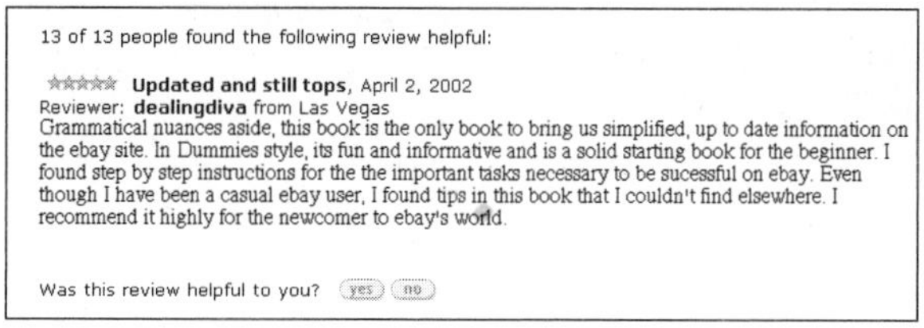

Figure 8-7:
Customer reviews are one of the best ways to find out whether something may be worth owning!

13 of 13 people found the following review helpful:

★★★★★ **Updated and still tops**, April 2, 2002
Reviewer: **dealingdiva** from Las Vegas
Grammatical nuances aside, this book is the only book to bring us simplified, up to date information on the ebay site. In Dummies style, its fun and informative and is a solid starting book for the beginner. I found step by step instructions for the the important tasks necessary to be sucessful on ebay. Even though I have been a casual ebay user, I found tips in this book that I couldn't find elsewhere. I recommend it highly for the newcomer to ebay's world.

Was this review helpful to you? (yes) (no)

Although customer reviews are relatively unbiased, it's important to know whether the customer whose views you're reading is someone you'd agree with. Fortunately, when you're checking out an individual customer review, you can do more than just read it. You can also do the following:

✔ **Look at the reviewer's status.** If that customer is rated a Top Reviewer, the odds are better that the review is good info.

✔ **See whether other people found the review helpful.**

✔ **Look at the reviewers' Friends & Family bio.** If there is one, it's worth checking out. Who the heck are these people? What other things have they bought or reviewed? Do you have anything in common with them?

You should also consider reviews as a whole. Here are a few guidelines:

✔ **Take note of how many reviews an item has.** If an item has hundreds of reviews, it may or may not be great, but it's definitely *popular*. And it's got enough oomph that lots of people chose to write about it.

✔ **Look at the overall stars.** This is, of course, an obvious thing to do, but I'm a control freak and I can't help myself. I had to mention it.

✔ **Read the bad ones.** Keep in mind that if an item has a handful of reviews — let's say ten or fewer — a couple of bad reviews can bring its score down significantly. So scan the list for negative reviews. If you find just one or two, read them. Sometimes kooks get online and write reviews too. It'd be a shame to pass up a good product because of one or two grouchy reviews.

Spotlight Reviews

You may have noticed that the Customer Reviews section starts out with the *Spotlight Reviews* header (as in Figure 8-8). These reviews are chosen daily by Amazon's editorial staff from the pool of reviews deemed most helpful by other customers. Spotlight Reviews are always shown first, above the other customer reviews, as long as there are enough really good reviews to qualify.

For items that have more than a few, Amazon doesn't show all reviews on the detail page. To see them all, click the <u>See all customer reviews</u> link at the bottom of the list showing the reviews.

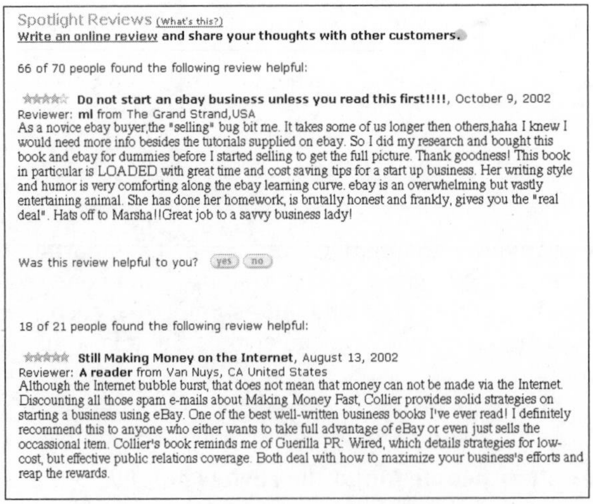

Spotlight Reviews (what's this?)
<u>Write an online review</u> and share your thoughts with other customers.

66 of 70 people found the following review helpful:

★★★★☆ **Do not start an ebay business unless you read this first!!!!**, October 9, 2002
Reviewer: **ml** from The Grand Strand,USA
As a novice ebay buyer,the "selling" bug bit me. It takes some of us longer then others,haha I knew I would need more info besides the tutorials supplied on ebay. So I did my research and bought this book and ebay for dummies before I started selling to get the full picture. Thank goodness! This book in particular is LOADED with great time and cost saving tips for a start up business. Her writing style and humor is very comforting along the ebay learning curve. ebay is an overwhelming but vastly entertaining animal. She has done her homework, is brutally honest and frankly, gives you the "real deal". Hats off to Marsha!!Great job to a savvy business lady!

Was this review helpful to you? (yes) (no)

18 of 21 people found the following review helpful:

★★★★★ **Still Making Money on the Internet**, August 13, 2002
Reviewer: **A reader** from Van Nuys, CA United States
Although the Internet bubble burst, that does not mean that money can not be made via the Internet. Discounting all those spam e-mails about Making Money Fast, Collier provides solid strategies on starting a business using eBay. One of the best well-written business books I've ever read! I definitely recommend this to anyone who either wants to take full advantage of eBay or even just sells the occassional item. Collier's book reminds me of Guerilla PR: Wired, which details strategies for low-cost, but effective public relations coverage. Both deal with how to maximize your business's efforts and reap the rewards.

Figure 8-8:
Spotlight
Reviews are
the cream of
the crop.

Chapter 9

Window-Shopping on the Web

*I*n the early days of Amazon, there was a favorite expression used by the higher-ups. They liked to refer to the site as a "discovery machine." While I always thought that sounded oddly Wonka-esque and a little embarrassing, I agree with the sentiment. Amazon is a great place to discover things. Unlike a brick-and-mortar retailer, Amazon never cleans house. It doesn't have to. Instead, it gets bigger — like an onion, growing layer after layer of products and content. Those layers make it a great place to explore and to find things that you didn't even know were out there. Things like Book Accessories (which includes everything from bookmarks to Bible covers) or the Artisan Gallery (a collection of handmade garden art and fixtures in the Outdoor Living store).

But not everyone uses the site that way. Most new customers who come to Amazon are *searchers* — they have an item in mind, they use the Search feature to find it, and they're done. Once they spend a little bit of time at Amazon, though, they find there's a lot more than quick searching to be done. That's where Browse — the Web equivalent of window-shopping — comes in. Amazon is set up for it — and it's far more than just a leisurely e-stroll.

At Amazon, *browse* isn't just a verb. It's an adjective too (as in *browse node*), and it's a noun (as in *doing a music browse*). In this chapter, I explain the meaning of (and some of the thinking behind) all three usages. I show you how to browse around the store, point out some interesting stops along the way, and explain how browsing different stores can be a different experience. This is the part where you find out how to have some fun at Amazon, but be warned! Browsing the site is a really good way to make an hour or two (and yeah, okay, some of your cash) magically disappear.

The Basics of Browse

If you've ever gone to Amazon and found yourself clicking around the site on stuff that catches your eye, then you've already browsed. It's not difficult. In fact, browsing comes naturally to us shoppers. But there are a few things to know that can make you a better browser:

- **Scroll!** The pages at Amazon are loooong. If you're not scrolling down well below the fold (and by "below the fold" I mean any area beneath what's immediately visible when you come to the page), you're missing more than half of the good stuff. (I'll get to that good stuff later in the chapter.)

- **Go the whole nine yards.** At least once, browse from the top to the bottom. By that I mean, check out every layer offered within a store. For example, your breadcrumb trail — the series of links that show your path to your current location — might look like this: Kitchen & Housewares ⇨ Categories ⇨ Coffee, Tea & Espresso ⇨ Coffee Machines ⇨ Drip Coffee Machines. That way, you'll have a better sense of how many layers of detail there are in a given store.

- **Use the info centers.** Amazon is plumb full of excellent information and lots of it lives in the info centers. (See Chapter 8 for a list of topics and locations.) Spend some time browsing those. It's like reading a good magazine and shopping at the same time.

What's a browse node and should I have it removed?

The short answer to that question is, "No." As for what it *is*, the simplest explanation is that a browse node is Amazon's term for any of the various groupings that make up the site structure — sort of like the e-commerce equivalent of departments, aisles, and shelves.

Think of the millions of products at Amazon.com. If all anyone ever wanted to do was search for things, those products could all float around in the ether in no particular order at all. It wouldn't matter because the Search feature would use keywords to pull up products that matched. But just as people like to shop in physical stores, people want to wander the electronic aisles of Amazon. So products are organized into meaningful groups and each of those groups is a browse node.

But not all browse nodes are created equal. There are different levels of browse nodes. The stores are the highest level, and every page beneath them (until you get down to the detail page) is another browse node. Lots of products appear in a variety of different nodes. Of course, you can find them in their actual category (for example, jazz music). But they might also be on an Essentials list — which is a node of its own. Or they might be in a Specialty Store (another kind of node). When you're exploring the site, you're jumping from node to node. Here's another way to think of it: The Search feature deals with individual products; Browse deals with groups of like products.

Figure 9-1:
A bread-
crumb trail
in the
Bookstore.
Click the
links to
access
nodes
higher up in
the store.

✔ **Use the breadcrumb trail.** You are *not* lost! At the top of browse node pages there's a breadcrumb trail (pictured in Figure 9-1) so you always know where you are.

✔ **Sort it!** You can actually sort browse lists. For example, go to the mystery section in Books and you'll find that you can sort your browse list by "featured," "recommendations," "top sellers," "new releases," and "used." It's a good way to get a different look at the category you're exploring.

✔ **Bookmark it.** If you find something nifty during your browsing adventure, use your browser's bookmark feature to bookmark it. There's nothing more frustrating than trying to find something and coming up blank. Bookmark it and you'll always be able to get there.

Don't forget to scroll: Juicy tidbits below the fold

Back in the day, everything worth anything had to be "above the fold." The phrase comes from the newspaper world — where there actually was a fold. In terms of the Web, "above the fold" encompasses everything you see on the page when you open up your browser, but before you scroll. It's still a good place to be if you're someone trying to sell something on Amazon, but if you're a shopper, limiting yourself to things above the fold is a travesty!

Lots and lots of good stuff lives below the fold. It varies depending on what type of page you're on — store page, category page, detail page, and so on — but one juicy morsel that's always below the fold is the Bottom of the Page Deals (See Figure 9-2). This is a random assortment of deeply discounted products. They change daily, so remember to take a look each time you visit.

Bottom of the Page™ Deals for September 18
Amazon.com = **low prices**. Save up to **50%** on these **one-day-only** deals.

	Our Price	You Save	
Sabatier Precision 14-Piece Stainless-Steel Knife Block Set Save over 80% on Sabatier's Precision 14-piece cutlery block set.	$29.99	$210.01 (88%)	☐
ThermaCare Air-Activated HeatWraps (18 Wraps) Wear these heat wraps under your clothes for hours of powerful pain relief.	$49.50	$13.41 (21%)	☐
SOLD OUT FOR TODAY Kodak Max Versatility Plus 800 Color Print Film, 16 Rolls (384 Exposures) Save 60% on the versatile film that combines the benefits of low and high speed.	$35.98		
Memorex 80 Minute/700 MB 48X CD-R Discs (100-Pack Spindle) Get 100 Memorex 80-minute CD-Rs--shipped to your door free.	$27.99	$12.00 (30%)	☐
Starbucks Espresso Roast Whole Bean Coffee, 6 12-Ounce FlavorLock Bags (72 ounces total) A delicious caramel-sweet espresso blend at an irresistible price.	$39.99	$5.00 (11%)	☐
HoMedics ES-1 Envira-Spa Aroma & Sound Machine Save 40% and transform your home into a tranquil aromatherapy spa.	$29.99	$15.01 (33%)	☐
Memorex 4.7 GB DVD+RW Discs (10-Pack) Ideal for pre-mastering, high-volume data recording, and archiving.	$29.99	$20.00 (40%)	☐
Ray-O-Vac C Alkaline Batteries (36 Batteries) A great low price on high-quality Ray-O-Vac batteries.	$35.97	$35.85 (50%)	☐
Nicorette 2mg Stop Smoking Aid, Mint Flavor (192 Pieces) Enjoy a smoke-free future with low-cost Nicorette!	$59.88	$24.68 (29%)	☐

 FREE Super Saver Shipping on orders over $25. See details.   [▶ Add selected items to cart] [● Buy selected items with 1-Click®]

Figure 9-2:
Bottom of the Page Deals — just one juicy tidbit below the fold.

Here are some other good things you'll find when you scroll:

✔ **Recommendations:** When you're on the detail page for any product, you'll find the Customers Who Bought This Also Bought feature just below the fold. This feature is a good way to find like products that you might enjoy. If an entire group of people bought a book that you loved, you might also love another book that the same group purchased.

✔ **Reviews:** Both product and customer reviews live below the fold.

✔ **Expert Advice:** You'll find this header sprinkled throughout the site on category and subcategory pages. This is how you can access Amazon's info centers and other fun information.

✔ **Your Recent History:** As you shop, Amazon keeps a log of your journey and records it in a box that sits almost at the bottom of the page. You can use the links in the Your Recent History box to get back to something you looked at earlier in your shopping trip.

The list versus the slide show

As you browse along, you'll notice that not all browses (and I'm using the words as a noun here) look the same. Amazon displays browse nodes in two ways: the list and the slide show. Figure 9-3 shows an example of each.

Why one versus the other? The answer has to do with giving customers the right kind of information. When you shop for books, music, or DVDs, you probably want written product information, because knowing what the cover art looks like doesn't really help you. On the other hand, when you shop for hard goods — kitchen products, TVs, cordless drills, or sweaters — seeing the product informs you faster than written information would. Plus, with the slide show, they can fit more products above the fold.

Figure 9-3: Different stores use different kinds of browse displays. The Kitchen store uses the slide show, while the Bookstore uses the list.

Using the Subnav to Find Goodies

Poor subnav. It's ever the sidekick. The best supporting actress. It's one of the most underrated parts of Amazon.com. (To review, the subnav is the strip of buttons at the top of the page just below the store tabs.) But the subnav deserves a fair shake. There are actually lots of goodies to be found by using the subnav, and unlike lots of other things at Amazon, it's always there so you can always find it.

Here are a few subnav ground rules:

- ✔ **Subnavs differ from store to store.** All subnavs at Amazon serve the same purpose — to help you get to places within that store in one click — but they're not the same store to store.

- ✔ **The subnav is always the same within a given store.** So no matter what page you're on in the Books store, for example, your subnav will look the same. You can access the same areas from the Books store home page as you would from a book detail page.

- ✔ **Subnavs offer a mix of choices that you can find elsewhere in the store as well as choices that are unique to the subnav.** Though they differ from store to store, all subnavs offer the same kind of choices. There are always Browse Categories buttons, a few featured categories, possibly an Advanced Search option, and then some goodies.

- ✔ **The subnav on the Welcome page is unique.** This is the only subnav that allows access to the Top Sellers and Today's Deals directory pages as well as Target and the international stores.

And here are some of the goodies you'll find on the subnav:

- ✔ **Top Sellers:** You'll find a Top Sellers button on the subnav of every store at Amazon (in Books it's called Bestsellers). They are Amazon's most popular items and the lists are updated hourly! You'll also notice a subset of Top Sellers listed by category in boxes on the right side of the page, as shown in Figure 9-4.

- ✔ **Today's Deals:** Every store except Books, Toys, and Baby features this subnav item. The deals are a combination of those advertised by Amazon in Sunday circulars, and some regular deals that just show up on the site.

- ✔ **New & Future Releases:** You'll find New and Future Releases in Music, Video, and DVD. In this section you can not only check out all the new releases by date, but you can also preorder items that haven't been released yet.

- ✔ **Resource Center:** Alas, the only subnav that features a Resource Center is Baby. But there are several other centers on the site and I'm lobbying to get them up on that subnav!

- ✔ **Used:** This shows up in several of the stores — Books, Music, DVD, Kitchen — to name a few. If you don't need it sparkly new, you can find great deals here.

Top Sellers in Electronics

1. Linksys WMP11 Wireless-B PCI Card
2. Koss KTX1 Portable Stereophone
3. Sony MDRCD180 Traditional Home Style Headphones...
4. Sennheiser MX-500 Stereo In-Ear Headphones (Blue)
5. HP DSCA21 Digital Camera Accessory Kit

▸ **All Electronics top sellers**

Figure 9-4:
Top sellers are in the nav and in boxes on the side of the store home page.

✔ **Store-Specific Goodies:** Check out the subnav in each store and you'll find that they all have their unique sweet spots — Shop by Age in the Toys Store, Newspapers and Professional/Trade magazines in the Magazine store, Maternity in the Apparel store, and so on.

No matter where you are within a given store, you can click on the store's main tab — the one that says Electronics or Books or whatever — to get back to that store's home page.

Movers and Shakers

Movers and Shakers are fun. They're the 25 biggest daily gainers in Amazon sales ranking. In other words, they are what's hot right now. I would never suggest that you buy things just because the other kids are doing it, but it is cool to check out who's buying what — in almost-real time.

You'll find Movers and Shakers for the following products: Books, Music, Videos, DVDs, Electronics, Software, Toys & Games, Video Games, Kitchen & Housewares, Magazine Subscriptions, Outdoor Living, and Tools & Hardware.

Now here's the tricky part. As far as I can tell, you can only access the various Movers and Shakers lists from two places: the Welcome page and the Your Recommendations area in Your Store. In both places, it's at the bottom of the page, so you have to scroll down a bit.

Chapter 10

Clicking Your Way to Purchase Paradise

· ·

In This Chapter

▶ Signing in

▶ Using your shopping cart

▶ Shipping your stuff

▶ Paying: Giving Amazon your credit-card information

▶ Canceling an order

▶ Buying with 1-Click

· ·

*A*t last you've found it! You searched. You browsed. You discovered. And now you want to buy. But how? If you're new to Amazon.com, buying may be mysterious and a little bit scary. Where's my shopping cart? Where's the checkout lane? Is it safe to give them my credit-card info?

Don't fret. Buying at Amazon is as easy as shopping at Amazon — safe too. In this chapter, I show you how to buy like a pro — from signing in to consolidating orders. I walk you through the buying process step by step — putting items in your shopping cart, entering your shipping and credit-card information, double-checking your order, and taking the leap to being an official Amazon customer.

You've Found It, Now How Do You Buy It?

Buying at Amazon is pretty easy — really easy after you've made one purchase and can buy with 1-Click. But that first purchase does take a little bit of effort. And it's during that first purchase that you set up certain areas of your account that you continue to use down the line. Don't worry! You can always make changes to your account. But that first purchase helps you set up things like a default shipping address and default credit-card information.

Here are a few things you should know about buying at Amazon.com:

✔ **Buying changes after your first purchase.** Once you've bought from Amazon and they have your information, buying gets much simpler. When you have an active account, buying with your shopping cart is a 4-step process: Sign In, Shipping & Payment (all on one page), Gift Wrap (optional), and Place Order. You can also buy with 1-Click, which is, literally, a 1-Click process.

✔ **You can cancel or return an item ordered from Amazon, but not necessarily from an Amazon merchant.** As long as it hasn't entered the shipping process, you can cancel any item ordered *from* Amazon, but not any item ordered *at* Amazon. If you buy from an Amazon merchant, you are subject to their cancellation policies. Same goes for returns.

✔ **Your credit-card information is safe.** Amazon uses the industry standard SSL technology (that stands for Secure Sockets Layer) to encrypt your credit-card info as you send it. They also promise safe shopping — shopping free from credit-card fraud — and cover any fraudulent shopping on your credit card over what your bank will cover.

Signing in

Any time you want to buy, whether you're a newbie or an old hand, you have to sign in. If you don't already have an account, don't worry about it. You create one as part of the buying process. (If you're interested in creating an account before you buy, check out Chapter 3.)

If you do have an account, you're asked to sign in before you can add an item to your shopping cart. To do that, simply enter the e-mail address you used to set up your account, enter your password, and click the sign-in button.

If you've forgotten your password, don't worry. Click the <u>Forgot Your Password</u> link below the sign-in button and Amazon walks you through a 3-step process to create a new one. They e-mail your new password to your e-mail address of record instantly. The entire process won't hold up your shopping for more than a minute or two.

Adding it to your shopping cart

So where is this fabled shopping cart? There are two good ways to access your shopping cart. One is by clicking the <u>View Cart</u> link in the Shopping Tools menu at the top of every page. The other is by adding something to your cart from a detail page.

You can stuff your cart to the brim — there's no limit — and adding to your cart doesn't mean you have to buy. Once you add something, it stays there for 90 days unless you take it out. So if you decide you don't really feel like buying it right now, you can exit the order pipeline and it will still be there later.

Ship it. Ship it good.

Once you've added the item to your cart, you have to arrange the shipping. Amazon makes this very easy for you. You have three choices:

- ✔ **Standard shipping:** This takes 3-7 days and is the cheapest option.
- ✔ **Two-day shipping:** This takes 2 business days and they won't deliver on Saturday.
- ✔ **One-day shipping:** This takes 1 business day and, again, no Saturday delivery. This is the most expensive option.

One thing to keep in mind is that these shipping times refer to just that: the shipping from the distribution center to your house. They don't include the availability time. That's the time listed on the product's detail page, something like, "usually ships within 24 hours" or "usually ships within 1 to 2 weeks." Be sure to take that into account so you're not disappointed when your item doesn't arrive the next day.

You may also be eligible for Amazon's free Super Saver shipping. It's for orders over $25 but excludes certain things like toys, video games, baby items, and things sold by Amazon merchants or marketplace sellers. The rub is that Super Saver shipping takes an additional 3-5 days. But if you're not in a hurry, you can save a bundle on shipping costs.

For more details on Super Saver shipping, plus a complete list of shipping rates and some other good shipping info, go to the Shipping section of the Help department.

Relatively painless paying

I say "relatively" because although the process is simple, you still have to give them your money. That said, paying at Amazon is pretty painless. You give them your credit-card information, they keep it on file — and don't worry, it's 100 percent safe — and every time you shop, it's ready for you to use. You do have to enter it again (for security reasons) if you ship to a new address, but it's worth it in the name of safety!

If, at any point, you want to use a different credit card, you can change your credit-card information either by accessing it through Your Account (see Chapter 3) or during the buying process — but not if you're using 1-Click.

Amazon.com also accepts other methods of payment. To find out what they are, check out Chapter 3 or visit the Payment Methods We Accept section of the Help department. You can find it under Ordering.

To get to the Help department, simply click on Help in the Shopping Tools menu at the top right of almost any page on the site.

Shooting the order pipeline

When you're ready to place an item in your shopping cart, you're about to enter what Amazonians call, The Order Pipeline. Radical. You're ready to buy.

Buying on Amazon for the first time is really just a few steps start to finish. Here's how you do it:

1. **Click the Add to Shopping Cart button on the detail page of the item you want to buy.**

   You find a Ready to Buy? box, looking very much like the one in Figure 10-1, on every detail page in the site. When you're a new customer, before you've made your first purchase, your only option in the Ready to Buy? box is to "add to shopping cart."

2. **In the new page that appears — see Figure 10-2 — confirm or Edit the content of your shopping cart.**

   Only the box labeled "Your Shopping Cart" is your shopping cart. The rest is made up of recommendations based on your purchase history and the purchase histories of other people who've bought what you're buying. Confirm that you want to buy the items in your cart. (No stress, though. This isn't the moment of truth. You can delete items later in the buying process.) If you've had second thoughts, click the Edit Shopping Cart button, delete or change the necessary items, and proceed to Step 3.

Figure 10-1:
The New
Customer
version of
the Ready to
Buy? box.

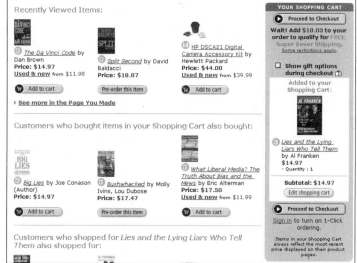

Figure 10-2:
Your
shopping
cart as it
looks during
the buying
process.

3. **Keeping on the same page, choose whether you want to show gift options during checkout, and then click Proceed to Checkout.**

   If your item is a gift, you may want to include a card and gift wrap, or at least a gift note (which is free). That way, your recipient will know that the gift is from you. Without at least a gift note, it's tough for them to tell. To show gift options, check the box next to Show Gift Options During Checkout. If not, leave the box unchecked.

4. **In the new page that appears — appropriately named New Customer Sign In — enter your e-mail address in the field provided.**

   If you are the proud owner of several e-mail addresses, be sure to enter the e-mail address you want listed as your user ID at Amazon.com. You get to create a password later. The next page asks you to enter your shipping address.

5. **Enter your shipping address and phone number in the fields provided and then click Continue.**

   They also ask whether you're shipping and billing addresses are the same. If they are, make sure you click the Yes radio button. It saves you time later on.

6. **In the new page that appears, choose your shipping speed — Standard, 2-Day, or 1-Day — and then click Continue.**

   You might also be eligible for Super Saver shipping (free shipping on *certain* orders over $25). If so, you'll see that option listed as well. Remember, though, that it takes 3-5 extra days. For shipping rates, click the Learn More link next to the header. You notice that you have another chance here to edit the contents of your shopping cart. Again, this is not your last chance. You also notice that you have another chance to check the gift options button — just in case.

7. **In the new page that appears — a page that looks a lot like the page in Figure 10-3 — enter your credit-card information into the appropriate fields of the Payment Method section, scroll down and create a password in the sensibly named Create a Password section, and then click Continue.**

   The page you see in Figure 10-3 is one of the most important pages at Amazon, because it's where you give up your credit-card digits and create your password. You're asked to enter your password twice to ensure accuracy.

Figure 10-3:
Enter your
credit-card
information
and create a
password
on the same
page.

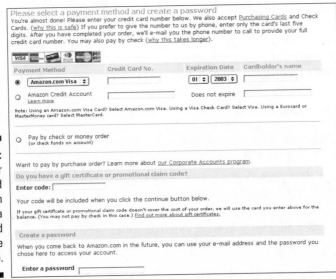

8. In the new page that appears, review your order and click the Place Your Order button!

This is the moment of truth: You come to a page that looks like Figure 10-4. Notice that you have the opportunity to edit every part of your order from shipping address to credit-card information. If you see something incorrect, just use the appropriate edit button to make a change. If all's well, place it!

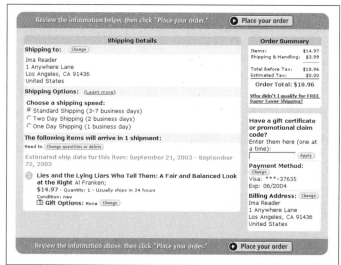

Figure 10-4:
The final step in the buying process!

Whenever you buy with your shopping cart, you should review your order carefully before placing it. Remember that when you put something in your cart, it stays in the "active" part of your cart for 90 days. If within 90 days, you add something else to your cart and proceed through the buying process, that first item will be included in your purchase. To avoid this happening, you have to actively designate it "save for later." If you don't, you might accidentally buy it.

E-Mail Confirmation

Any time you make a purchase at Amazon.com, they send you an e-mail confirming your buy. In fact, it shows up in your inbox about two minutes after you make that final click.

Though not all confirmation e-mails are identical, they all contain the same critical information.

Figure 10-5 is a confirmation e-mail I received for a purchase I made in the Apparel store. The e-mail is broken down into a few different sections. At the top — not shown in Figure 10-5 — is the "many splendors of your account" plug (my name for it, not theirs). It's followed by purchasing information, an order summary, and some housekeeping-type stuff at the bottom. This e-mail is more than just a hey-we-got-your-order note. It's also a tool. Here are the things you can do from your confirmation e-mail:

- ✔ **Access your account.** Some of the more popular order-related links are in the e-mail, or you can just go to the main "Your Account" page.

- ✔ **Access the order summary page for that item.** Do that by clicking the hot linked order number in your e-mail. You can cancel or change orders from the order summary page.

- ✔ **Change your e-mail status from HTML to text-only.** If your e-mail client (the program you use to send and receive e-mail) isn't set up to handle them, HTML e-mails will look like a bunch of gibberish. Also, because they're image heavy, they take a bit of time to download. So if you're on a slow connection, you may prefer a text-based e-mail. At the bottom of the e-mail (not shown in Figure 10-5) is a link that says <u>Prefer not to receive HTML mail? Click here.</u> Clicking that link takes you to your Customer Communications Preferences page where you can change your e-mail receiving status.

Figure 10-5:
Your confirmation e-mail reviews your order and gives you access to your account.

Purchasing Information:

E-mail Address: mara@smartypantscomm.com

Billing Address: Shipping Address:
Mara Friedman   Mara Friedman

Seattle, WA 98116   Seattle, WA 98116
USA   USA

Purchase Grand Total: $ 18.47

Order Summary:

Shipping Details: Footlocker.com, Inc.

Have questions about your this order? Please contact the seller.
Order #:   058-3647108-5726734
Shipping Method: Standard Shipping (4-14 business days)
Subtotal of Items: $9.99
Shipping & Handling: $6.99

Total before tax: $16.98
Estimated Tax: $1.49

Total for this Order: $18.47

Shipping estimate for these items: September 15, 2003
        1   "Kaepa Women's Classic (sz. 08.0, Red)"
             ;
             $9.99 each

Please note that Amazon Payments will charge your credit card at the time you place your order. You can expect to receive your item(s) in accordance with the shipping estimates

How to Cancel Your Order

If you're suddenly stricken with buyer's remorse before your order is sent out, you can cancel orders at Amazon.com — but be sure to do it by the book.

Two conditions apply to all cancellations: If you bought the item from Amazon, and not from one of its merchant or marketplace sellers, and if the items hasn't yet entered the shipping process, you can cancel. You may be able to cancel orders from merchants or marketplace sellers, but you have to deal with them directly and adhere to their cancellation policies.

To cancel an Amazon.com order, take the following steps:

1. **Click the Your Account link to access the Your Account page.**

   You can find the necessary link at the top of every page in the Shopping Tools menu.

2. **In the Your Account page that appears, click the Cancel Items or Orders link.**

   You arrive at your Open and Recently Shipped Orders page. You should see the order listed under the Open Orders heading.

3. **Click the View or Change Order button next to the item you want to cancel.**

   This takes you to the order summary page for that item. You can also access this page by clicking the order number in your confirmation e-mail.

4. **Click the Need to Cancel Order or Change Quantities? button.**

   First make sure that the order you want to cancel is actually under the Not Yet Shipped heading. Only these orders are eligible for cancellation. If it isn't, you can wait until it arrives and return it. For some help on how to do that, read Chapter 4.

5. **Check the Cancel Item box and then click Update Order.**

   The Cancel Item box is to the right of the item title.

When you're finished, you find yourself at a page that looks like Figure 10-6. You also receive an e-mail from Amazon.com that confirms your cancellation.

Figure 10-6:
Confirmation
that your
order
cancellation
was
successful.

Better Buying with 1-Click

After you've made your first purchase, assuming you paid with a credit card, you're set up for 1-Click shopping. 1-Click is the patented Amazon.com technology that lets you make a purchase with just one click of your mouse. After you've made that first purchase, the Ready to Buy? box on the detail page changes to include the 1-Click option (as in Figure 10-7).

Figure 10-7:
The Ready
to buy? box
is now
1-Click
enabled.

Unless you change your 1-Click settings, Amazon uses the shipping address and credit-card information you used for that first purchase. As you continue to buy from Amazon, you may buy gifts and have them shipped to other people. Those people become options in the drop-down menu in the Buy box — so you can 1-Click gifts as well.

1-Click is very easy to use. So easy, in fact, that it makes my husband a little bit sad. (But you know what they say . . . how can you really experience joy if you don't sometimes experience sadness?) But there are a few things you should know about using 1-Click ordering:

✔ **You can't use 1-Click to buy products from Amazon merchants.** Remember that often, when you buy *at* Amazon, you're not buying *from* Amazon. So many Amazon merchants, like the ones in the apparel and sporting goods stores, aren't compatible with 1-Click. Only two exceptions to this rule: Toys 'R' Us and Babies 'R' Us.

✔ **1-Click won't work if you're using cookie-blocking software.** If you think your 1-Click settings are turned on and the 1-Click option isn't showing up in the Ready to Buy? box (and you're buying from Amazon itself, rather than from a merchant) it may be that the computer fairy (or a techie-geek spouse?) has decided to protect you by adding this software without your knowledge. Just a thought . . .

✔ **You can change your 1-Click settings to use a different credit card or shipping address.** Do this in the Personal Information section of Account Settings on the Your Account page.

✔ **You can link specific shipping addresses with specific credit cards.** Again, access the Personal Information section of Account Settings in Your Account. You'll notice that the 1-Click Settings page is also the Address Book Management page (as in Figure 10-8). Next to each entry in your address book, you have the 1-Click settings associated with that address. Use the Edit button to change the credit-card information associated with that person or address. This comes in handy if you use different credit cards for different purposes — say, work versus pleasure, and so on.

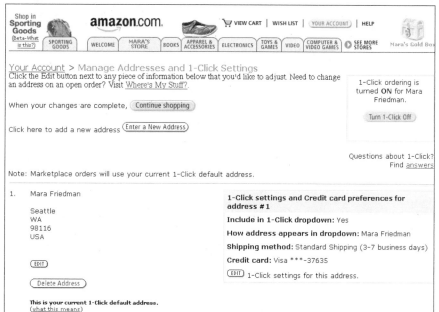

Figure 10-8: You can change the 1-Click settings for each address in your address book.

Order Consolidation

If you use 1-Click to buy several items in one visit, Amazon.com does their best to automatically consolidate your order and send things together in one package. There are, however, a few things that affect automatic order consolidation:

- ✔ **Items have to be shipping to the same address.** Okay. All right. Duh. But I felt like I had to mention it.

- ✔ **Items have to be bought within a 90-minute period.** I don't know what's behind this Cinderella-esque rule. But I do know that after 90 minutes, it's out of the automatic consolidation loop. You can sometimes consolidate them yourself through Your Account. The window for manual consolidation is wider — more like a few hours or even a day — though not entirely concrete. In other words, after the 90 minutes is up, nobody is making any promises.

- ✔ **Items bought from Amazon.com can't be consolidated with items bought from merchants, marketplace sellers, zShops, or Auctions.** Why? Simple: Those people do their own shipping.

- ✔ **Item availability times affect consolidation.** You may have noticed availability times listed on the detail page. They usually say something like, "Availability: usually ships within 24 hours." This little note affects consolidation as follows: Items that ship within 3 days or fewer are consolidated and items that ship in more than 3 days are consolidated as they become available. In other words, if one items ships in a week and another in 3 weeks, they won't make you wait 3 weeks so they can ship them together.

- ✔ **Items bought using the shopping cart won't be consolidated with items bought using 1-Click.** Again, not sure why, but those are the rules.

- ✔ **No consolidating with Super Saver.** You can't consolidate any orders that are shipping for free under free Super Saver shipping. In other words, no lumping an ineligible item with a Super Saver to score some free shipping.

Part III

The More the Merrier: The Amazon.com Community

The 5th Wave — By Rich Tennant

Did I mention I found a set of balloon-folding videos for a steal on Amazon?

In this part . . .

There are more than 30 million people shopping at Amazon.com. It may seem idealistic to think of people who shop at the same store as a community, but they are. And Amazon.com is no ordinary store.

Amazon breeds community. It brings people together in the name of their shared passions — books, music, cooking, gardening, woodworking, whatever — and lets them share information about those passions (or at least information about the products associated with those passions). Amazon also fosters that sense of community by using the information they collect from the entire group to point us individuals toward new products.

Any time you come to the site and make a purchase, you are participating in the community. But there's more to be done at Amazon than just shop. In this part, I cover the cool features this community has to offer and show you how to get the most out of them. You get the lowdown on how to become a real part of — and engage — the Amazon. com Community.

Chapter 11

It's All About You! Cool Stuff That Happens Automatically

*Y*ou may not think you have anything in common with an accountant from Cleveland, or an interior decorator from Taos, or a barista from Irvine — and in the physical world, you may never cross paths with those people to find out. But in the world of Amazon, any of them could be your shopping soul mate.

More than 37 million people are shopping at Amazon — and Amazon is collecting data on every single one. They use that data in a host of different ways, one of which is to point us shoppers to other products we might like. But it's not as simple as, "Hey, Mara! Read this book." Amazon's recommendation features are far more elaborate and hardworking than that. Best of all, you don't have to do anything but shop to take advantage of them.

In this chapter, I cover all the cool recommendation features that Amazon offers. I explain what they know about you and how they use it. I also show you where to find your various recommendations and how to use some of the features associated with them.

What Amazon Knows About You That No One Else Knows (Revisited)

Amazon is not your all-knowing best friend. It doesn't know that you secretly yearn to be a professional ice dancer or an astronaut. Or that when you were

5 years old you put a button in your nose to see if it would come out the other side. Or that sometimes you cry during dog-chow commercials. Amazon doesn't know any of that. But if you've shopped with them once, even if you only gave them the required information, they do know a lot about who you are and what you like.

Here's what Amazon knows:

- ✔ **Your name and shipping address.** Because you gave it to them when you filled out your info in the order pipeline.

- ✔ **Your credit-card information and billing address.** Because in order to pay for your purchase you gave this to them as well.

- ✔ **What you like.** This they know because of where you looked when you shopped, and because of what you ultimately bought.

- ✔ **Who you like to send gifts to and what those people like.** If you use Amazon to send gifts, they remember that too.

It may seem obvious, but the nature of the Internet makes it easy to collect information — so when you shop at Amazon, that's what they're doing. They're collecting information, saving it, and using it. That information can be grouped into two categories: the info they collect as you shop and the (more personal and lasting) info they collect when you buy.

As-you-shop information

You're being watched. You may not even notice it, but as you click your way through the pages of Amazon.com, a little shopping fairy is watching you. That fairy (also known as "software" to those who created it) is taking note of where you stop and what you look at — so before you even buy anything, Amazon is tracking you and preparing recommendations.

You find this as-you-shop information put to use in two places:

- ✔ **Your Recent History:** This lives at the bottom of every page and travels with you as you shop. It's really just a log of the stores and items you've looked at, and you can use it to access those places quickly and easily.

- ✔ **The Page You Made:** The Page You Made lives in Your Store (and I talk more about both of these later in the chapter). This special category page is a combination of the items you've looked at and related items — updated in real time. So as you click around the store, The Page You Made changes accordingly.

When-you-buy information

When you buy at Amazon, you're not just improving your own recommendations, you're adding to the information pool for the entire Amazon community. As that information pool grows, everyone's recommendations improve. It's the circle of shopping life; think of it as a public service of sorts.

Amazon uses your buying history for two purposes: to give *you* better recommendations *and* to give the entire Amazon community better recommendations. They use your buying history to match you with other shoppers who share your taste. They use it to recommend specific items. They use it to link items on the site. Buying history is what makes Amazon a community rather than just a store.

So very many places and features on the site are shaped by buying history — and the best part is, you don't have to do anything to take advantage of them. All you have to do is shop and buy — and that's easy.

Here are some features that are products of buying history:

✔ **Recommendations:** These are the granddaddies of Amazon personalization features. The Big Kahuna of buying history put to use. Basically what happens is this: You buy something, Amazon finds out who else bought it, and then checks to see what other related things those people bought. Then Amazon recommends the items that were the most popular. The more you buy, the more honed Your Recommendations become. You can access your Recommendations any time by clicking on them in the subnav of Your Store.

✔ **Similarities:** You may have noticed these on the detail pages of the site. (You'll also find them on your shopping cart page.) They fall under the heading that begins, "Customers who shopped for this . . . " (as in Figure 11-1) or "Customers who bought this." Similarities function the same way that Recommendations do: People buy an item, then Amazon finds out what other related items those people bought and recommends the items that were the most popular. But instead of being directed at you, similarities are for everyone.

✔ **The Page You Made:** Okay, I know I said The Page You Made was a product of the as-you-shop information. It is, but it uses the community buying history as well. You click around the store, and that's how Amazon decides what items to base your page on. Then they beef up the page by using community buying history. It's really a joint effort! You can access The Page You Made either from the Welcome page (in the box on the right side) or from the subnav of Your Store.

✔ **Just Like You:** This nifty little feature takes the whole recommendation thing to a new level. Amazon reviews your buying history as a whole and finds other shoppers with similar buying histories. You can access Just Like You in the Browse box of Your Store under Your Community. There is one caveat: you have to have enough buying history in order for Amazon to find another customer Just Like You. How much? I can't say, but if you don't find the link in Your Store, keep buying and check back every so often. It'll show up.

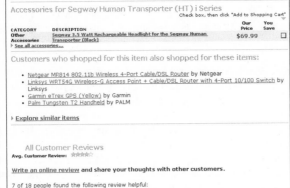

Figure 11-1:
Similarities
on the
detail page.

Your Very Own Store

As soon as you make one purchase at Amazon.com, you notice that a new tab with your name on it appears in the main nav, right next to the Welcome tab. It means you now have your very own store. It's called (drum roll, please) Your Store, and it's even named after you. (For example, Figure 11-2 shows a screen shot of my tab.) That tab will always be there and it's how you access Your Store.

Figure 11-2:
You can
always
access Your
Store from
your tab
in the
main nav.

So what is Your Store? It's a collection of features and recommendations based on your buying history and the related buying history of the Amazon community — put in a store template so it looks like the rest of Amazon.com. Check out my store "home page" in Figure 11-3.

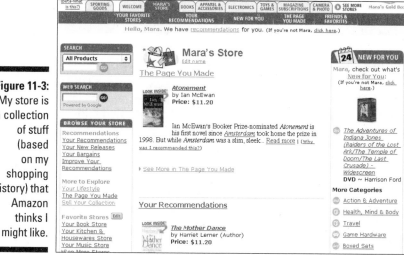

Figure 11-3:
My store is a collection of stuff (based on my shopping history) that Amazon thinks I might like.

What you find there: Subnav

You find lots of familiar things and a handful of new things in Your Store. What you may notice first is that Your Store has a subnav unlike any other subnav at Amazon.

Here's what you can access through Your Store's subnav:

- ✒ **Your Favorite Stores:** This is not just a series of links to the stores you visit most often. This feature takes the stores you visit most often, considers the kinds of things you buy there, throws in the community's buying history, and creates a unique "your favorite" kind of store.

- ✒ **Your Recommendations:** This is the home for all your recommendations. This is also where you can go to edit or change your recommendations.

- ✒ **New For You:** These are recommended new releases for all the categories you've shopped.

- ✒ **The Page You Made:** This is where the Page You Made lives full time.

- ✒ **Friends & Favorites:** This is the part of the site that allows you to create your own shopping network. (Check out Chapter 12 to find out more about what you can do in Friends & Favorites.)

What you find there: Other goodies

Your Store is chock-full of good stuff and most of it can be accessed from the subnav or from the Browse box on the left. But a few things that don't live in the subnav can only be accessed from the Browse box on the home page of Your Store (as in Figure 11-4):

- **Just Like You:** Here's where you get anonymously hooked up with a shopper who shares your taste. You find the link to Just Like You in the Browse box under the heading, Your Community.

- **Your Lifestyle:** Another form of recommendation, Your Lifestyle breaks into three categories — work, home, and play — and then offers up products you might like or need accordingly. You find it in the Browse box under the More To Explore heading.

- **Sell Your Collection:** Because Amazon records your shopping history, they also know some of the items you own that you might want to sell. Sell your Collection is a log of everything you've ever bought at Amazon, its used-price value, and a link to the appropriate marketplace selling area of the site. You find this feature in the Browse box under the More To Explore heading.

Figure 11-4:
The Browse box in Your Store is a good place to access certain special features.

BROWSE YOUR STORE

Recommendations
Your Recommendations
Your New Releases
Your Bargains
Improve Your
Recommendations

More to Explore
Your Lifestyle
The Page You Made
Sell Your Collection

Favorite Stores Edit
Your Book Store
Your Kitchen &
Housewares Store
Your Music Store
▶See More Stores

Your Community
Your About You Area
Friends & Favorites
Just Like You

Changing your store's name

It's true. You can change the name of Your Store and put your personal mark on the Internet. But there are rules. You only get to pick the first word (the second will be "store") and you can only use up to eight characters for the first word. In other words, I can't change my store's name to "Mara's Nasty Habit" because (*a*) that's too many characters and (*b*) that name doesn't include the word "store." But I could change it to, "Queenbee Store," and I just might.

You can't change the name of Your Store without changing your Amazon screen name — they're one and the same. This isn't the name associated with shipping and billing, but it's the name they use to greet you, it's the name that shows up in your public info, and so on. So make sure you choose something that you don't mind looking at and that you wouldn't mind other people seeing (or calling you by).

Here's how to change the name of Your Store:

1. **Click the Your Store tab on the main nav to get to Your Store and then click the Edit Name link.**

   You find the Edit Name link at the top of the page, directly underneath Your Store's current name. If you're not already signed in, you're taken to a sign-in screen.

2. **Sign in by entering your password in the field provided and then clicking the Sign in Using Our Secure Server button.**

   You come to a screen that looks like Figure 11-5. You notice that you can also change your e-mail address and password of record here. Don't do that unless you want to. It's not required.

3. **Enter your new name in the field provided and click the Submit Changes button.**

   A confirmation screen tells you that you've successfully changed your account. If you click any of the nav items, you notice that Your Store has its new name!

Figure 11-5:
You can change your account name, e-mail address, and password from this screen.

Your Favorite Stores

Your Favorite Stores is a good place to discover stuff at Amazon.com. You can access it by clicking on it in the subnav of Your Store. It's similar to Your Recommendations — many things there were chosen to reflect your buying history as it relates to the group buying history. This collection of items also includes popular things from the stores that you shop regularly.

The Your Favorite Stores home page looks a lot like Figure 11-6. It's really just a selection (about six) of your favorites and some corresponding products in the form of recommendations or features such as More to Explore. You'll notice that you can access more favorites from the Browse box on the left side of the page.

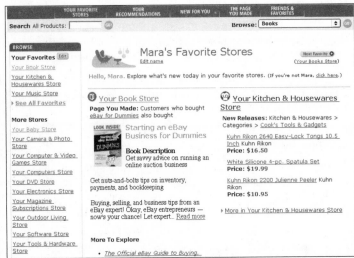

Figure 11-6:
Your Favorite
Stores home
page is the
gateway to
good
personalized
recommen-
dations.

When you click one of your favorite stores, you come to that particular Favorite Stores page. Each favorite store shows up on-screen in a category-page template, which looks like Figure 11-7. Somehow this makes it more fun — it feels more like your own store. You find your favorite categories and subcategories in the Browse box, as well as sections like New Releases, Top Sellers, and so on.

If you go to Your Favorite Stores and find they aren't really tickling your fancy, you can edit them. Here's how to do that:

1. **Click the See All Favorites link in the Browse box on Your Favorite Stores home page.**

   It's a mystery to me that this is the right link, but it is. You come to the Favorite Stores edit page, which has a series of categories and subcategories next to corresponding check boxes.

2. **In the Favorite Stores edit page, click the boxes next to the subjects that interest you.**

   You notice that the list is broken down by store — and that the bottom of the page offers you Other Stores. Okay, these aren't currently the stores you shop — not yet. But if you want to add them to your favorites, you can click the appropriate boxes.

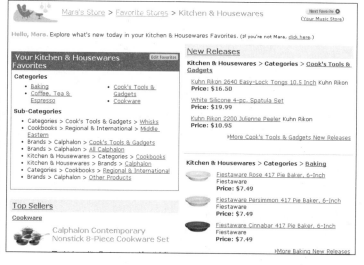

Figure 11-7:
Each of Your
Favorite
Stores is
like a
category
page in one
of Amazon's
other stores.

If there are categories within a store that you'd like as a part of your Favorite Stores, but that aren't there, don't dismay. Adding them is a bit tricky (or, at least, unintuitive) but possible. What you need to do is add them into your Recommendations when you select your favorite areas (see the next section of this chapter for more on this). Once you do this, they'll show up in your Favorite Stores.

3. **Still in the Favorite Stores edit page, click the boxes to uncheck items that you want excluded from your favorites, and then click the Submit button.**

   After you submit your changes, you come to a page that looks like Figure 11-8. It's basically the Favorite Stores edit page all over again, but with a personalized message at the top. If you want to continue to edit, repeat Steps 1 through 3. If you're finished, move on to Step 4.

4. **Click the Your Store link in the personal message.**

   This takes you back to Your Favorite Stores home page, where you notice that your editing has already been taken into account.

Figure 11-8:
After you've
edited your
favorites,
you see a
personal
message at
the top of
the page.

May I Suggest . . .
Recommendations 101

The Your Recommendations page is always being updated — not only by you (when you buy), but also by the shopping community as their habits change — and you can access Your Recommendations from either the Welcome page greeting or from the subnav on the Your Store page.

From the vantage point of the Your Recommendations page, you notice a variety of ways to view Your Recommendations. You can look at them by favorites, by store, by bargains, or by used items. To do that, just click the appropriate link in the Browse box.

If your recommendations aren't inspiring, you can improve them to make them more accurate. There is an Improve Your Recommendations box — looking a lot like Figure 11-9 — right there on the Your Recommendations page.

There are three ways to improve your recommendations. You can "edit your Amazon history" by rating items you've bought or excluding them from your recommendations altogether. You can "select your favorite areas" by choosing the stores (and the categories within them) that interest you. And you can rate items you already own, but didn't necessarily buy at Amazon, by searching for and then rating them.

If you click the Improve Your Recommendations link in the Improve Your Recommendations box, you're asked to sign in, and to confirm that you want to improve your recommendations. Then you're taken to the general Improve Your Recommendations page, where you can access any of the three choices.

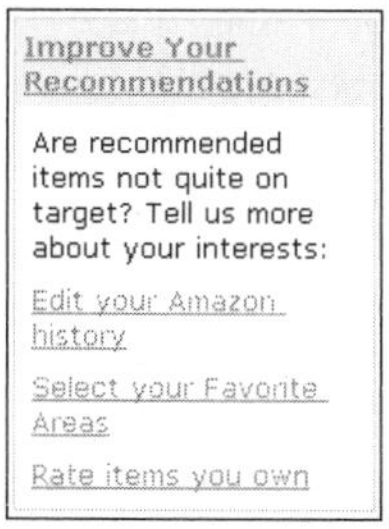

Figure 11-9:
The Improve
Your
Recommen-
dations box
is the place
to start
editing or
changing
your recs.

Improve Your
Recommendations

Are recommended
items not quite on
target? Tell us more
about your interests:

Edit your Amazon
history

Select your Favorite
Areas

Rate items you own

Here's how to edit your Amazon history:

1. **From the Your Recommendations page, click the Edit Your Amazon History link in the Improve Your Recommendations box.**

   If you're already signed in to your account, you are taken directly to the Edit Your History page. If not, you come to a sign-in screen.

2. **Sign in by entering your password in the field provided and clicking the Sign In button.**

   Unlike other sign-ins, this sign-in takes you to an acknowledgment screen.

3. **Click the Continue button.**

   You come to the Edit Your History page. You notice the Edit Your Info box on the left side of the page. The default setting for the Edit Your History page is Items You Own.

4. **Choose the items you'd like to edit in the Edit Your Info box.**

5. **Rate each item by clicking the appropriate number value.**

   You can give each item a rating that ranges from a question mark to 5. As you probably guessed, 5 is the best and "?" is the default for items you've bought but haven't yet rated. You should also choose the question mark if (for some reason) you don't feel you can rate the item.

6. **Check or uncheck the appropriate box to determine if that item will be used to make recommendations.**

   You find the Use To Make Recommendations option underneath the number ratings.

   Items purchased as gifts do not offer this option.

7. **Click the Save or Save and Continue button at the bottom of the page.**

   If you have more than 25 items in the list of items you're rating, you will click the Save and Continue button to move to the next page. However, you don't have to rate every item. Whenever you're finished, just click the Save or Save and Continue button to have Amazon record your changes.

8. **Use the site nav to exit the Edit Your History section.**

   There is no "You're Finished" page in the Edit Your History section. You decide when you're finished. At any point in the process, you can save your changes and leave the area by using the main nav.

Here's how to select your favorite areas:

1. **From the Your Recommendations page, click the Select Your Favorite Areas link in the Improve Your Recommendations box.**

   If you're already signed in to your account, you're taken directly to the Select Favorite Stores page. If not, you come to a Sign-In screen.

2. **Sign in by entering your password in the field provided and clicking the Sign In button.**

   This sign-in takes you to an acknowledgment screen.

3. **Click the Continue button.**

   You come to the first page of the Select Your Favorite Areas section. Notice the graphic at the top of the page — right there below the bread-crumb trail — that shows you where you are in the 4-step process.

4. **Check the stores that interest you and then click the Continue button.**

   In addition to checking the check boxes for stores that interest you, be sure to deselect the boxes for any stores you *don't* find — or no longer find — interesting. If a particular store strikes you as pretty dull but it has a check mark in its box, click the box to make that check mark disappear.

5. **In the new page that appears, check the categories that interest you and then click the Continue button.**

   For each store you chose in the previous step, you're offered a separate page of category choices. If (for example) you chose three stores in Step 4, you have three pages of category choices to work through. When you've completed your last page and clicked Continue, you come to the Add Details page.

6. **In the Add Details page, enter the requested information in the fields provided and click Continue.**

   For each store you chose in Step 4, you're asked to enter one favorite or Soon To Be Purchased item. So if you chose four stores in Step 4, you have to fill in four fields — one for each store.

7. **Choose the appropriate number rating for each item, check the box if you own the item, and click Rate More Items or Finish.**

   Amazon displays items from each store you've chosen based on the information you give them in Steps 4 through 6. If you're unfamiliar with an item, leave it as a question mark. If you click Rate More Items, Amazon will simply offer up another list. You can rate as many items as you like. When you do hit Finish, you're taken back to the Your Store home page with your recommendation changes recorded.

You can also change your recommendations by rating items you already own. These don't have to be items that you purchased at Amazon, just items that are in their catalog. You locate them by searching for them from the Your Recommendations feature itself (as opposed to using the Search box).

Here's how to rate items you already own:

1. **From the Your Recommendations page, click the Rate Items You Own link in the Improve Your Recommendations box.**

   If you're already signed in to your account, you are taken directly to the general Improve Your Recommendations page — Figure 11-10 gives you an idea what it looks like. If not, you come to a sign-in screen.

Figure 11-10:
Rate items
you own
from the
general
Improve
Your
Recom-
mendations
page.

2. **Sign in by entering your password in the field provided and clicking the Sign In button.**

   This particular sign-in takes you to an acknowledgment screen.

3. **Click the Continue button.**

   You come to the general Improve Your Recommendations page. Unlike the other two recommendation features, there is no beginning page for this feature.

4. **Enter the item you'd like to rate in the field provided, use the drop-down menu to narrow your search, and click Continue.**

   You come to a page that offers up search results along with rating options. You may not find an exact match, so be sure to enter solid key-words when initiating your search. (See Chapter 8 for more on key-words.) If your search is fairly nonspecific, you are given search results per store with the option to view all the results from that store.

5. **Choose the appropriate number rating for each item, check the box if you own the item, and click Save and Continue.**

   You will be taken back to the general Improve Your Recommendations page, but there will be a personal message at the top acknowledging your changes.

TIP

You can also improve your recommendation item by item. On every detail page, you'll see a box on the left side of the page called "Rate this item." (You'll have to scroll a bit to find it.) Use it to tell Amazon how much you like that item and that info will be incorporated into your recommendations.

Amazon on Line 1: Your Message Center

You may not have noticed that you have a message center on Amazon.com, but you do. Every customer with an account also has a message center. (Mine looks like Figure 11-11.) You can access it from the New For You box on the Welcome page or from the New For You section of Your Store.

So what is it? You know that Amazon isn't much for spam. So this is basically a way for them to tell you about new products that you might like without having to spam you. The messages in your message center are generated based on your shopping history and any other information you've given Amazon about stuff you like. They're basically recommendations in the form of a "message." You are under no obligation to ever look at them, and they will disappear from your message center 30 days after they show up. Occasionally, something interesting crops up.

amazon.com
VIEW CART | WISH LIST | YOUR ACCOUNT | HELP
Search All Products:
Browse: Books
New for You > Your Message Center
Hello, Mara. Check out what's New for You today. Learn More. (If you're not Mara, click here.)
Date Subject Delete
09/23/2003 1 New Release in Video: Action & Adventure
The Lord of the Rings - The Two Towers
09/23/2003 1 New Release in Computer & Video Games: PlayStation2
Silent Hill 3
09/23/2003 15 New Releases in DVD: Comedy
A Mighty Wind, and more...
09/24/2003 6 New Releases in DVD: Classics
Sleeping Beauty (Special Edition), and more...
09/24/2003 15 New Releases in Computer & Video Games: PC Games
SimCity 4: Rush Hour Expansion Pack, and more...
09/24/2003 15 New Releases in Books: Science Fiction & Fantasy
The Sandman: Endless Nights (The Sandman, 11), and more...
09/24/2003 15 New Releases in Books: Travel
1,000 Places to See Before You Die, and more...

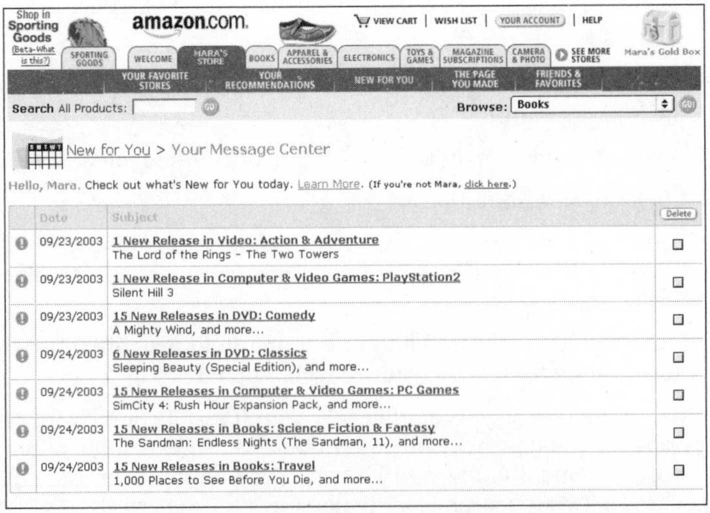

Figure 11-11: My Message Center.

It's easy to get rid of unwanted messages in your message center. To delete messages, simply click the boxes to check the message you want to get rid of and click the Delete button. Your message center will reflect the change immediately.

The Page You Made Without Even Trying

Anyone who tells you shopping isn't productive is lying. When you shop at Amazon, you are secretly hard at work. You are busy making a page that you can then visit to do more shopping.

The Page You Made is one of the coolest features at Amazon. It's a collection of the places you've shopped mixed with some recommendations based on the products you looked at all wrapped up in a neat little store-like page. And it's all built in real time. So if you start shopping now, in about five minutes you have made a page.

You can access The Page You Made from the subnav of Your Store. It will look something like Figure 11-12 — The Page I Made while shopping at Amazon today.

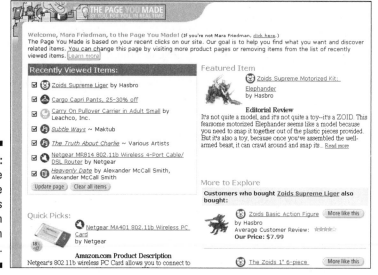

Figure 11-12: The Page You Made collects information and builds in real time.

Your Recent History on steroids

The Page You Made is like Your Recent History (Chapter 2) on steroids (but I mean that in a good way). While Your Recent History tracks where you've been and presents it to you in shorthand — by products, categories, and searches — The Page You Made takes that information and beefs it up. When you poke around the site, you are creating a shopping profile — a quick picture of what you're interested in. Amazon takes that profile and uses it to build a mini store just for you. In some ways, The Page You Made is like Your Recent History on steroids but before it got so big that it became Your Store.

Here's what you find on The Page You Made:

- **Recently Viewed Items:** You find this series of product links in the blue box at the top left. This is the nerve center of The Page You Made because these are the products you actually looked at — the products on which the rest of the page is based.

- **Featured Item:** This sits right next to the recently viewed items on the page — if it's there at all. The Featured Item is something that fits your shopping profile and that's also been getting some attention on the site. If nothing fits the bill, you won't have a featured item.

- **More to Explore:** Here Amazon takes some of the items you've looked at, finds people who bought those items, and shows you other relevant items that those people bought.

- **Quick Picks:** These are more products that fit your profile.

- **Listmania:** Amazon has a feature that lets customers put together their own lists of products. It's called Listmania and I talk more about it in Chapter 12. Here Amazon includes several Listmania lists that fit your profile.

- **Explore Related Categories:** These are handy links to other categories that might interest you but that you haven't visited in this shopping trip. (Because, remember, The Page You Made happens in real time so it doesn't take into account any of your shopping past.)

Don't want it? Turn it off

Some people don't like The Page You Made. These are the stealth shoppers who prefer anonymity. They shop in the shadows, preferring the cover of nightfall. (Either that, or they're husbands shopping for gifts for their occasionally nosy wives.) If you're one of those, you can easily turn off The Page You Made.

Here's how to do that:

1. **Go to Your Store and click The Page You Made in the subnav.**

   You come to The Page you Made and there will be a paragraph of text at the top that welcomes you and explains a little bit about this feature. At the end of that paragraph is a link that says, <u>Learn more</u>.

2. **Click the Learn More link.**

   You will now find yourself at the help-like Learn More page that looks like Figure 11-13. There's a longer explanation of what The Page You Made is all about (and an on/off button) in the upper-right corner.

3. **Click the Turn Off button.**

   You will remain on the same page, but the button will have changed from a Turn Off to a Turn On. Now if you go to Your Store and then click The Page You Made, you're taken directly to the Learn More page.

If you want to turn the feature back on, simply click the Turn On button from the Learn More page. But don't be alarmed when The Page You Made is empty. When you turn the feature off, your data is lost and you're starting from scratch. Spend a few minutes shopping, and you have a brand new page.

Figure 11-13:
You can turn The Page You Made off from the Learn More page.

Finding Your E-Commerce Twin

I have certain friends who I trust to recommend good books, movies, products, and so on. I'd say that seven out of ten times I like what they suggest. But those three times, those misses, can be a little painful. And frankly, I have unusual taste. I loved *Moby Dick* and *Old School*. I listen to Wham! and to The Flaming Lips. And to tell you the truth, I've felt a little bit alone. Like a shopping island.

But Amazon knows that no woman is an island. They know that there is someone out there that likes the same things I like — and they've matched us up.

You too have a shopping doppelgänger and Amazon knows who it is. In fact, you probably have *several* kindred shopping spirits and you can tap into them through Amazon's Just Like You feature.

You have to have enough shopping history for Amazon to make a match. If you don't, you won't find a Just Like You link in Your Store. Don't lose the faith! Keep shopping and eventually Amazon will match you with your shopping soul mate.

How Just Like You works

Just Like You is a feature that matches you with other customers who bought or rated several of the same products you've bought or rated. It's totally anonymous, so you don't see any of their personal info and they don't see yours, and it allows you to view 25 of their most recent purchases. (Which, of course, may be tempting for you because these people are Just Like You.)

Just Like You is something of a buried treasure. You can access it only from the Browse box on the home page of Your Store. You find it under the Your Community heading, below the fold.

Like all personal areas of Amazon.com, Just Like You is protected. So when you click the link in the Your Store Browse box, you're asked to sign in to your account (unless you're already signed in). Just enter your password in the field provided and you're taken to your Just Like You page.

Odds are your Just Like You page looks something like mine (shown in Figure 11-14), though it's perfectly okay if your interests are different. I mean, it's a free country. Honest.

Figure 11-14:
Just Like
You
matches
you with
customers
who share
your tastes.

Here's a quick anatomy of what you find on the page:

- **The Intro.** You find this at the top center of the page. It tells you a tiny bit about the person who is "just like you." Sometimes it tells you where that person is from (Arizona, New York, Uranus, and so on); other times it just says, "an Amazon.com customer." But you knew that.

- **The Drop-Down Menu.** You can use the drop-down menu to sort the 25 products you're looking at by store.

- **Left Column.** This column shows the items that both of you own or have rated positively.

- **Middle Column.** In the middle area you find the items that the customer like you owns or likes but that you don't own (as far as Amazon knows). These entries are essentially recommendations.

- **Right column.** On the right are items only you own. You can use this as a reference point to identify where your tastes *don't* overlap.

- **Next Customer button.** You find this at the top right of the right column. You thought there was just one customer like you? Au contraire! There are several and you can use this button to see them all, one by one. You notice that once you move past the first page another button will appear at the top left. Use the Previous Customer button to get back to customers you've already looked at.

- **Next and Previous.** At the bottom of the page, but above the Bottom of the Page Deals, you find the links that will get you to the second chunk of products owned by your Just like You customer. (See Figure 11-15.) Click Next to access the rest of that customer's products.

Figure 11-15:
Use these links to move within a particular Just Like You customer's products.

How to turn it off

For those of you who like to believe you're a 100 percent original (and you are, honey, you are), you can turn off Just Like You. Here's how to do it:

1. **Click the Just Like You link in the Browse box of Your Store.**

   If you aren't already signed in, you're asked to.

2. **Sign in by entering your password in the field provided and clicking the Sign In Using Our Secure Server button.**

   You will come to your Just Like You page. At the top of the page, underneath the customer info, is a sentence that says, "How do we determine customers 'just like you'? Learn more."

3. **Click the Learn More link at the top of the page.**

   You're transferred to a page in the Help Department. (Check the breadcrumb trail to locate yourself if you want.) The Just Like You on/off button is at the bottom of the page.

4. **Click the Turn Off button at the bottom of the page.**

   You will remain on the same page, but the button will have changed from a Turn Off button to a Turn On button. Now if you go to Your Store and then click Just Like You, you're taken directly to the Just Like You page in the Help Department.

To turn Just Like You back on, go to Your Store and click the Just Like you link in the Browse box. You're taken to the Just Like You page in the Help Department. Just click the Turn On button at the bottom of the page.

Because Just Like You is fueled by buying history, whereas The Page You Made is built on immediate shopping or clicking activity, Just Like You saves all your data so the page will still be fully stocked.

One Man's Treasure Is Another Man's . . . Treasure?

One of the most basic and most common things that Amazon does to help customers find products is identify similar products. Amazon calls this feature, fittingly enough, Similarities.

Similarities are basically open-ended recommendations. While Your Recommendations focus on you and your buying history, Similarities are product focused and use everyone's buying history. They start with a product, find all the people who bought that product, and then find the most popular other things that those people bought.

You'll notice that Similarities show up all over the site, but their most common spot is on the detail page. You may have noticed them sandwiched between the product image and the customer reviews. Figure 11-16 shows the Similarities for *Ebay For Dummies*.

Customers who bought this book also bought:
The Official eBay Guide to Buying, Selling, and Collecting Just About Anything by Laura Fisher Kaiser (Author), et al (Paperback)
eBay the Smart Way: Selling, Buying, and Profiting on the Web's #1 Auction Site by Joseph T. Sinclair (Paperback)
How To Sell On eBay: An Instructional Guide by Annette Graf (Paperback)
Online Auctions at eBay, Bid with Confidence, Sell with Success by Dennis L. Prince (Paperback)
The Official eBay Bible by Jim Griffith (Paperback)
Explore Similar Items: 18 in Books, 3 in Video, and 20 in DVD

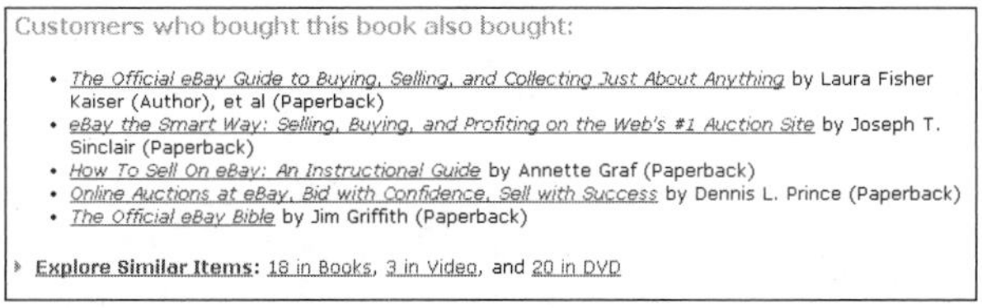

Figure 11-16: Similarities on the detail page.

You notice that Amazon identifies both other books and recommendations for other products. If you click the Explore Similar Items link, you're taken to a cornucopia of Similarities goodness (as in Figure 11-17). Scroll through the page and do a little exploring. Some products they recommend are closely related to the original item you looked at; others are totally unrelated — just other stuff that people liked. You can even use the drop-down list to sort items according to how closely they're related to the original item.

Also bought these items...
More results
Show items from:
All Products
Books (18)
Camera & Photo (1)
Computer & Video Games (1)
DVD (20)
Electronics (5)
Kitchen & Housewares (5)
Magazine Subscriptions (2)
Music (20)
Software (5)
Video (3)
Show items that are:
Closely Related
Starting an eBay Business for Dummies
by Marsha Collier (Author)
More like this
The Official eBay Guide to Buying, Selling, and Collecting Just About Anything
by Laura Fisher Kaiser (Author), et al
More like this
eBay the Smart Way
by Joseph T. Sinclair
More like this
How To Sell On eBay
by Annette Graf
More like this
Online Auctions at eBay, 2nd Edition
by Dennis L. Prince, Dennis L. Price
More like this
The Official eBay Bible
by Jim Griffith
More like this
The Unofficial Guide to eBay and Online Auctions
by Dawn E. Reno (Author), Bobby Reno (Author)
Selling Used Books Online
by Stephen Windwalker
Getting Started in Internet Auctions
by Alan C. Elliott (Author)

Figure 11-17: Good stuff on the Explore Similar Items page.

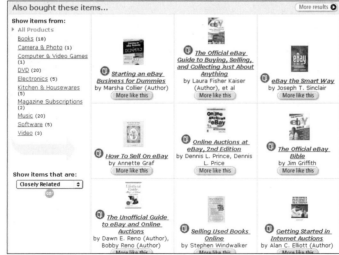

Chapter 12

Putting Your Two Cents In: Reviews, Lists, & Cool Features

. . . .

In This Chapter

▶ Writing customer reviews

▶ Using Friends & Favorites

▶ Creating Listmania lists

▶ Using Share the Love

▶ Getting the hang of Purchase Circles

. . . .

Amazon.com is interactive, and not just because you click buttons and things happen. It's truly interactive — the way only a real community can be. You can give and receive information along with thousands of other people through Amazon.com. You can create your own personalized area. You can generate lists that live publicly on the site. You can include your friends and family in your Amazon experience. You don't just have to be a "user" at Amazon. You can also be a participant.

Amazon is a place that encourages you to put your two cents in. Now most people who use Amazon know that they let you write reviews of the things they sell, but I'm guessing that not that many people know that reviews are just the tip of the iceberg. (And only about 1 million of their 37 million customers actually write them.) There are many more "community" features at Amazon.com. You just have to dig a little to find them.

In this chapter, I show you how to write your first customer review, help you set up your Friends & Family area, and walk you through your first Listmania list. I also cover Share the Love and Purchase Circles. I show you how to take advantage of these "community" features so you can make the most of your Amazon shopping adventure.

Loved It? Hated It? Writing Customer Reviews

Customer reviews have been a part of Amazon.com since (almost) the very beginning and including the customer review feature on the site was a stroke of genius. Remember, Amazon launched as an online bookstore in the mid-90s. That was just after man discovered fire, but before every preteen on earth owned a cell phone — people were still very wary of this thing they called "the Net." But allowing customers to put their opinions on the site dispelled some of the suspicion. What better way to get the straight scoop on whether something was good or not? And what better way to give to people a sense of ownership in the site?

More than eight years later, there are several million reviews on the site. Ask any of those devout Amazon users, and they tell you that they never buy from Amazon without first checking the reviews. If you spend some time on the site, you start to recognize reviewers by name — especially the goods ones. Spend enough time writing reviews yourself and you may become one of them.

What you can and can't say

Though anyone with an Amazon account can write a review, there is some protocol involved, because after all, reviews are supposed to help other shoppers make a buying decision.

Amazon is pretty laissez faire about what you can say. A good Amazon review focuses on the specifics — product features, a book's content, and so on. A good review is also meaty. Don't just praise or condemn; explain *why* you like or dislike something. This is your chance to pipe up, so use it!

Amazon is much more particular about what you *can't* say. Here's the list:

- **No potty mouth.** This includes both foul language and general meanness. Amazon is not a place to slam that fourth-grade bully who somehow ended up writing a book.

- **No one-word reviews.** Remember, reviews are there to help people. So if you just say, "rocks!" or "sucks!" you're not really doing that.

- **No giving it away.** This applies to books, DVDs, and videos, of course. You will not be a popular reviewer if you give out the ending. This is called a "spoiler," and if you do it, Amazon will pull your review from the site.

- **No personal contact info.** I don't know why anyone would want to give out info such as personal phone number, e-mail address, or mailing address to 37 million strangers. But if you've got a yen to do it, refrain — it's against the rules.

- ✔ **No competitive shopping info.** Hey, everyone, even Amazon, wants to protect his or her turf. So Amazon doesn't allow you to advertise its competitors on its site.

- ✔ **No trolling for good votes.** As an author, I can understand the temptation to solicit Amazon's massive customer base to boost my sales ranking, but, alas, it's just not kosher.

- ✔ **No commenting on other reviews on the page.** I admit that I have occasionally enjoyed witnessing a review spat. There's nothing like a public forum and a little anonymity to make people feisty. But that's not what this forum is for — and besides, really useless reviews are regularly dropped from the site. So no matter how insane a review looks to you, don't comment on it. You may be referring to some aspect of it that's not actually there (and then, guess what, you look like the nut job).

How to write your first review

Writing a review isn't as challenging as writing a *good* review. You can review any product at Amazon in just a few minutes, but you have to have an Amazon.com account. If you aren't signed in to your account, they ask you to sign in before allowing you to write a review. So, assuming you have an account, and you're signed in, here's how to do it:

1. **Go to the detail page of the product you want to review.**

   Once you're there, you need to scroll down below the Editorial Reviews to where the Customer or Spotlight Reviews begin.

2. **Click the Write an Online Review link.**

   If you're not already signed in, you're taken to a sign-in screen. Enter your e-mail address and password and click the Sign In button. On the next screen, click the Continue button. Once you're signed in, you're taken to that item's review page, which will look something like Figure 12-1. If you're younger than 13 years, use the kid's review form. (The link for that is at the top of the page.)

3. **Use the drop-down menu to select the number of stars that you want to give the item.**

   5 stars is the highest rating; 1 is the lowest. If you're reviewing a toy, you'll get to rate it three ways: how fun it is, how educational it is, and how durable it is.

4. **Enter the title for your review in the field provided.**

   It's not necessary, but it's nice to give your title a little bit of substance.

5. **Type your review in the field provided.**

   Remember the rules. No swearing. No giving away the ending. And try to be helpful in 1,000 words or less.

Figure 12-1:
Every item
on the site
has a
review page
that looks
something
like this.

6. **Click the appropriate option to choose whether or not to display your screen name with your review.**

   Amazon will offer two choices: You can display your review with your screen name (that's the name they use to greet you) or you can remain anonymous.

7. **Enter the name of your city in the field provided and click the Preview Your Review button.**

   Telling them where you're from is actually optional. Stars, a title, and a review are not optional and if you forget to do one of them and click the Preview Your Review button, you're taken to a screen that looks like Figure 12-2. The missing info shows up in bold, red font. Just enter the missing piece and click the Preview Your Review button again. You're taken to a page that shows your review as it will look on the site. Make sure it looks the way you want it to. If you need to change it, you can click the Edit button to get back to your review page.

8. **Check your review thoroughly and click Save.**

   The last page in the process thanks you and confirms that your review was submitted. It may also ask you to enter some information to build or update your About You area. This is 100 percent optional. Do it if you like — no harm will come of it — but don't feel obligated. You've written your first review and you are free to return to shopping!

Reviews can be fun to write, but don't expect immediate fame and glory. It takes some time for your review to go live on the site. Amazon gives themselves a 5-to-7 day window. More often than not, it's up there in a couple of hours, but you won't be able to write it and then immediately go check it out. Patience, Grasshopper, patience.

Figure 12-2:
The "whoops" page tells you what information is missing from your review.

When you've written a review and submitted it, you are agreeing to Amazon's terms and conditions. One key thing to note is that your review becomes their property and they can use it as they like. That means that it might show up on other sites on the web. For example, both AOL and Target use Amazon's reviews on their sites.

Was the review helpful?

Not only are we allowed to review items, but we're also allowed to vote on whether other people's reviews were good. You may have noticed that underneath each review is a sentence that says, "Was this review helpful to you?" — and then you get to click a Yes or No button to vote on reviews. When you do so, you come to a screen that looks like Figure 12-3.

Amazon counts the votes and posts them above the review. This tally helps you determine which reviews to take seriously and which you may be able to disregard.

The Top Reviewers

You may have noticed that some customer reviews have little icons next to them that look like the icon in Figure 12-4. These are the proud, the few, the Top Reviewers.

Figure 12-3:
Your vote
counts
toward the
reviews
total.

☆☆☆☆☆ **DIVERTING AND ENTERTAINING**, October 11, 2003
TOP 10
Reviewer Reviewer: <u>G. Cooke (see more about me)</u> from TX
"The Pleasure Of My Company" is "Shopgirl (Mr. Martin's previous foray into literature) with pathos. Rather than an older man intrigued by a younger store clerk, we meet a neurotic; indeed, one who is almost certifiable.

Daniel Pecan Cambridge (we can only assume his middle name to be a reference to his nutty mental state) is a man whose age varies, depending upon his feelings on a particular day. He's a transplanted Texan who now rarely leaves his Santa Monica apartment. After all, there are 8 inch curbs everywhere and the chance that he might be forced to endure seeing a garage attendant in a blue hat.

Now, there are one or two enticements that will draw Daniel out of the comfort of his apartment - one is the attractive clerk, Zandy, at the Rite Aid. Two might be a sale on ear plugs or the purchase of over a dozen lip balms (a practical purchase, he notes).

Due to these ventures into the outside world our hero finds himself embroiled in a murder, and, of all things, an unsuccessful wooer.

Mr. Martin again depicts loneliness and love with poignancy and humor. In addition, we'd expect him to read his story superbly, and he does. "The Pleasure Of My Company" is a diverting and enjoyable listening experience.

- Gail Cooke --*This text refers to the* <u>Audio Cassette</u> edition

*** Thanks for the valuable feedback you provided to other Amazon.com readers and reviewers. Your vote will be counted and will appear on the product page within 24 hours. ***

(Add) this reviewer to your list of Favorite People. Whenever one of them writes a new review, you'll see it on the Friends & Favorites home page.

Figure 12-4:
The Top
Reviewer
icon means
"good
advice
ahead."

☆☆☆☆☆ **In pursuit of a life list**, May 28, 2002
TOP 100
Reviewer Reviewer: <u>michaeleve (see more about me)</u> from Miami, Florida
I don't doubt that persons uninitiated in the brotherhood of birding and who may have may picked this book up out of curiosity, after reading it may very well be tempted to say "life-list? forget that! Please, get a life!". Cocker understands and he has all the traits of a serious birder instantly recognizable to other members of the species. We are just a little bit defensive at times, especially when having to explain our obsession. And yes, we may be a touch overly sensitive but we do tend to react negatively to those goggle-eyed, mouth-slightly-agape ostrich-like stares of total incomprehension that usually greet us when describing our wondrous hobby. Cocker though is a great advocate because he has an abundance of that vital birding necessity - a self-deprecating wit - and a sense of humour that prevents taking oneself or their sport too seriously. That his adventures and "Tales of a Tribe" about BIRDERS are very well written just adds to the enjoyment of this book.

Top Reviewers are (according to the opinions of other customers) the best reviewers at Amazon.com. In addition to the Top Reviewer icon, you may also have noticed that you can vote on whether a review was helpful — and that vote is how Top Reviewers are born. Theirs are the reviews deemed most helpful, most often, by other Amazon customers.

There are six classes of Top Reviewers: Top 1,000, Top 500, Top 100, Top 50, Top 10 and the reviewer's reviewer, El Numero Uno. Today, the number-one reviewer at Amazon.com is Harriet Klausner, a former acquisitions librarian who has written 5,617 reviews and gotten 34,701 "helpful" votes. (And all I can say about that is "Oh, my God.")

So what can you do to become a Top Reviewer? Write good reviews for popular items and hope that people find them helpful and vote accordingly. You can check on the status of the Top Reviewers list from the Friends & Family section of Your Store. You find a link to the list in the Explore browse box on the left side of the page. But I warn you, Harriet is going to be tough to unseat.

And another thing: customer advice

There is yet another way to give your fellow shoppers a hand. In the last year or so, Amazon has introduced a feature called Our Customers' Advice. It lives on the detail page just above the Editorial Reviews. (See Figure 12-5.)

Customer Advice is actually a recommendation. Say you own a digital camera. You love it, but it only has enough room for two print-quality pictures. You might recommend that other shoppers buy it along with a new memory card. With Customers Advice, you can suggest that people buy something in addition to — or instead of — the item shown on the detail page. To do that, you have to know what the ASIN or ISBN is for your recommended item (and, of course, you have to recommend something that Amazon sells).

What are ASINs and ISBNs? An *ASIN* is something that Amazon made up. It stands for Amazon Standard Information Number and it's a multidigit code used to identify products. Each product on the site has a unique ASIN, unless it's a book and then it has an *ISBN*. ISBN numbers are the industry-standard ID for every published book that's in the Library of Congress.

To find your recommended product's ASIN or ISBN, just go to that item's detail page. The number is in the section of the page called Product Details (or sometimes Product Information). (Figure 12-6 shows the *eBay For Dummies* ISBN.)

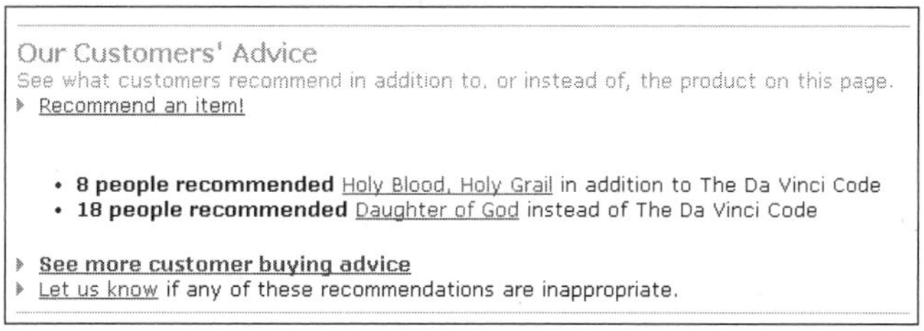

Figure 12-5:
Customer Advice recommends products in addition to (or in place of) the item on the detail page.

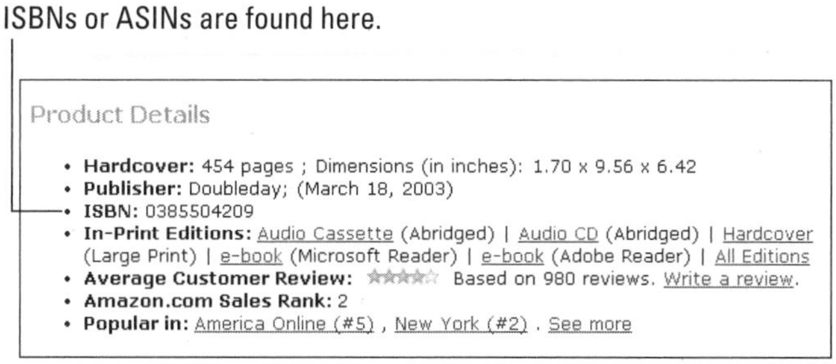

Our Customers' Advice
See what customers recommend in addition to, or instead of, the product on this page.
▸ Recommend an item!

- **8 people recommended** Holy Blood, Holy Grail in addition to The Da Vinci Code
- **18 people recommended** Daughter of God instead of The Da Vinci Code

▸ **See more customer buying advice**
▸ Let us know if any of these recommendations are inappropriate.

Figure 12-6:
ASINs and ISBNs are used to identify each product on the site.

ISBNs or ASINs are found here.

Product Details

- **Hardcover:** 454 pages ; Dimensions (in inches): 1.70 x 9.56 x 6.42
- **Publisher:** Doubleday; (March 18, 2003)
- **ISBN:** 0385504209
- **In-Print Editions:** Audio Cassette (Abridged) | Audio CD (Abridged) | Hardcover (Large Print) | e-book (Microsoft Reader) | e-book (Adobe Reader) | All Editions
- **Average Customer Review:** ☆☆☆☆☆ Based on 980 reviews. Write a review.
- **Amazon.com Sales Rank:** 2
- **Popular in:** America Online (#5) , New York (#2) . See more

After you've found the ASIN or ISBN for your recommendation, you're ready to give some customer advice. Here's how you do it:

1. **Go to the item's detail page where you want your recommendation to live.**

   In other words, this is the item you're commenting on, not the additional (or "in place of") item you're recommending. When you get there, scroll down below the product information until you reach the Our Customers' Advice header.

2. **Click the <u>Recommend an Item</u> link.**

   You're taken to a page that looks remarkably like the detail page you just came from. Scroll a tiny bit, though, and you see the advice field.

3. **Enter the ASIN or ISBN of the item you want to recommend in the field provided.**

   The easiest way to do this is to copy and paste.

4. **Click the appropriate circle to choose whether to recommend it in addition to or instead of the item on the detail page.**

5. **Click the Submit button.**

   If you're not already signed in, you're taken to a sign-in screen. Enter your e-mail address and password and click the Sign In button. On the next screen, click the Continue button. Once you're signed in, your recommendation is submitted. You'll notice an Important Message box on the detail page, acknowledging your recommendation. Notice, too, that it will take a day or so for your recommendation to be posted.

If you find some Customer Advice that is completely misguided and bizarre, you *can* actually do something about it. You may have noticed that at the bottom of the Customer Advice section there is a line that says "Let us know if any of these recommendations are inappropriate." Click on the Let Us Know and a series of No buttons will show up next to each piece of Customer Advice. Click on the No button for the wonky advice, and you'll be alerting the appropriate editorial team. If they agree with you, they'll remove the advice from the site within a week or so. If not, it stays, but at least you put your two cents in.

Shopping with the Ones You Love

Shopping at Amazon.com can be something of a family affair if you choose to make it that way. Amazon has lots of features that you can use to loop people in to your shopping experience — review writing, list creation, registries, and so on. — and all those cool features have one thing in common: They have a home in your Friends & Favorites area.

You find your Friends & Favorites area in Your Store. To get there, click the Friends & Favorites link — it's the last item on the subnav. When you first start out at Amazon, your Friends & Favorites looks a little bare. But as you shop and participate in the community, your Friends & Favorites fattens up (so to speak) to offer a bounty of fun extras.

But before you create your Friends & Favorites, you should know the difference between a "friend" and a "favorite."

✔ **Amazon Friend.** At Amazon.com, an Amazon Friend is someone who has access to the private view of your About You area. You have to create your About You area, and it may contain personal information such as your e-mail address. You determine who your Amazon Friends are, so you don't have to worry about suddenly having "friends" you don't want (spammers, troglodytes, your 6th grade boyfriend) know too much.

✔ **Favorite People.** Favorite People at Amazon are also people you select, but they don't have access to your private About You area. Typically, they're people whose opinions you trust; when you pick them, Amazon uses any reviews they've written to populate your Friends & Favorites page.

In short, Friends have access to your About You Area; Favorites don't.

Friends & Favorites highlights

Friends & Favorites is the roosting place for lots of the personalization features offered at Amazon.com. For the record, most of those features also have other homes on the site, but Friends & Favorites is an easy way to revel in their glory because they're all in one place.

In the beginning, before you add to it, your Friends & Favorites area will look something like Figure 12-7. In it, you find all kinds of goodies:

✔ **An invitation to get started.** In the center of the page you find three blocks of text. The first invites you to create your About You area, the second invites you to create a Wish List, and the third invites you to find and add people to your Favorites list (this third is actually a repeat of the search box that only shows up on this Starter page — see the next bullet).

✔ **A special Search box.** It's true that there's a Search box at the top left of every page, but the one in your Friends & Favorites area lets you search for people. By this I mean that you can search for other Amazon customers who may have public profiles, wish lists, registries, and so on. You can search by name, nickname, or e-mail address.

TIP

✔ **The master list of cool personalization features.** You find these on the left side of the page in the Explore box. This really is the most convenient catalog of all that's cool and free and personal on Amazon.com.

✔ **Friends & Favorites management tools.** Below the fold is a very important box. It's the Manage Your Friends & Favorites box — the easiest (but of course not the *only*) access you have to these management/editing links.

Figure 12-7:
Friends &
Favorites
houses all
the links to
the fun
personal-
ization
features at
Amazon.
com.

After you've spent some time with your Friends & Favorites, it'll look more like mine (as in Figure 12-8) and some new things will appear on the page:

✔ **Content based on stuff you picked.** In the center of the page you find an assortment of content based on the information you've entered in your Friends & Favorites area. In Figure 12-8, you notice that I have a review from one of my Favorite People and some Purchase Circle content based on where I live. (I talk more about Purchase Circles later in the chapter.)

✔ **Your Favorite People list.** This you have to create, but after you do, it's conveniently located on the left side of the page below the Explore box.

✔ **A list of the things you're participating in at Amazon.** This is also known as the Your Participation box; you'll find it on the right side of the page just below the nav. If you've set up a registry, written a review, created a list, done anything Amazon-ey, it shows up in this box and you can access it by clicking the link.

Figure 12-8:
Your Friends
& Family
area
changes as
you add
information.

Tell me about yourself: Creating and building your About You area

Your About You area is your own little Amazon club house — your own space on the site that could include a profile, a wish list, a photo, and so on. Before you can beef up your About You area, you have to create it. Here's how:

1. **Go to your Friends & Favorites area by clicking the link in the subnav of Your Store.**

   You notice a bevy of solicitations to create your About You area. Any will work.

2. **Click the Create Your About You Area link.**

   Any time you're trying to access what can be considered private information, Amazon asks you to sign in. So when you try to access your About You area, you're taken to a sign-in screen.

3. **Enter your e-mail address and password in the fields provided and click the Sign In Using Our Secure Server button.**

   You will come to a confirmation screen.

4. **Click the Continue button.**

   You come to a page that looks like Figure 12-9. After you complete it, you have a functioning About You area. From there, you can edit and add to it to make it more your own.

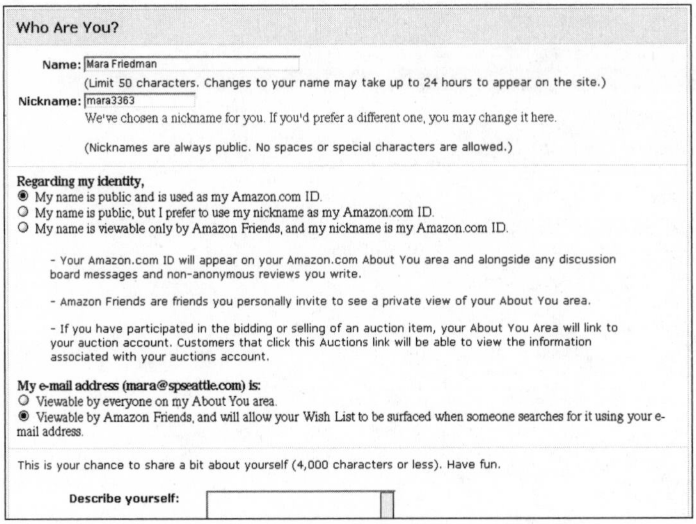

Who Are You?

Name: [Mara Friedman]

(Limit 50 characters. Changes to your name may take up to 24 hours to appear on the site.)

Nickname: [mara3363]

We've chosen a nickname for you. If you'd prefer a different one, you may change it here.

(Nicknames are always public. No spaces or special characters are allowed.)

Regarding my identity,
- ● My name is public and is used as my Amazon.com ID.
- ○ My name is public, but I prefer to use my nickname as my Amazon.com ID.
- ○ My name is viewable only by Amazon Friends, and my nickname is my Amazon.com ID.

- Your Amazon.com ID will appear on your Amazon.com About You area and alongside any discussion board messages and non-anonymous reviews you write.

- Amazon Friends are friends you personally invite to see a private view of your About You area.

- If you have participated in the bidding or selling of an auction item, your About You Area will link to your auction account. Customers that click this Auctions link will be able to view the information associated with your auctions account.

My e-mail address (mara@spseattle.com) is:
- ○ Viewable by everyone on my About You area.
- ● Viewable by Amazon Friends, and will allow your Wish List to be surfaced when someone searches for it using your e-mail address.

This is your chance to share a bit about yourself (4,000 characters or less). Have fun.

Describe yourself: [   ]

Figure 12-9:
The About You area form.

5. **Enter a name and nickname in the fields provided.**

   Because you've gotta have an account before you can have an About You area, Amazon already knows your name — and will use it as the default here. You can change it if you like, but any new name can't have more than 50 characters. As for nicknames, Amazon automatically gives you one (mine was mara3363 — very *Blade Runner*). You can change this as well.

   Nicknames are always public in your About You area — you can make your actual name private and viewable only by Amazon Friends.

6. **Choose your identity status by clicking the appropriate circle.**

   The thing to keep in mind here is that your "name" and "nickname" are whatever you entered in the fields provided. They're not necessarily your real name or real nickname (unless, of course, you want total strangers to know you as "Private Sassy Pants"). That said, the choices grow more private as you move down the list. So if you're a very private person, choose the third option.

7. **Choose your e-mail status by clicking the appropriate circle.**

   Again, the choices grow more private as you move down the list. If you want more privacy, choose the second option.

8. **Enter a description of yourself in the field provided and click the Submit button.**

   Here's your chance to get personal. You've got 4,000 characters to tell people about yourself (that's about 300 words). Remember, you can choose to make this viewable only by Friends.

Once you hit that Submit button, you're taken to your About You area. Now it's time to spruce the place up a bit. Here are the things you can add to your About You area:

- ✔ **A photo.** To upload a photo to your About You area, you just click the Add an Image Here link and then paste the URL for your photo in the field provided. But (and this is a pretty big but) it necessitates you posting a photo somewhere on the Web first in order for that photo to have a URL. If this is too techy for you, you can use one of the "zany" images that Amazon provides. You find these when you click that Add Image link.

- ✔ **A Wish List.** When you create a Wish List, it shows up in your About You area. (To find out how to create one, check out Chapter 13.)

- ✔ **A Listmania List.** Listmania lists are thematic lists of products that you (and any other customer) can create. They also appear in your About You area and you can find out how to create one later in this chapter.

- ✔ **A So You'd Like To . . . guide.** These are user-created how-to guides. They, too, find a home in your About You area and you can discover how to create one later in the chapter.

- ✔ **Friends.** Now that you've got an About You area, you can invite Amazon Friends to come check it out. (Adding friends to your list is a good, and somewhat subtle, way to get them to look at your Wish List.)

Enough about you: Adding Friends and Favorite People

A quick review: Friends can view your private stuff, Favorite People can't, but Amazon will use your Favorite People to populate your Friends & Family area with content you appreciate.

Friends

Adding Friends is marvelously simple. You can do it in one fell swoop, or bit by bit as you use the site — because each time you view a Wish List or Registry, you have the option to add that person to your Friends list. Here's the one-fell-swoop method:

1. **Go to your Friends & Favorites area by clicking the link in the subnav of Your Store.**

2. **Scroll down the page until you see the Manage Your Friends & Favorites box.**

   You find the Manage Your Friends & Favorites box on the left side of the page.

3. **Click the Add Amazon Friends link.**

   You come to the Invite Friends page, which explains, one more time, what Friends are all about.

4. **Enter the e-mail addresses of the people you want to add in the field provided and click the Add button.**

   You can enter more than one e-mail address at a time, so long as you separate them by commas. These people don't have to have an Amazon account. And don't worry about Amazon spamming these people to death — or selling their names to someone who wants to spam them to death. Amazon doesn't and won't.

That's it! Amazon sends those people an e-mail, telling them that they're officially your Amazon Friends and can view your About You area as they please. If they accept your invitation to become a Friend (by clicking the link in the e-mail) they show up on your list with a star by their names. If they don't accept, they become a mere Favorite Person. To access your Amazon Friends list, just click on the Amazon Friends link in the Your Participation box on the right side of the Friend & Favorites page.

Your Friends list and your Favorites list live together in one big list. You can differentiate between the two within the list because Friends have a star next to their names.

Technically, all your Amazon Friends are *also* Favorite People. You notice this as soon as you create your Friends list (which you can access by clicking on the Amazon Friends link in the Your Participation box on the right side of the Friend & Favorites page). Those people will also show up on your Favorite People list. So I recommend creating your Friends list first. That way, if you run out of steam, you'll have populated both lists and your Friends & Family area will have a little life.

Favorite People

Adding Favorite People is trickier than adding Friends. Unfortunately, there isn't a "one-fell-swoop" method. Instead, there are two sort of roundabout methods for adding Favorite People: By clicking reviewer names on the detail page and by using the Search box at the top left of the Friends & Family page (if you're still on that Starter page, you can also use the Search box in the middle of the page — the two are the same).

Using the Search box to add people to your Favorites list is the premeditated method. It's the method of choice if you know the name, nickname, or e-mail address of the person you're searching for.

Only people who have participated in some kind of community feature will show up in People search results. In other words, they have to have a Wish List, an About You area, shared purchases, and so on.

Here's how to add Favorite People using the Search box:

1. **Go to your Friends & Favorites area by clicking the link in the subnav of Your Store.**

   You see that the Search box at the top left of the page — right below the nav — is already set on People as a default.

2. **Enter the name of the person you're searching for in the search field and click Go.**

   Be as specific as you can be. (For example, don't enter *Smith* unless you have time to sift through 32,000 results.) Also, keep in mind that the search field is not case sensitive.

3. **Click the name of the person you want to add.**

   You notice that underneath each name are links to that person's "stuff" — Wish List, reviews, shared purchases, and so on (as in Figure 12-10). You should know that if the person has only a Wish List showing and you click the name, you're taken straight to that Wish List. And here's the rub: You can't make someone a Favorite from his or her Wish List. You can make the person a Friend (and so automatically a Favorite), but you can't make the person *only* a Favorite. In other words, if someone only has a Wish List in the People search results, you can't add that person to your Favorites unless you're also willing to make him or her a Friend.

4. **Click the Add To Your Favorite People List link.**

   You're taken to that person's About You page; the person's name is then officially added to your Favorites list (which you can access by clicking on the Amazon Friends link in the Your Participation box on the right side of the Friend & Favorites page).

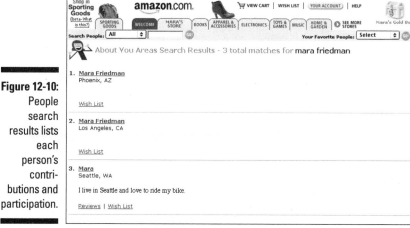

Figure 12-10: People search results lists each person's contributions and participation.

Adding people via the reviews on a detail page is a little bit easier and probably makes more sense. After all, the purpose of Favorites is to provide you with content from people whose opinions you trust. So if you're cruising the site and read a good review, it makes sense that you'd seize the moment and add that person to your Favorites list.

Here's how to add someone to your Favorite People list from a review:

1. **Click the person's name.**

   I'm assuming three things here: One, that you're on a detail page, two, that you have found a review you like, and three, that the reviewer's name is a hot link. If all three are true, you're taken to the Reviews page in that reviewer's About You area.

2. **Click the About (Their Name) link in the breadcrumb trail.**

   You find it at the top of the page under the nav. This link takes you to the person's About You area.

3. **Click the Add To Your Favorite People List link.**

   This is right next to the name at the top and center of the page. Once you click it, you've added someone to your Favorite People list. To access this list, just click on the Favorite People link in the Your Participation box on the right side of the Friend & Favorites page.

Everybody's Got Listmania!

What are the 20 essential items you have to have if you call yourself a sci-fi fan? If you were a contestant on *Survivor* and could bring five luxury items instead of only one, what would they be? What are the ten all-time greatest hair-band albums? If you've given things like these some thought, Listmania is going to float your boat.

Listmania is a feature that allows you to create thematic lists of products that Amazon sells. They don't necessarily have to be things you bought at Amazon. You don't even have to own them. You can create any kind of list you want, as long as the items on it are in Amazon's catalog.

How to create a list

Creating a Listmania list is pretty simple and very fun. To do it, you have to have an Amazon account, but otherwise, no requirements. The very first thing you have to do is have an idea — "Cookbooks and Kitchen Equipment for the Novice," "Gifts for Dog Lovers," and so on. Once you've got that nailed down, you're set.

Here's how to create a Listmania list:

1. **Go to your Friends & Favorites area by clicking the link in the subnav of Your Store.**

   You notice a link to Listmania in the Explore box on the left side of the page. You may have to scroll down a bit.

2. **Click the Add a Listmania List link in the Explore box.**

   If you haven't used your About You area, you may come to a "Who Are You" page that will ask you to confirm your information — screen name versus real name, e-mail address, and so on. (If not, you'll be taken directly to Step 4.) Make sure it looks as it should or make the appropriate changes.

3. **Click Submit.**

   You'll come to a sign-in screen.

4. **Enter your e-mail address and password in the fields provided and click the Sign In Using Our Secure Server button.**

   You're taken to the Listmania page shown in Figure 12-11.

5. **Before filling in any of the fields on the Listmania page, click the Open Another Browser link in the middle of the page.**

   The link automatically opens another browser window and goes straight to the Amazon Welcome page. Amazon recommends that you do this to make the search easier when you're looking for the items on your list. You can find their ASINs or ISBNs (refer to Figure 12-6) and then copy and paste them into the Listmania fields in the other browser window.

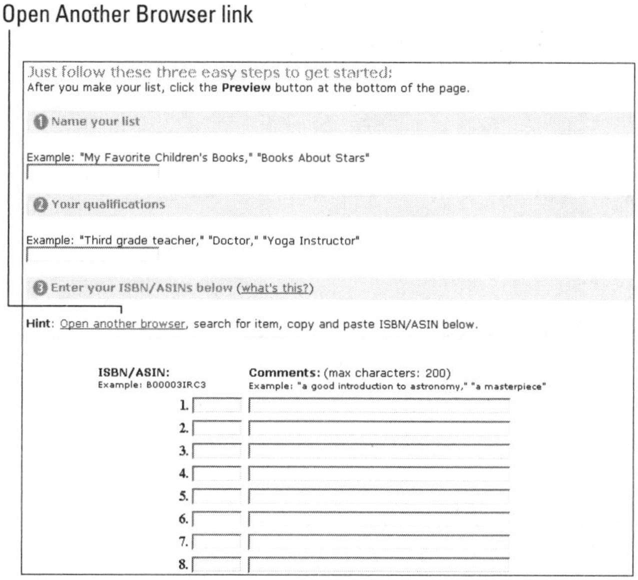

Open Another Browser link

Figure 12-11:
The
Listmania
form.

6. **Go back to the open list form in your first browser window and enter the name of your list in the field provided.**

   It's good to be descriptive and okay to have some fun.

7. **Enter your qualifications in the field provided.**

   You don't have to have real qualifications here — no one is checking. But if you're writing a list and you do have relevant qualifications (for example, you're writing a list on good art books and you're a curator for a museum), list your credentials. They're helpful to people.

8. **Use the special Search box to find an item on your list.**

   Do this in the "other" window — the one with the Amazon welcome page. Once you find an item, go to its detail page, scroll down to its product information, and find its ASIN or ISBN (again, refer to Figure 12-6).

9. **Select the ASIN or ISBN and copy it.**

   Do this by double clicking the ASIN or ISBN and then going up to "edit" in your browser's menu and selecting "copy."

10. **Paste the ASIN or ISBN into the field provided on the list form.**

    To paste, you put your cursor in the field you want to fill, go back up to your browser's menu, and select "paste."

11. **Enter your comments for that item in the field provided.**

    These aren't required, but they add something.

12. **Repeat Steps 6 through 9 until your list is complete and then click the Preview button.**

    You list must be at least 3 items long, and no longer than 25 items (and be sure to separate each item on the list with a comma). When you click Preview, you're taken to a page that shows you what your list will look like on the site. Make sure it's okay — and if it isn't, click the Edit button to make changes.

13. **Click the Publish This List button.**

    You did it! You're taken to a confirmation page and your list makes its way onto the site.

Where your list lives and who's gonna see it

You've done it. You've created a Listmania list and it's a thing of beauty. So who gets to feast their eyes on your handiwork? Your list will definitely show up in your About You area. That means that anyone who has access to that area can see your list.

Your list may also show up in various other places on the site — search results, in the marketing section of the shopping cart, on info-type pages, and so on. This is not an act of favoritism on Amazon's part. In fact, it has nothing to do with who they like and everything to do with what's in your list. When you put ASINs and ISBNs in your list and then submit your list to the site, Amazon registers those ASINs and ISBNs and pulls up lists for relevant situations based on those numbers. So if you wrote a list about bird-watching essentials and someone buys a birdfeeder, your list may end up in the marketing section of that person's shopping cart.

Share the Love

It's always a good idea to share the love, but it's a *really* good idea at Amazon.com. Share the Love is essentially a referral program — except instead of referring people to Amazon and getting a bonus, you refer products to people — and if they buy them, you get a bonus.

You can be both a giver and a receiver of Love at Amazon. When you make a purchase, you have the option to share with your friends and give them the option to buy whatever you've bought, but at a discount. When your friends make a purchase, they can share with you and you get the discount. Either way, Love is Shared.

Love . . . That's Entertainment!

So true. Especially at Amazon. There are a few rules associated with Amazon's Share the Love program. The biggest is that you can only share love with purchases made in the Books, Music, Video, and DVD stores. Here are some other important rules you should be familiar with:

- ✔ **Friends have to buy within one week.** When you're the shar*er* (as opposed to the shar*ee*), your recipients have to buy whatever you're sharing within a week of getting the Share the Love e-mail from Amazon in order for you to get a credit. Conversely, when you're the sharee, *you* have to buy within one week to get the discount. So the buying heat is on!

- ✔ **You can only get one credit per item.** Sad but true. Even if you share an item with 500 of your closest friends and all 500 buy it within a week, you still only get one credit.

- ✔ **You must use your credits within 30 days of receiving them.** After 30 days, your credits expire. You can use a bunch of credits at once, but they all have to be within their valid period. So, again, the buying heat is on. I admit, it's not as hot, but still . . . it's heat.

✔ **You can only use your credit at Amazon.com.** The good news is you aren't limited to just books, music, and movies. The bad news is you can't use your credit at any of the international stores or with any third-party sellers.

✔ **You can't return The Love.** You can return items you bought with Share the Love credits, but you won't receive a refund for the amount of the credit. So plan to keep The Love.

✔ **You can't redeem The Love for cash.** Share the Love is a credit only situation. You either apply it to an Amazon purchase or you lose it.

✔ **You have to use your shopping cart when you apply your credit.** There is a step in the shopping cart process that asks you to include promotional credits. This is where you apply your Share the Love. So don't buy it with 1-Click if you want to apply credits.

How to be a sharer

Sharing the Love is wonderfully easy. You get to look like such a lovely, giving person and you hardly have to lift a finger. Here's how to be a sharer:

1. **Make a purchase from the Book, Music, Video, or DVD store using your shopping cart.**

   You go through just about the whole process — from adding it to your cart through payment — before you hit the Share the Love screen. When you do, you're at a page that looks like Figure 12-12. If you need some help with using the shopping cart, refer to Chapter 10.

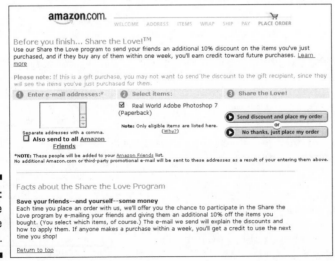

Figure 12-12:
The Share
the Love
page.

2. Enter the e-mail addresses of the people you want to share with in the field provided.

You can enter multiple addresses if they're separated by commas. You can also Share the Love with your entire Friends list by clicking the box next to "Also send to all Amazon Friends." But if you don't want to share it with the whole group, you have to enter e-mail addresses from the list individually in the field provided.

There are times when you don't want to be sharing that love. If you're buying a book, CD, or DVD as a gift for an Amazon.com Friend, don't accidentally "Share the Love." If you do, say, "bye-bye surprise."

3. Click the box next to each item you want to share.

Unfortunately, you can't pick and choose who gets what. Every item you click is shared with every person you enter in the field provided.

4. Click the Send Discount and Place My Order button.

Your order is not placed unless you click this button (or the "No, thanks . . ." button beneath it). So even if you change your mind about sharing, you have to click one of the two buttons to complete your order. When you're finished, you're taken to a page that includes Figure 12-13, where you're offered lots of optional things to do. These are just options. Your order is complete and you have successfully shared.

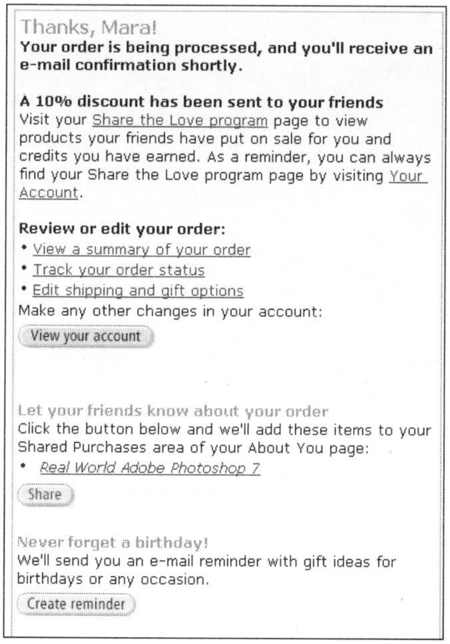

Figure 12-13:
Confirmation —
you have
successfully
Shared the
Love!

Thanks, Mara!
Your order is being processed, and you'll receive an e-mail confirmation shortly.

A 10% discount has been sent to your friends
Visit your Share the Love program page to view products your friends have put on sale for you and credits you have earned. As a reminder, you can always find your Share the Love program page by visiting Your Account.

Review or edit your order:
• View a summary of your order
• Track your order status
• Edit shipping and gift options
Make any other changes in your account:
[View your account]

Let your friends know about your order
Click the button below and we'll add these items to your Shared Purchases area of your About You page:
• *Real World Adobe Photoshop 7*
[Share]

Never forget a birthday!
We'll send you an e-mail reminder with gift ideas for birthdays or any occasion.
[Create reminder]

If you get any takers, your credit shows up in the Credits You've Earned section of your Share the Love page. You can access this page from the Explore box on the left side of your Friends & Favorites area in Your Store.

How to be a sharee

Being a sharee is even easier than being a sharer. Here's how to do it:

1. **Click the link to the item from the Share the Love e-mail.**

   When someone Shares the Love with you, you receive an e-mail that looks like Figure 12-14. You can click the item's link or image and you're taken to a Sign In screen.

2. **Enter your e-mail address and password in the fields provided and click the Sign In Using Our Secure Server button.**

   You come to the Discounts for You section (or tab) of your Share the Love page. To get the discount, you have to buy the item from this page, using the shopping cart. The language on the Share the Love page is ambiguous about this, but if you go to the Help Department they confirm that all Share the Love discounts must be redeemed from the Share the Love page.

3. **Click the Add to Cart button.**

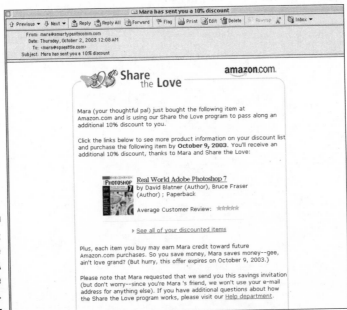

Figure 12-14:
Someone loves you! A Share the Love e-mail.

You're taken to your shopping cart, which will show the item at its non-discounted price. Don't be alarmed. Scroll a tiny bit and you notice that the subtotal reflects the discount.

4. **Click the Proceed to Checkout button.**

You're taken to another Sign In screen.

5. **Enter your e-mail address and password in the fields provided and click the Sign In Using Our Secure Server button.**

This time you come to the Order Placement page. Notice that the Share the Love discount is reflected as a line item in your order summary.

6. **Click the Place Your Order button.**

You, too, are encouraged to Share the Love. The next screen is the Share the Love screen.

7. **Click one of the two buttons to complete your order.**

Your order isn't complete until you either share love and click that button, or decline and click the "No, thanks . . ." button.

Applying credits

Now for the fun part. If you're a big shopper and a big sharer, you can build up a hefty lot of credits. But to use them, you have to activate them! Here's how:

1. **Go to your Friends & Favorites area by clicking the link in the subnav of Your Store.**

2. **Click the Share the Love link in the Explore box on the left side of the page.**

You're taken to your Share the Love page.

3. **Click the Credits You've Earned tab.**

You will see a list of the items that have earned you credits and your total credit amount in red.

4. **Click the Apply Credits button.**

You have officially activated your credit.

You don't have to use your credit right when you activate it. But if you don't use it within 30 days of receiving it, you forfeit it. When you're ready to apply it to a purchase, just make sure you use the shopping cart instead of 1-Click. When you come to your order summary page, you see your Share the Love credits listed. Make sure you check them if you want to apply them to that order.

The People in Poughkeepsie Love Pokemon

I made that up. Maybe the people in Poughkeepsie don't really love Pokemon, but they do love Kasey the Kinderbot. It's their 13th favorite toy. (And who can blame them? If Kasey the Kinderbot and Pokemon ever came to fisticuffs, I'd put my money on the Kinderbot too.)

How do I know all this? Because I checked out Poughkeepsie's Purchase Circle on Amazon.com.

You, too, can check out Purchase Circles. You can go to Amazon and find out what the people in your city are reading or which CDs your fellow college alumni are buying. You can find out what movies your co-workers are watching and which toys their kids are playing with. Purchase Circles are Amazon bestseller lists based on commonalties — geographic, educational, organizational, corporate, and governmental affiliations. So you can go check out Purchase Circles that are relevant to you or take a gander at Purchase Circles that have nothing to do with you but are just fun to look at. (The latter isn't an act of illicit voyeurism. It's perfectly acceptable and entirely *anonymous* voyeurism.)

But Purchase Circles are more than just a curiosity. In some ways, they're better than regular, old bestsellers. If you're looking for good ideas on what to buy, it makes sense to get those recommendations from people you have something in common with. That's what Purchase Circles are all about.

Purchase Circles — getting around

Purchase Circles are most easily accessed from the Friends & Favorites section of Your Store. You find a link to Purchase Circles in the "Explore" box on the left side of the page.

There are hundreds of Purchase Circles on Amazon.com. In fact, one of my favorites is the Amazon.com Purchase Circle. (This is a Purchase Circle for my former co-workers, not the 37 million people shopping at Amazon.) Here's how you would access it:

1. **Go to your Friends & Favorites area by clicking the link in the subnav of Your Store.**

2. **Click the Purchase Circles link in the Explore box on the left side of the page.**

3. **Click the Companies link in the Browse Purchase Circles box.**

4. **Click the A-Z link in the Browse Companies box.**

5. **Click the A link in the Browse Companies A-Z Purchase Circles box.**

6. **Click Amazon.com.**

The average Purchase Circle page looks like Figure 12-15. (Ooh, Web Development with Apache and Perl — those Amazonians sure know how to party!) You can navigate the Purchase Circle by using the links just above the first bestseller. Those links will also tell you which categories you find best-seller lists for in that Purchase Circle.

You can also create a list of favorite Purchase Circles. To add a Purchase Circle to your favorites just click the Add to Favorites button on the right side of the page. Don't see a button? In some cases, if a Purchase Circle isn't well populated, there won't be an Add to Favorites button. If you go up one level (back to the page you clicked from), you're likely to find the button there — and you can add that page to your Favorites. To access your list of favorite Purchase Circles, just click on Purchase Circles in the Explore box on your Friends & Favorites page. That'll take you to the Purchase Circles page and, if you've created one, your Favorite purchase Circles list.

Figure 12-15:
The
Purchase
Circle for
Amazon.
com Inc.

Purchase Circles and privacy

Purchase Circles are completely private. According to Amazon's Purchase Circle FAQ, they are created by "aggregating anonymous data." So you don't have to worry about protecting your privacy. No one will know that you love Air Supply unless you say so.

If you're still worried, you can remove yourself from the circle. By changing your Purchase Circle settings, you will remove your data from the aggregate. Here's how to do it:

1. **Go to your Friends & Favorites area by clicking the link in the subnav of Your Store.**

2. **Click the Purchase Circles link in the Explore box on the left side of the page.**

3. **Click the link that says, Purchase Circles FAQ.**

   You find this under the Have More Questions? header on the right side of the page. You can also click the Here link in the intro paragraph on the Purchase Circles page. Both will take you to the FAQ.

4. **Scroll to the bottom of the page and click the Purchase Circles Settings link under the Privacy heading.**

   You're taken to a Sign In screen.

5. **Enter your e-mail address and password in the fields provided and click the Sign In Using Our Secure Server button.**

   You come to your Manage Your Purchase Circles Favorites page. Scroll down below the fold to find the Participation check box.

6. **Uncheck the Participation box and click the Update button.**

   You come back to the Manage Your Purchase Circles Favorites page, but there's a message above the Participation box acknowledging the changed status.

So You'd Like to Write a "So You'd Like To . . ." Guide

Do you have a special, secret talent? Have you recently finished up a hefty project? Did you recently take a fabulous trip? Share your knowledge with the rest of the Amazon community by writing a So You'd Like To . . . guide.

Creating the guide is similar to creating a Listmania list. Here are a few quick rules to know before you get started:

- ✓ **The items in your guide have to be available at Amazon.** You're not limited to items that you've purchased at Amazon. You're not even limited to items you own.

- ✓ **The items in your guide have to have an ASIN or ISBN number.** This excludes certain products, like Auction and zShops items.

- ✓ **You have to recommend at least 3 and no more than 50 items.** If you write a guide with 50 items, then hats off to you!

- ✓ **Your guide has to be at least 100 words long and no more than 1,500 words long.**

✔ **The first three items you recommend are your featured items in the guide.** So choose them wisely!

Those are the rules, here's how you use them:

1. **Go to your Friends & Favorites area by clicking the link in the subnav of Your Store.**

   The Friends & Favorites area duly appears.

2. **Click the <u>Write A So You'd Like To . . . Guide</u> link in the Explore box.**

   It's the last one in the Explore box — right there on the left side of the page.

   Note: As always, if you're not already signed in, you're taken to a Sign In screen.

3. **In the Sign In screen, enter your e-mail address and password in the fields provided and click the Sign In Using Our Secure Server button.**

   You should now be at the first of two So You'd Like To . . . creation pages (as in Figure 12-16).

4. **Click the <u>. . . open another browser</u> link.**

   You find it in the second bullet under the Enter Text and Product ASINs header. It will automatically open another window and go straight to the Amazon Welcome page. Amazon recommends that you do this to make it easy for you to search for the items on your list and find their ASINs or ISBNs (as in Figure 12-6) in one window, and copy and paste them into your guide in the other window. So you'll be jumping back and forth between the two windows as you write your guide.

5. **Create a title for your guide in the field provided.**

   You do this in the "guide" window, not the second window you opened in order to search for items. They automatically plug in the "So You'd Like To . . . " part. You just need to complete the sentence.

6. **Enter your qualifications in the field provided.**

   You are a world traveler writing a travel-related guide. Or a new dog owner writing a puppy-related guide. You get the drift.

7. **Enter the text for your guide, excluding the item titles.**

   Don't worry; we get to item titles in Step 8. You notice that there are special instructions on the page that tell you how to enter items into your guide. You don't need to enter item titles, just ASINs or ISBNs.

8. **Switch to your second browser window and use the Search feature to find the first item in your guide.**

   Once you find an item, go to its detail page, scroll down to its product information and find its ASIN or ISBN. (Refer to Figure 12-6.)

9. **Select the ASIN or ISBN and copy it.**

   Double-click the ASIN or ISBN and then go up to Edit in your browser's menu and select Copy.

10. **Switch back the your other open browser window and paste the ASIN or ISBN into the appropriate place in the text of your guide.**

    To paste, put your cursor where you want the number to appear, go back up to your browser's menu, and select Paste. Make sure you use the proper format outlined on the So You'd Like To . . . page. Each item entered should look like this: `<ASIN: B00003IRC3i>`. Even if you're entering an ISBN, the letters after the less-than sign should be `ASIN`. This stuff (the greater and less-than signs and the ASIN rule) is important. It has to be exact because it's actually going to become a part of the HTML that makes up the web page.

11. **Repeat Steps 8 through 10 until your guide is complete.**

    Remember, at least 3 items and no more than 50. If you want to add a section heading to your guide, make sure it's in the proper format. Headings should look like this: `<HEADING: "heading here">`.

12. **Click Save and Continue.**

    If you've spent a while constructing your guide, you may need to sign in again. If so, just enter your e-mail address and password and click the Sign In Using Our Secure Server button. You're taken to the preview of your guide. Check to make sure it looks the way you want it to look. If you need to make changes, click the Edit button to go back to the first So You'd Like To . . . page.

13. **Click the Publish button.**

    You come to a page that acknowledges receipt of your guide. You did it!

Figure 12-16:
The So You'd Like To . . . creation page.

So You'd Like to...
Share Your Advice with Others at Amazon.com
(Under 13? <u>Click here</u>.)

Have you recently become an expert at buying a DVD player? Do you know all of the books or products someone must have to learn how to make the perfect pizza? Did you just finish building a deck? Share your advice, experiences, and product recommendations with others. Your guide will appear on your About You page and other places on the site. See a <u>sample So You'd like to... guide</u>. Questions? Go to our <u>Help</u> page.

➊ Step 1 out of 2: Get started

Enter a title, tell us your qualifications, and write your text. After you're finished, click the "Save and continue" button at the bottom of the page.

Create a title
Examples: "Buy the best digital camera," "Build a house," "Create the perfect BBQ feast"
So You'd Like to... |
(Minimum of 8 characters and maximum of 60 characters)

Enter your qualifications
Examples: "Photographer," "Amateur Movie Critic," "Chef Extraordinaire"
|
(Minimum of 10 characters and maximum of 60 characters)

Enter text and product ASINs or ISBNs (<u>what's this?</u>) in the box below.

▸ <u>View sample So You'd Like to... guide</u>
Follow these helpful instructions:

- There is a 100-word minimum and 1,500-word maximum.
- To insert ASIN/ISBN numbers, <u>click to open another browser</u>, search for a product, and copy and paste the ASIN/ISBN where you want the product's title to appear in the text in the following format: `<ASIN: B00003IRC3i>`. Please note: use

Chapter 13

Giving (and Getting) Good Gifts

- -

- -

I love gifts. I love giving them. I love getting them. I love holidays and occasions that involve giving and getting them. When I was little, I would write out long, elaborate Christmas lists — and I'm Jewish. I'm gift-centric. I'm a Giftist. And there's no better place for a Giftist than Amazon.com.

Amazon is set up for good gift getting. They have registries, Wish Lists, gift-matching tools — everything you need to ensure that you're not going to get *another* dickie from your Great-Aunt Lany. Conversely, it's equally easy to give good gifts using Amazon's registries, lists, and matching tools. So you'll never be compelled to give another dickie to your great-niece or nephew.

In this chapter, I show you how to use all of Amazon's gift-related lists, set up your own Wish List, and set up wedding and baby registries. I help you hunt for other people's Wish Lists and registries so good gifts go where they're most wanted (whether you're giving or getting them). I also show you how to use Amazon's Gift Explorer in case the person you're giving to doesn't have a Wish List or registry. Finally, for those of you who are like me and find it difficult to remember important dates, I reveal the glory of Amazon's Special Occasion Reminders. They help you actually remember to use those other gift features in time for your gift-giving events.

I Really Wish You'd Look at My Wish List

Have you ever seen that episode of *Sex and the City* where Carrie, disenchanted by the giftless plight of the single girl, decides to marry herself — and registers at the Manolo Blahnik store? I think she sold herself short. I agree that a $475 pair of shoes can make a girl feel giddy, but one pair of shoes does not a gift bonanza make. Carrie should have gone to Amazon.com and created a Wish List for herself. Then she could have signed herself up for shoes *and* a handbag *and* a nice home entertainment system.

An Amazon Wish List is the grown up equivalent of the Christmas list — only better because it sticks around all year. And unlike wedding and baby registries, Wish Lists are good for any gift-giving occasion.

If you've got a Wish List you can access it any time by clicking on Wish List in the Shopping Tools menu at the top of most pages on the site. (And if you don't have one, click Wish List to get started on making one.)

There's more to know about Wish Lists than what you find here in this chapter. I'm going to cover the basics — the things you absolutely need to know — but if you want to find out more, you can do so on Amazon's site. Just go to the Help department by clicking on Help in the Shopping Tools menu at the top of the page. Then click the Wish Lists & Gift Registries link, and then click Wish Lists. You find lots of good information!

Creating your Wish List

Before you can populate your Wish List, you have to have an Amazon.com account. Then it's automatic; once you have an Amazon.com account, you have a Wish List. It may be bare, but it's there, so you may as well fill 'er up.

Adding items to your Wish List is a wonderfully simple process. The hardest part may be deciding on what to add. If you have an Amazon account, you only need to complete Steps 1 and 2. If you don't, you need to complete all the steps. Here's how to do it:

1. **Search or browse the site for the item that you want.**

   Don't hold back. No one is required to buy the things on your Wish List, so have some fun. Put that gigantic plasma TV on your Wish List. Add the Segway Human Transporter. Why not? You might get lucky. If you need help with searching or browsing, read Chapters 8 and 9, respectively.

2. **Click the Add to Wish List button.**

   You find this button on the right side of the item's detail page, just below the fold (see Figure 13-1). If you already have an Amazon.com account, that's it! You come to a screen that looks like Figure 13-2, where you're shown the item you've added, along with options to view your Wish List or keep shopping. If you don't have an account, just go on to Step 3, where you enter your e-mail address on a sign-in screen.

3. **In the new page that appears, enter your e-mail address in the field provided, click the New Customer radio button, and then click the Sign In Using Our Secure Server button.**

A *New to Amazon.com?* page appears, asking you to register. This is just to set you up with an account so you can have a Wish List. You won't need to give your credit-card information; only your name, e-mail address, and password.

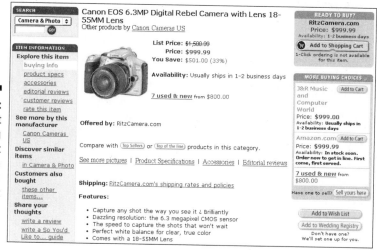

Figure 13-1: Just about everything for sale at Amazon.com has an Add to Wish List button on its detail page.

Figure 13-2: Confirmation that you've successfully added an item to your Wish List.

4. **Enter your name, e-mail address (twice), and password (twice) in the fields provided and then click the Continue button.**

   They also ask for your birthday, but that's optional. When you complete this step, you get your first peek at the Your Wish List page — which looks something like Figure 13-3.

5. **On the Your Wish List page, click the Enter Address button.**

   After you complete Step 4, you've created an account and you can populate your Wish List. But if you want those Wish List items to arrive at your house (what a concept), you'd better enter a shipping address. Don't worry. Nobody can see your address — just your city and state.

6. **Enter your full name and address in the fields provided and click the Submit button.**

   You're taken to a page that confirms your Wish List address has been saved. You'll also get an e-mail confirming the creation of your Wish List.

Figure 13-3:
You have a
Wish List
but you still
have to
enter your
address so
people can
send you
gifts!

Success! You officially have a Wish List, complete with a shipping address. But let's say you were in a big hurry and you just didn't have time to enter your shipping address. Don't despair. You can always add your shipping address later. Just go to the Your Wish List page by clicking on Wish List in the shopping tools menu. Then click the Enter Shipping Address link in the Wish List Information box on the right side of the page. Also, people buying from your Wish List will be notified that you haven't supplied a shipping address and will be given the opportunity to enter it themselves during the checkout process.

Now that you've inaugurated your Wish List, you can pack it full of goodies. To add more items to your Wish List, simply repeat Steps 1 and 2.

I've been telling you to access the Wish List from the Shopping Tools menu, but that's not the only way to do it. Here are a few other ways to get at your list of goodies:

- ✔ **Through the Wish List link in the Shopping Tools menu.** This is the fastest way to get there. The Shopping Tools menu is at the top right on every page of the site.

- ✔ **From the Gifts store.** There's a Wish List choice in the subnav of the Gifts store.

- ✔ **From your Friends & Favorites area.** There's a nice little link in the Explore box on the home page of your Friends & Favorites area.

If there are items on your Wish List that are available used, Amazon will also created a Used Wish List for you. You can access that on the main page of Your Store and on the Your Favorite Stores page within Your Store.

You won't necessarily know when someone buys you something off of your Wish List (until you get it, of course). Amazon.com doesn't make it obvious to keep from spoiling the surprise. When you're logged in to your account, your Wish List will look as it always does — as you created it — whether or not someone has purchased from it. But you can find out what's been purchased by making the appropriate selection from the drop-down list.

Telling people about it

Once you've created a Wish List, you need to spread the word. Say it loud and say it proud and watch the goodies roll in. Here's how to tell people about your Wish List:

1. **Click Wish List in the Shopping Tools menu.**

   You can access your Wish List in any number of ways. How you get there doesn't actually matter.

2. **Click the Share Your Wish List link.**

   You find the link just above the items on your Wish List. When you click it you come to a page that looks like Figure 13-4.

3. **Enter the e-mail addresses of the people you want to notify in the field provided.**

   You can enter as many as you like. Just separate the addresses by commas.

4. **Click the appropriate box if you want to notify your Amazon Friends.**

   This sends an e-mail to the entire group. For more on Amazon Friends, read Chapter 12.

5. **Enter a message in the field provided or use the default message and click the Send E-Mail button.**

   You notice that Amazon has supplied a default message explaining what your Wish List e-mail is about. Feel free to delete this and type your own. When you send the e-mail, you come to a confirmation screen that tells you who your Wish List e-mail has been sent to.

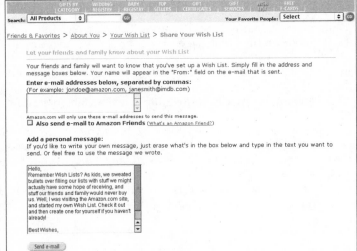

Figure 13-4: The Share Your Wish List page.

Finding someone else's Wish List

If you know you have a gift-giving occasion coming up (and if you use Special Occasion Reminders, you'll know), you can get on Amazon.com and search for the giftee's Wish List. Finding a Wish List is easy. Here's how you do it:

1. **Click Wish List in the Shopping Tools menu.**

   Of course, this isn't the only way to access your Wish List, just the fastest way.

2. **Click the Find a Wish List link.**

   You find the link just above the items on your Wish List.

3. **Enter the name or e-mail address of the person you're searching for in the field provided.**

   If you're going with a name search, try entering the full name. You can enter just first or last, but unless that person has a very unusual name, you're going to end up with a host of search results. Also, this page has lots of good search information, so it wouldn't hurt to read it.

4. Enter the city or state in the field provided.

Entering the city or state is optional, but it can help narrow your search results. When I enter just *Friedman,* I get 2,581 search results. When I enter *Friedman* and *Seattle,* I get 10 results (and 2 of them are mine).

5. Click the Find It! button.

If your search is specific enough, you end up right at that person's Wish List and you're done. If not, you come to a Search Results page that looks something like Figure 13-5. (Notice that doing a Wish List search may also turn up registries.)

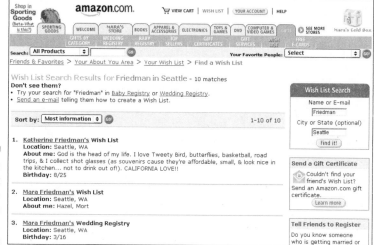

Figure 13-5: A Wish List search results page.

6. Click the name of the person whose Wish List you want to view.

This will take you to their Wish List (see mine in Figure 13-6 — and feel free to use me as a test subject). You can buy items from the Wish List by using the Shopping Cart and 1-Click buttons to the right of each item.

What if you search and search and can't find the person you're looking for? You can send that person an e-mail encouraging him or her to create a Wish List. There's a link on the Wish List Search Results page (Figure 13-5) that says, "Send an e-mail telling them how to create a Wish List." If you click that link, you come to a page that looks like Figure 13-7. Sending an e-mail to tell someone to set up a Wish List is basically the same as sending an e-mail to tell someone about *your* Wish List (instructions for how to do that appear earlier in this chapter).

Figure 13-6:
My Wish
List.

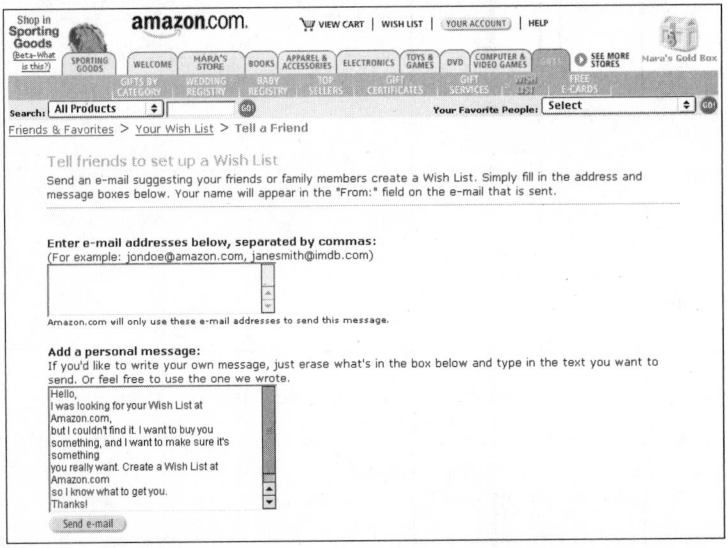

Figure 13-7:
Send friends
and family
an e-mail
and tell
them to
create their
Wish Lists.
It sure
makes your
gift-giving
life easier.

What Anniversary? Setting Up Special Occasion Reminders

Knowing what to get someone is no good unless you also know when to get it.
I know. I'm a consummate occasion-misser. They created the word "belated"
for me. But it doesn't have to be that way.

Amazon's Special Occasion Reminders are a good way to stay in the good graces of the ones you love. And they're easy to set up. Here's how you do it:

1. **Click the See More Stores link.**

   You find this link above the nav on the right side of the page. It takes you to the Store Directory.

2. **Click the Gifts Store link under the Gifts & Registries heading.**

3. **Click Gift Services in the Gifts Store subnav.**

4. **Click the Special Occasion Reminders link.**

   You should now be on the first Special Occasion Reminders page. It's nothing more than a quick paragraph about what Reminders are and a place to put the Create New Reminder button.

5. **Click the Create New Reminder button.**

   You're taken to a Sign In screen.

6. **Enter your e-mail address and password in the fields provided and then click the Sign In Using Our Secure Server button.**

   You come to the Create a Special Occasion Reminder page you see in Figure 13-8.

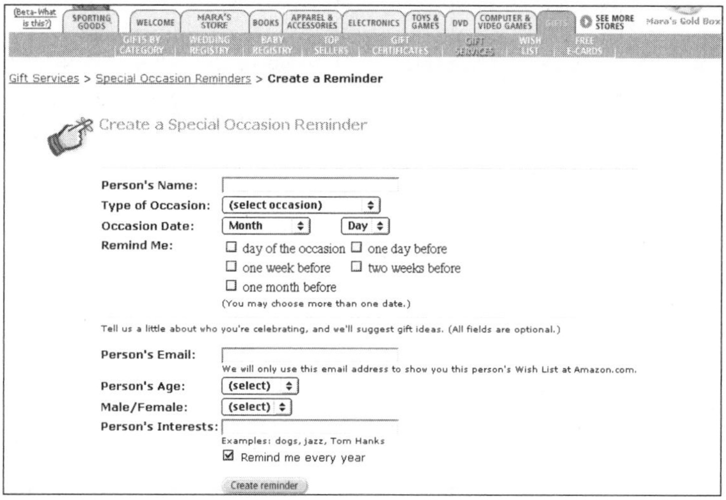

Figure 13-8: You create your Special Occasion Reminders by using this form.

7. **Enter a name in the field provided.**

   This should be the name of the person associated with the event or occasion. Ostensibly that's the person who would receive the gift.

8. **Use the drop-down menus to specify both the type and date of the occasion.**

You have plenty of choices for type — anniversary, birthday, wedding — and if none of those work, choose Other.

9. **Click the appropriate box or boxes to tell Amazon when to send your reminder.**

   You can choose as many boxes as you like. You're sent a Reminder e-mail for each box you choose.

10. **Fill out the optional info.**

    If you want, you can tell Amazon a little bit about the person you're gifting. Enter their e-mail address in the field provided and when the occasion is drawing near, Amazon will surface their Wish List for you (assuming they have one). You can also use the drop-down menus to give the age and gender of the recipients, and you can even enter some of their interests (separated by commas, please). The last optional choice is a box that's automatically checked; it offers to remind you of this occasion every year. If you don't want a yearly reminder, just uncheck the box.

11. **Click the Create Reminder button.**

    You're taken to your Special Occasion Reminders page, which now shows one entry. To add more reminders, click the Create New Reminder button and repeat Steps 6 through 10.

You access your Reminders from your About You area. Go to your Friends & Favorites area, click on your About You Area in the Browse box, and then click on Your Reminders under Gift Helpers in the Browse box.

Going to the Chapel: Wedding Registries in Detail

If you've ever gotten married and had a registry, you know how great it is to pick out all the stuff you need and actually get it. Amazon is an especially good place to register because you won't be limited to just kitchen and household items. If you want to register for CDs, you can. If the happy couple wants a new cell phone, they can register for it. You can register for just about anything Amazon sells with the exception of used goods or Auctions items.

Amazon offers a lot good information on their Web site on how to get the most from their registry service. Here I cover the basics of setting up and updating your registry, and also show you how to find someone else's registry — but if you need more information, I encourage you to go to the Amazon Help department (just click on Help in the Shopping Tools menu at the top of most pages on the site). Once there, just click the Wish Lists & Gift Registries link, and then click Wedding Registry.

Everything you ever need: The Info Center

When you get married, you get advice from everyone. Everyone wants to share (or at least tell you) wedding stories. Everyone's got an opinion. Things can get heated. Some people go a little insane. Getting married can be confusing and stressful. That's what happens when we gather all those space aliens we call our family members and ask them to sit together and make nice for an entire day. (Or maybe I'm projecting here.)

Anyway, registering doesn't have to be confusing and stressful. But in case you start to feel that way, visit Amazon's Wedding Info Center (shown in Figure 13-9). You find it in the Wedding section of the Gifts store. Here's how to get there:

1. **Click See More Stores.**

   You find this link above the nav on the right side of the page. It takes you to the Store Directory.

2. **Click Wedding Registry under the Gifts & Registries heading.**

3. **Click Info Center in the new subnav.**

   This is one of the few times Amazon breaks one of its own rules. Notice that the subnav in the Wedding section is different from the subnav in the Gifts store, even though the wedding section is actually *in* the Gifts store. Strange but true.

Figure 13-9:
The
Wedding
Info Center
has
answers
galore!

The Info Center has more than what you need in the way of information. You find a thorough FAQ, checklists, buying guides, and more. Even if you don't think you need help, the Info Center is a good place to browse. You may get some good ideas and find some things to register for that you didn't even think about. Remember, you're only going to get married once (in theory, at least), so you may as well make that registry a work of art.

Creating your wedding registry

Creating your wedding registry at Amazon is much like creating your Wish List, but with a little extra work up front. It helps to know what you want on your registry, but if you don't, you can use Amazon's Quick Start registry (more on that in a minute).

Here's how to create your Amazon.com wedding registry:

1. **Click the See More Stores link.**

   Remember, it's at the top right of every page on the site.

2. **Click the Wedding Registries link.**

   You find it under the Gifts & Registries header.

3. **Click the Create Your Registry button.**

   You're taken to a Sign In screen.

4. **Enter your e-mail address and password in the fields provided and then click the Sign In Using Our Secure Server button.**

   You should now be on the Create Your Registry page. Entering your registry information and shipping address is mandatory; the optional information is not.

5. **Enter your registry information in the fields provided.**

   You need to give your full name, your partner's full name, and a name for the registry. Notice that Amazon completes your registry name by making whatever you enter a possessive and adding the word "Registry" at the end.

6. **Enter your shipping address in the fields provided.**

   People viewing your registry will only be able to see your city and state. No need to worry about privacy here.

7. **Add optional information in the fields provided at your discretion.**

   In the comments section, you might add something like, "Please buy us something from our registry as we don't really *want* a ceramic Dalmatian candlestick holder." (Or maybe I'm projecting again.) You can also add a photo, but keep it clean, people, keep it clean.

8. **Click the Create Registry button.**

   You come to a page that confirms that your registry has been created.

9. **Search for items that you want in your registry.**

   Now it's time to add items. You can do this in two ways: by clicking the Start Adding Items button on the confirmation page and using a Registry Checklist, or by hopping around the site and finding things you want.

10. **If you're using a Registry Checklist, click the check boxes next to the items you want to add and then click the Add to Registry button. If you're "hopping around the site," click the Add to Wedding Registry button next to each item on its detail page.**

    You find the Add to Wedding Registry button on the right side of the detail page underneath the Ready to Buy? box. After you add items to your registry (regardless of how you added them), you come to a screen that is ⅔ marketing and ⅓ acknowledgment that the item has been added to your registry. You'll also receive an e-mail confirming your registry.

A quick word about registry checklists. These may be the most convenient way to add items to your registry. They're broken out by category and each one lists a host of options. (Figure 13-10, for example, shows the Cookware Registry Checklist.) You can check as many options as you like and add them all to your registry at once. You can access the Registry Checklists on the Wedding Registry main page.

Figure 13-10: Registry Checklists make adding to your registry a snap.

The Quick Start registry

The Kitchen & Housewares Quick Start registry is an all-categories registry checklist. There's a little bit of everything here — from cookware to small appliances. Just enough to stock a happy kitchen with your sweetie.

You can get to the Quick Start registry from the Wedding Registry page. To access the registry, just click either the link in the paragraph or the Get Started button.

Using the feature is a cakewalk (pun alert!). Check the boxes for the items you want on your registry. You can check as many or as few as you like, and then click one of the two Add to Registry buttons on the page (there's one at the top and another at the bottom). That's it. The items are added to your registry.

Updating your registry

You're not stuck with your registry as is when you've created it. Your registry is extremely flexible; it can change as quickly as your mood if you want it to.

To update or change your registry, first you have to access it. To do that, simply go to the Wedding Registry page and then click the View/Update Your Registry button. You'll notice that there are several ways to update your registry.

Figure 13-11 shows a sample wedding registry — Congratulations, Muffy! — ready for updating. Here are some key things you can do from this page:

- **Share your registry.** You find the link to do this just above the items in your registry. This is the same feature that you may have used for your Wish List. Amazon will send an e-mail out on your behalf informing people of your registry. All you need to do is enter the e-mail addresses of those folks you want notified and then click the Send E-Mail button. Easy!

- **Edit your registry information.** This lives in the About Us box on the right side of the page. Use this to change your name, your partner's name — it can happen! — or the name of your registry.

- **Change your shipping information.** This also lives in the About Us box. It's where you can change the address that registry items will be shipped to.

You can also change the status of individual items on your registry. You'll find these options under each item in your registry:

- **Change quantities.** The default for the Desired box is 1. Enter whatever number you like, and make sure you click the Save Changes button.

- **Delete.** Do this by simply clicking the "delete" button underneath he item.

- **Move an item to another list.** You can move an item from your wedding registry to either your Wish List or baby registry. Use the drop-down menu to choose where you want the item to go and click the "go" button.

Wedding > **Your Registry**

Welcome to your Wedding Registry, Muffy.
(If you are not Muffy, click here.)

Share Your Registry | Browse Brands | Wedding Home

Total Items: 3   Page 1 of 1

Sort: [Date added ▼] (GO)   Hide edit options

Items will ship to: Muffy Muffin - Muffinsville, CA

1.   **Bissell 6700 Butler Revolution Canister Vacuum**   Buy new: $64.99
     Bissell
     In stock soon. Order now to get in line. First come, first served.
     Date added: October 3, 2003   (🛒 Add to cart)

     Desired: [1]
     Comment: [   ]
     (Save Changes)   (Delete)

     Move to: [Wish List ▼] (GO)

2.   **Tupperware Rock'N Serve 6-Piece Set, Gemstone**   Buy new: $49.49
     Tupperware
     In stock soon. Order now to get in line. First come, first served.
     Date added: October 3, 2003   (🛒 Add to cart)

     Desired: [1]
     Comment: [   ]   Used & new from
     (Save Changes)   (Delete) $48.98

About Us

Registry Information

Couple: Muffy Muffin and Cookie Cookin
Wedding Date: March 16, 2004
Your Comments:
Please enter your comments.
Name of Registry: Muffy and Cookie

(Edit info)

Shipping Address

Muffy Muffin - Muffinsville, CA

(Change)

Your Wish Lists & Registries

• Wish List
• Create a Baby Registry

Wedding Registry Search

Name:
[   ]
City or State:
(of shipping address -- optional)
[   ]

(Find it!)

More to Explore

▸ Registry Checklists

Figure 13-11:
A wedding registry (for a make-believe person).

Finding someone else's Wedding Registry

Finding a registry is a lot like finding a Wish List. Here's how you do it:

1. **Click Wedding Registry in the Store Directory.**

   You can access the Store Directory by clicking the See More Stores link above the nav on any page of the site.

2. **On the Wedding home page, enter the name of the person you're searching for in the field provided in the Wedding Registry Search box.**

   The box is on the right side of the Wedding home page. Enter the full name of either member of the couple. Remember, anyone who sets up a Wedding Registry is required to enter his or her partner's name.

3. **Enter the city or state in the field provided.**

   This helps you narrow your search results if the person you're searching for has a common name.

4. **Click the Find it! button.**

   If you hit the nail on the head, you go directly to the registry itself. If not, you come to a Search Results page.

5. **Click the name of the person whose registry you want to view.**

   When the registry appears, you can buy items by clicking the Add To Shopping Cart button.

   You can also access a handy Find a Registry page from any place in the Wedding area by clicking Find a Registry in the subnav.

Oh Baby! Baby Registries in Detail

Baby registries at Amazon are the kissing cousins of wedding registries with one critical difference: Many of the items you're likely to put on your registry are going to come from Babies 'R' Us because Amazon's Baby store is actually a cobranded store. Type either **babiesrus.com** or **amazon.com** and you end up at the same place. So baby registries are actually *cobranded registries* (which can go either route, businesswise) as opposed to just Amazon.com registries.

So what? Well, one thing that is affected by this partnership is returns. Here is the nutshell version of the rules:

✔ **Babies 'R' Us items.** You can return them to Amazon.com or a Babies 'R' Us store, but they're subject to the Babies 'R' Us return policy.

✔ **Amazon.com items**. These can only be returned to Amazon and are subject to Amazon's return policy.

Privacy is also an issue to consider. You should be aware that when you shop the Baby store, you're sharing your personal info with the "'R' Us family." This matters because their policies are not as stringent as Amazon's are (for example, they will solicit you over the phone to tell you about "special offers"). Here's how to find out more about the 'R' Us family's privacy policies:

1. **Click Help in the Shopping Tools menu.**

2. **Click the Baby Registry link.**

   You find it under the Gifts & Gift Certificates heading.

3. **Click the Click Here link.**

   You find the link in the second paragraph of text.

4. **In the new page that appears, click the Privacy Policy link.**

   Nope. You're not there yet. One more click . . .

5. **In the *new* new page that appears, click 'R' Us Family Privacy Policy.**

   The lengthy, lumpy truckload of legalese that appears on your screen is the 'R' Us Family Privacy Policy. If you're particularly concerned with privacy, you should read it.

There is one piece of good news about the partnership (other than that you can buy all kinds of great stuff online): When you create a baby registry online, it also exists in the 'R' Us stores — which means people can shop your registry virtually *or* walk into a brick-and-mortar store and do it the old-fashioned way. Also, if you already have a registry with the 'R' Us stores, you can activate it online. (Tips on how to do this appear later in the chapter.)

Everything you ever need: The Resource Center

The Resource Center in the Baby store is one of the best collections of information you find at Amazon.com. They're not just selling here. They're providing valuable information.

To access the Resource Center, go to the Baby store and click Resource Center in the subnav.

Here are the kinds of information you find in the Baby store's Resource Center:

- ✔ **Buying Guides.** You find Buying Guides on everything from baby shower gifts to safety gates. There are 13 Buying Guides in all.

- ✔ **Checklists.** These are not like the checklists in the wedding registry section. They are, in fact, just simple lists with links to category pages for the items that are available at Amazon/Babies 'R' Us. There are 12 different checklists.

- ✔ **Articles and Information.** These are often taken from magazines or other expert sources. There are nine different categories of information and several articles within each. You'll find everything from articles on fertility to info on behavior and development.

- ✔ **Expert Advice from Your Baby Today.** Here's where Amazon excerpts several pieces of content from Your Baby Today, an organization created by Nestlé Carnation to "offer tips for mother and baby on health, nutrition, and care; review baby and maternity products; and provide interactive tools to chart pregnancy and baby's development." The advice in this section appears in a question-and-answer format.

Creating your baby registry

If you've created a Wish List and/or wedding registry, then creating a baby registry will be child's play (pun alert!) — and here's how to do it:

1. **Click the See More Stores link.**

   Remember, it's at the top right of every page on the site.

2. **Click the Baby Registries link.**

   You find it under the Gifts & Registries header. You can also access the baby registry from the subnav of the Baby store.

3. **Click the Create Your Registry button.**

   You're taken to a Sign In screen.

4. **Enter your e-mail address and password in the fields provided and then click the Sign In Using Our Secure Server button.**

   You come to a page that looks like Figure 13-12. Don't worry about the Activate Registry business. I talk about that later in the chapter.

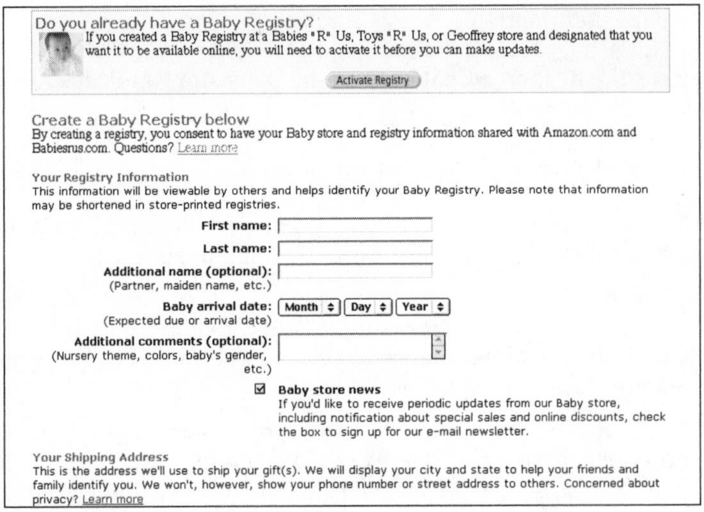

Figure 13-12:
The Baby
Registry
form.

5. **Enter your registry information.**

   Enter your first and last names in the field provided, and then use the drop-down menu to enter the due date. Your partner's name is optional and so are any comments you might want to make (such as, "Please don't touch my belly.") Also, notice that the Baby Store News box is checked as a default. If you don't want to receive e-mail about the Baby store, uncheck the box.

6. **Enter your shipping address in the fields provided.**

   People viewing your registry will only be able to see your city and state. No need to worry about privacy here. Also, in-store employees won't be able to see the second line of your address; if you possibly can, put your address info on line one.

7. **Click the Submit button.**

   If you've taken a bit of time, you may be asked to sign in again. Enter your e-mail address and password in the fields provided, and click that yellow button! You come to a page that confirms that your registry has been created.

8. **Search for items that you want in your registry.**

   Add items to your registry by using one of the two Quick Start Registries or by shopping the Baby store.

9. **If you're using a Quick Start Registry, click the uncheck boxes next to the items you don't want to add and then click the Add to Baby Registry button. If you're shopping the Baby Store click the Add to Baby Registry button next to each item on its detail page.**

After you create your registry, you'll get an e-mail from Amazon confirming it.

Activating an existing registry

If you already have a registry with an 'R' Us store, and indicated that you wanted to be able to see it online, you can view it and buy from it at Amazon. You won't, however, be able to change or edit it. To do that you have to activate it. If you gave the 'R' Us folks your e-mail address when you created your registry in the store, they should have sent you an e-mail with instructions on how to activate your registry. If not, you can request another e-mail by clicking the Activate Registry button on your registry page. Enter your e-mail address and your registry number and click the Send E-Mail button. Amazon will send the 'R' Us store an e-mail requesting that they send you instructions.

Quick Start registries

The Baby store has two Quick Start registries: Bestsellers and Top of the Line. They function the same way the Kitchen & Housewares Quick Start registry does for Wedding Registry types, but with one critical difference: instead of checking what you want, you *uncheck* the items you don't want. Tricky, I know.

You can access the Quick Start registries from your registry page. You find the Quick Start Registries link at the top center of the page, just below your greeting. Click it and then choose which registry you want. Within the registry, just uncheck the boxes for the items you don't want on your registry and click one of the two Add to Baby Registry buttons on the page. (Again, there's one at the top and another at the bottom.)

Updating your registry

You update your registry right on your registry page. You can access your registry directly from the subnav of the Baby store.

Here are some key things you can do from this page:

 ✔ **Share your registry.** This link sits at the top center of the page along with the Quick Start Registries and New Parent's Checklist. Amazon sends an e-mail on your behalf, informing your list of your registry. All you need do is enter the e-mail addresses of the potential gift givers.

✔ **Edit your registry and shipping information.** You can do this from the Your Information box on the upper-left side of the page.

✔ **Access the New Parent's Checklist.** This is a good resource. It's a very comprehensive list and can help jog your memory lest you forget something.

And you'll find these editing options under each item in the registry:

✔ **Change quantities.** The default for the Desired box is 1. Enter whatever number you like, and make sure you click the Save Changes button.

✔ **Delete items.** Do this by simply clicking the Delete button underneath the item.

✔ **Find someone else's baby registry.** The Baby Registry Search box sits just below the Your Information box.

Finding someone else's baby registry

Finding a registry is a lot like finding a Wish List. Here's how you do it:

1. **Click Baby Registry in the Store Directory.**

   You can access the Store Directory by clicking See More Stores above the nav on any page of the site. You can also access the Baby Registry by clicking it in the subnav of the Baby store.

2. **Enter the information for the person you're searching for in the fields provided in the Baby Registry Search box.**

   You can search by name and location, registry number, or e-mail.

3. **Click the Find It! button.**

   Even if there's only one match, you come to a Search Results page.

4. **Click the name of the person whose registry you want to view.**

   Notice that the registry is broken down by items available online and items that you have to buy in the store. You can use the store locator to find a store near you that has that item in stock. You can also view the items on the list that have already been purchased.

When All Else Fails: Gift Explorer

You've searched tirelessly for a Wish List or registry. You've sent them an e-mail asking them to create a Wish List or registry. But there's no Wish List and no registry. It's time for the Gift Explorer — a handy, fun feature that helps you find gifts that match the recipients' interests.

You can access Gift Explorer from the Search box on the Gifts store home page. That particular Search box is set up with the Gift Explorer function ready to go. Just enter a keyword in the field provided, make sure the Use Gift Explorer box is checked, and click Go. You get search results that look like Figure 13-13. The results are broken out by store and you can use the More Like These buttons to help refine your results further.

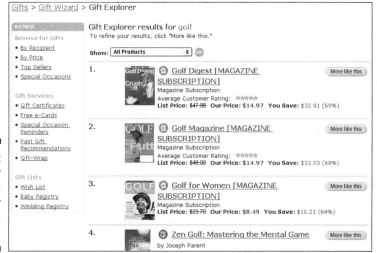

Figure 13-13:
Gift Explorer
gives you
gift-ready
search
results.

Part IV
Making Money at Amazon.com

The 5th Wave   By Rich Tennant

"For 30 years I've put a hat and coat on to make sales calls and I'm not changing now just because I'm doing it on the Web from my living room."

In this part . . .

Everyone knows you can buy things at Amazon.com. There are more than 30 million people doing it! But not everyone knows that you can use the site to make money — lots of money.

In this part, I show you how to use Amazon.com to make money. I cover Marketplace, Auctions, and zShops — selling programs that anyone can use. I talk about Amazon.com Advantage — a program for independent publishers, labels, and studios. And I give you a complete overview of Associates — Amazon's 1,000,000-member Web-referral program.

Chapter 14

The Basics of Using Amazon.com to Build Bucks

In This Chapter

▶ Discovering the different venues for making money at Amazon.com

▶ Signing up for Amazon Payments

▶ Giving and receiving feedback

▶ Finding out about advanced money earning techniques and opportunities

▶ Getting a handle on the rules

Few people know just how many moneymaking opportunities there are at Amazon.com. Amazon is an actual store. It's true. But it's also a store that allows you, the customer, to become a merchant. With a hefty dash of the right stuff and enough time to spare, you can actually make a living using Amazon.com. There are two ways to do that: You can sell stuff yourself or you can partner.

Selling stuff is pretty simple in concept. You have something you want to sell; you post it on the site using one of Amazon's selling venues; Amazon takes a cut when someone buys it. For those of you who are thinking, "I don't want to give them a cut! I'm going to sell it on my own." Just remember, they have a store all set up for you — and (more important) 37 million customers. Take my word for it. It's worth it!

Partnering is a little bit less defined but can be equally lucrative. Amazon has a couple of different partnering opportunities that are something like referral programs — you put links to Amazon on your site and if people use them and buy, you get paid. These are for people who have their own Web sites and want to use them to earn extra cash (and you'd be amazed at how much extra cash some people earn!).

In this chapter, I cover the basics of all of Amazon's moneymaking opportunities. I give you a general overview of each, talk about how you get paid, cover the rules and regulations, and point you to some advanced techniques to make the most of your efforts.

A Quick Look at the Venues

There are six moneymaking venues at Amazon.com — Marketplace, Auctions, zShops, Advantage, Associates, and Honor System — and you've probably come across at least half of them without even realizing it. In fact, some of them are woven into the site seamlessly.

Each program falls into one of the two categories I've described — a selling opportunity or a partnering opportunity. If you don't have a Web site of your own, you won't be able to take advantage of the partnering opportunities. But the selling is for everyone.

Marketplace

Marketplace is Amazon's consignment program. If you've shopped at Amazon, you've seen Marketplace in action. You find Marketplace items on the detail pages. Maybe you've noticed the invitation to buy an item used (as in Figure 14-1). Those items are being sold through Marketplace.

Figure 14-1:
The More
Buying
Choices box
houses the
link to
Market-
place items.

Marketplace is the "Everyman" selling tool. Anyone can use it and it's relatively simple to set up. Also, you can sell in any quantity — one-offs or bulk loads. It's the most flexible of Amazon's selling programs. Of course, there are some rules and restrictions associated with Marketplace (you can scope them out in Chapter 15). But if you're just looking to try out some Amazon opportunities — just dipping your foot in the online selling pool, as it were — Marketplace is a good place to start.

Here are the basics of the program:

> ✔ **The item you sell has to be in Amazon's catalog.** They feature the item on the detail page, right next to the brand-new one they're selling. So if they don't sell the item already, there isn't a page in the catalog, and that means no place to feature your product. You can even sell collectible versions of items they have in their catalog.

✔ **You set a fixed price.** Marketplace is not an eBay-style online auction. It's a fixed-price sale. If you're uncertain as to how to price your items, Amazon makes a suggestion.

✔ **Amazon takes a cut.** They charge a 99-cent-per-item flat fee plus a percentage commission. (In effect, it's not worth your while to sell an item for $1.50.)

✔ **You do the shipping, but Amazon gives you a shipping credit.** Amazon gives you a shipping credit based on the item you sell — different items earn different amounts — and where and how quickly you ship. You ship the item directly to your buyer. Amazon has clear guidelines about how to pack and ship appropriately posted on their site.

✔ **All payments happen through Amazon.** You won't receive money directly from your buyer. They pay Amazon and Amazon pays you.

Auctions

This is Amazon's version of the eBay concept — online auctions of just about any item you'd care to sell. Unlike Marketplace, you don't have to auction off an item that's identical to items already in Amazon's catalog, though you could if you wanted to.

Auctions offers more freedom in terms of what you can list, but less exposure. Because Marketplace items are featured in the stores on regular detail pages, they get all the exposure that those items get. Auctions are in a store of their own — slightly buried — and each item has its own detail page. So when you auction an item at Amazon, you are relying on customers to look for that item specifically.

In many ways, Marketplace has upstaged Auctions. Amazon offers so many different products now, it's hard to imagine what you might sell that you couldn't find in their catalog. Still, Auctions can be a good place to sell certain things — most notably, collectibles that aren't already in Amazon's catalog — because you can sell such collectibles at a fixed price through Marketplace. (In other words, you're better off selling a collectible book through Marketplace than you are through Auctions, because in Marketplace you have the benefit of the bookstore's exposure — more potential customers looking for what you're offering.)

The basics of Auctions are simple:

✔ **You post an item on the Auctions site.** There are rules about what you can and can't sell. See Chapter 16 for the details.

✔ **Amazon customers bid on your item.** Of course, it goes to the highest bidder.

✔ **You collect payment through Amazon or on your own.** All Amazon sellers sign up for Amazon Payments, but Auctions sellers are also allowed to accept other methods of payment. More on Amazon Payments later in this chapter. (More on other methods of payment in Chapter 16.)

✔ **You do the shipping.** Alas, no shipping credit here, but most Auctions sellers have the buyer pay for shipping as part of the deal.

✔ **Amazon takes a cut.** They charge a ten-cent listing fee per item that is not refundable, even if the item doesn't sell. If the item does sell, they also charge a percentage as a closing fee.

Amazon's fees are generally lower than eBay's, but fewer customers shop Amazon's auctions, so the final price you get may well be lower too. Just a thought. . . .

zShops

zShops are mini stores created by independent sellers. They're a trickier proposition in terms of set-up. Normally you would only want to set up a zShop if you had several items you wanted to sell — ideally, a selection of items that would make sense together all in one online store. To find out more about setting up a zShop, check out Chapter 16.

The basics of zShops are as follows:

✔ **You create a storefront on Amazon.com.** When you sign up for zShops, you actually have your own storefront that may look something like Figure 14-2. You upload images and/or descriptions of your products to your storefront.

✔ **You sell items at a fixed price.** These can be items that are also in Amazon's catalog, or unique items that aren't.

✔ **You collect payment through Amazon or on your own.** Like Auctions sellers, zShops sellers are allowed to accept other methods of payment in addition to Amazon Payments.

✔ **You ship.** Again, no credit here, but you can have the buyer pay for shipping.

✔ **Amazon takes a cut.** All zShops merchants are required to become Pro Merchant subscribers. There is a monthly fee of $39.99 for up to 40,000 items. (See? They really do intend for you to have your own store!) They also charge a percentage as a closing fee.

Figure 14-2:
A zShops
storefront.

Advantage

Advantage is a program that Amazon developed to help independent publishers, studios, and labels sell their work. So if you have independently produced videos, albums, or books and you need some help with distribution, Advantage is for you.

Advantage is actually a very elaborate program and can make a huge difference in the life of an independent artist. But it's not as "autopilot" as other Amazon selling opportunities. For Advantage to work, you have to put in some effort — not just on setup, but in maintenance too.

One of the nice things about Advantage is that your products are sold on the site the same way any label's, publisher's or studio's products are sold. They show up in browse lists and search results — indistinguishable from bigger fishes titles. If they're especially good, they may get the attention of an Amazon editor who might feature them. But at the end of the day, you are responsible for marketing your titles. Amazon just takes care of the selling logistics and the fulfillment. To discover more about Advantage, look at Chapter 17.

Here are the basics of the Advantage program:

✔ **You apply to the Advantage program.** They don't accept just anybody. Your products have to have the appropriate codes: ISBN or UPC. They must also be appropriate in terms of content (that is, no porn or other unsavory material).

✔ **You send products to Amazon's distribution centers.** If you're accepted, they send you an order. When they get low on inventory, they let you know and you can send more goods.

✔ **Amazon does the shipping.** The nice thing about Advantage is that Amazon handles the fulfillment so you never have to worry about getting the goods to the customer.

✔ **Amazon pays you and takes a cut.** The program has an annual fee of $29.95. Each month, Amazon sends you a check for 45 percent of the list price of the items you've sold. In other words, they take a 55 percent cut. This may sound hefty, but keep in mind that you can list titles that aren't in Amazon's catalog, and they handle the fulfillment to individual customers.

Associates

Associates is Amazon's referral program and it's the largest Web-referral program in existence, with almost 1,000,000 members. It's a very basic concept: You put a link to Amazon on your Web site and whenever anyone uses it to go to the site and buy something, you get a referral fee.

Anyone with an appropriate Web site can be an Amazon.com Associate. The program is free and it's pretty easy to sign up. For more on Associates, read Chapter 18.

Honor System

This is the newest kid on the block. Honor System is a program that allows you to collect voluntary donations or ask for payments (for using your digital content) from the people who visit your Web site. They click a graphic that Amazon supplies, and the transaction occurs through Amazon.com. (To see one of these graphics, check out `www.recipesource.com`. Scroll down a bit — it's on the left side well below the fold.)

In terms of payment, Honor System is closer to Marketplace or zShops than it is to Associates. For each Honor System payment you receive, Amazon charges you a flat fee of $.15 and 5 percent commission.

The Check Isn't in the Mail: Getting Paid

There are lots of things that make selling or partnering with Amazon a good idea — tons of customers, giant store already in existence — but getting paid might be the best reason of all. When you deal with Amazon, you get paid.

They're all set up for it. It's easy for you. It's easy for your customers (because they're really Amazon's customers). It's great. And anyone who has ever had the unpleasant experience of trying to track down a customer for payment knows just how great it is to have someone else do it for you.

Signing up for Amazon Payments

Advantage, Associates, and Honor System have their own methods of payment. Basically, you have an account on Amazon's site that shows you how much you've earned and they send you a monthly check or you can elect to have the money moved directly into your bank account. (More on this in Chapters 17 and 18.)

Amazon Payments is what you use to get paid for your Marketplace, Auctions, and zShops sales. You don't have to use Amazon Payments for the latter two, but it's what makes getting paid so simple.

You're required to sign up for Amazon Payments when you list your first item or items in Marketplace, Auctions, or zShops. It's part of the process. You can also sign up for Amazon Payments without listing an item — just to get ready.

You don't have to have a preexisting account at Amazon to sell there, but you do need to set one up in the process of signing up for Amazon Payments. Here's how to sign up if you *don't* already have an Amazon account:

1. **Go to the Help Department.**

   Do this by clicking on Help in the shopping tools menu at the top of almost any page on the site.

2. **Click the Selling at Amazon.com link.**

   You have to scroll below the fold to find this header.

3. **Click the Amazon Payments Help link in the Browse box.**

   The Browse box is on the top left of the page.

4. **Click the Apply Now link in the first paragraph of text.**

   This is where the application process actually begins. The very first thing you're asked to do is sign in.

5. **Enter your e-mail address in the field provided, click the circle that says that you don't have a password, and then click the Continue button.**

   You come to a screen that asks you to create a password. Be sure to pick something easy for you to remember and very hard (heck, let's shoot for *impossible*) for someone else to guess.

6. **Enter your first and last names in the fields provided, enter your password twice, and then click Continue.**

7. **Enter your credit-card number and cardholder name in the fields provided.**

   Before you can use Amazon Payments, you have to give Amazon your credit-card info. They use it to deduct their share should you decide to have buyers pay you independently. It's totally secure, but if you're concerned, click the <u>Why This Is Safe</u> link in the introductory text.

8. **Use the drop-down menus to choose card type and expiration date and then click Continue.**

   You'll need to supply the billing address associated with the card you gave.

9. **Enter your name, billing address, and phone number in the fields provided and then click Continue.**

   You come to a page that looks like Figure 14-3. If you already had an Amazon.com account, this would be the first page you'd see after signing in. Confirm that all the information on this page is as it should be. If you want to change your nickname, do. Remember, this is the name that your buyers see, so if you don't want a bunch of crazy, unsolicited e-mails, don't use your e-mail address here. Also, if you're a preexisting account holder, you may need to fill in the phone number fields and the nickname box. Mine were empty when I signed in.

10. **Check the box that indicates that you've read and agree to the Participation Agreement and then click Continue.**

    I know it's not fun to read the agreement, but do it anyway. Also, you notice that at the bottom of the page there is the option to give Amazon your checking account number or do it later. The default is set at "do it later" and that's what I'd do. If you sell something, you can enter it then.

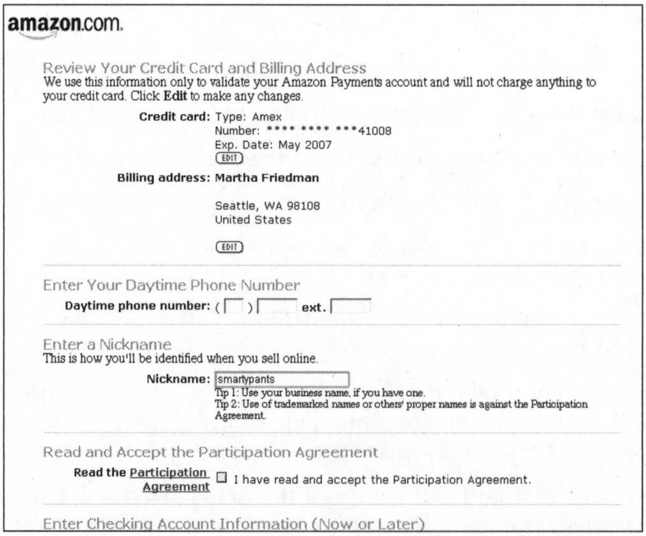

---

amazon.com.

Review Your Credit Card and Billing Address
We use this information only to validate your Amazon Payments account and will not charge anything to your credit card. Click **Edit** to make any changes.

     Credit card: Type: Amex
                 Number: **** **** ***41008
                 Exp. Date: May 2007
                 (EDIT)

     Billing address: Martha Friedman

                 Seattle, WA 98108
                 United States

                 (EDIT)

Enter Your Daytime Phone Number
     Daytime phone number: ([ ]) [ ] **ext.** [ ]

Enter a Nickname
This is how you'll be identified when you sell online.
         Nickname: |smartypants |
                 Tip 1: Use your business name, if you have one.
                 Tip 2: Use of trademarked names or others' proper names is against the Participation Agreement.

Read and Accept the Participation Agreement
     Read the <u>Participation</u> ☐ I have read and accept the Participation Agreement.
         <u>Agreement</u>

Enter Checking Account Information (Now or Later)

Figure 14-3:
The Amazon Payments registration form.

You come to a page confirming your account has been set up. Now you're ready to sell!

Setting up Amazon Payments if you *do* already have an Amazon account is much faster. Here's how:

1. **Click the Selling at Amazon.com link in the Help Department.**

2. **Click the Amazon Payments Help link in the Browse box.**

   Again, you find the Browse box on the top left of the page.

3. **Click the Apply Now link in the first paragraph of text.**

   This is where the application process actually begins. The very first thing you're asked to do is sign in.

4. **Enter your e-mail address and password in the fields provided and then click the Continue button.**

   Now is when you come to a page that looks like Figure 14-3.

5. **Enter your phone number and nickname in the fields provided.**

   These fields were empty when I signed in to the form.

6. **Check the box that indicates that you've read and agree to the Participation Agreement and then click Continue.**

That's it. You're done. You've just set up Amazon Payments.

Show me the money

Once your Amazon Payments application is accepted — and if you have a valid credit card, you shouldn't have any problem with that — you're ready to sell. Amazon deposits the money from your Amazon Payments account into your checking account every 14 days. If you didn't enter your checking account info in the application process, you're asked to do it after you make your first sale and they deposit the funds 14 days after that. If you want the funds transferred more regularly, you can arrange that through your seller account *after* the original 14-day cycle.

So how much do you get? That depends on what you sell and where you sell it. Table 14-1 gives you a quick overview of each moneymaking venue and the fees and commissions associated with it. Table 14-2 gives you the rundown on Amazon's shipping credit.

Sometimes, the shipping credit is more than it actually costs you to ship. That'll put a few extra coins in your purse!

Table 14-1	Amazon's Cut versus Your Profit
Venue	**Fees, Commissions, & Credits**
Marketplace	$.99 flat fee per listing Additional 6% of sales price on computers 8% on camera, photo, and electronics 15% on all other products. Shipping credit included *So if you charge $100 for a used camera, you walk away with $91.01 plus a shipping credit.*
Auctions	$.10 flat fee per listing 5% closing fee on items that sell for $0.01 to $25.00 $1.25 additional flat fee plus 2.5%closing fee on items that sell for $25.01 to $1,000.00 $25.63 additional flat fee plus 1.25% closing fee on items that sell for more than $1,000 No shipping credit *So if you auction off a vintage lunchbox for $100, you get $96.15.*
zShops	Pro Merchant monthly subscription of $39.99 No per item flat fees 5% closing fee on items that sell for $0.01 to $25.00 $1.25 additional flat fee plus 2.5% closing fee on items that sell for $25.01 to $1,000.00 $25.63 additional flat fee plus 1.25% closing fee on items that sell for more than $1,000 No shipping credit *So if you sell 10 vintage lunchboxes in a month at $100 each (and don't sell anything else), you get $922.51.*
Associates	No fees or commissions 5% of sales price for most Amazon products 2.5% of sales price for Marketplace products 15% of sales price on "direct link" books (If they go straight from your site to the book and buy it without looking around at all that's a direct link.) No more than $10 referral fee per item on items other than books, music, video, and DVD.
Advantage	$29.95 annual program fee 55% additional commission on sales price *So if you sell a CD for $15, you get $6.75. Sell 1000 in a year, and you get $6,450.50.*
Honor System	$.15 flat fee per payment Additional closing fee of 5% of payment amount

Table 14-2	Amazon's Shipping Credits		
Product	Domestic Standard	Domestic Expedited	International Standard
Books	$2.26	$5.05	$8.95
Music	$1.84	$3.85	$4.95
Videos	$1.84	$3.85	$4.95
DVDs	$1.84	$3.85	$8.95
Video Games	$2.26	$5.05	Not available
Software & Computer Games	$2.26	$5.05	Not available
Electronics	$4.04 + $0.45/lb.*	$5.84 + $0.89/lb.*	Not available
Camera & Photo	$4.04 + $0.45/lb.*	$5.84 + $0.89/lb.*	Not available
Tools & Hardware	$4.04 + $0.45/lb.*	$5.84 + $0.89/lb.*	Not available
Kitchen & Housewares	$4.04 + $0.45/lb.*	$5.84 + $0.89/lb.*	Not available
Outdoor Living	$4.04 + $0.45/lb.*	$5.84 + $0.89/lb.*	Not available
Computer	$4.04 + $0.45/lb.*	$5.84 + $0.89/lb.*	Not available
Sporting Goods	$4.04 + $0.45/lb.*	$5.84 + $0.89/lb.*	Not available
Everything Else	$4.04 + $0.45/lb.*	$5.84 + $0.89/lb.*	Not available

* Refers to the weight of the item, excluding the seller's packaging.

If You Don't Have Anything Nice to Say . . .

People know they can trust Amazon.com. But how do they determine if an individual seller on Amazon is going to be honorable and trustworthy? The answer is feedback.

Giving and getting feedback is a critical part of the Marketplace, Auctions, and zShops communities. The feedback star rating is a lot like customer review stars, except instead of rating the product, they're rating you!

Feedback basics

Every time you sell something at Amazon.com, your buyer has 60 days to give you a feedback rating. They fill out a form that looks like Figure 14-4 and their comments show up in your public Member Profile (see Figure 14-5). You also receive a score from 1 to 5 stars, with 1 being the worst and 5 being excellent. Each star rating you get figures in to your average and display with your nickname on both your Member Profile page and all your items' detail pages. As a seller, you should take care to make sure your rating is a good one. After all, it follows you wherever you go.

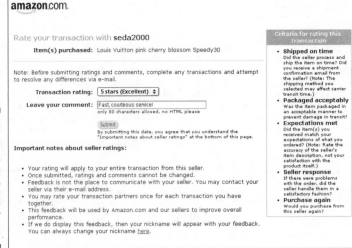

Figure 14-4:
The
feedback
form is
where your
reputation is
made or
broken!

Here's how to stay in good feedback graces:

✔ **Tell the truth.** There is nothing worse than misrepresenting your product. Tell the truth about what you're selling and be specific! Give an accurate description of the item's condition. Be truthful about its authenticity. Be straightforward and you avoid a lot of hassles and bad feedback. When it comes to selling on Amazon, honesty is definitely the best policy.

✔ **Ship it fast.** When people buy things from Amazon, they know when to expect them. Clearly you don't have the same distribution system at your fingertips, but you are still expected to uphold Amazon's tradition of timely shipping. People want their stuff, you know?

✔ **Pack it well.** If you don't, and it gets damaged en route, you're going to have an angry customer nipping at your feedback heels. Amazon has very clear guidelines about how to pack items on their site. (See Chapter 15 for more info.) Follow them and you should be fine.

✔ **Stay in touch.** Don't be a stranger. Contact your buyer quickly to arrange shipping. Be responsive if there's some kind of problem. Let them know when you've shipped the item. Pretend that you're Amazon.com, and provide the kind of good service they give their customers.

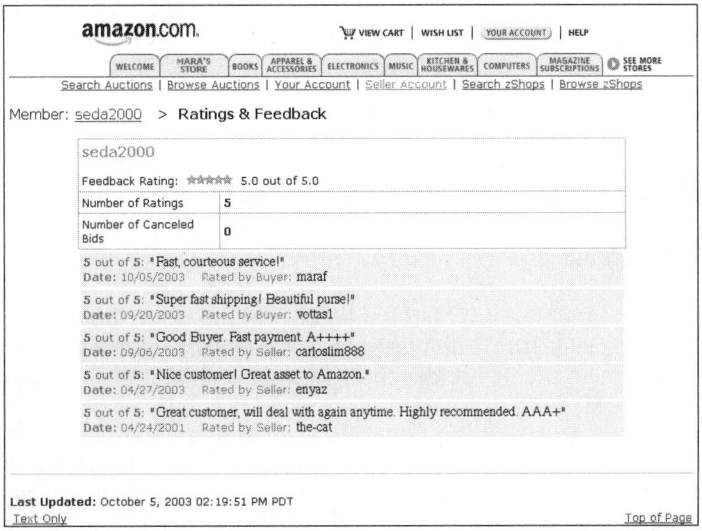

Figure 14-5:
Your
Member
Profile
shows
comments
as well as
star rating.

amazon.com. | VIEW CART | WISH LIST | YOUR ACCOUNT | HELP

WELCOME | MARA'S STORE | BOOKS | APPAREL & ACCESSORIES | ELECTRONICS | MUSIC | KITCHEN & HOUSEWARES | COMPUTERS | MAGAZINE SUBSCRIPTIONS | SEE MORE STORES

Search Auctions | Browse Auctions | Your Account | Seller Account | Search zShops | Browse zShops

Member: seda2000 > Ratings & Feedback

seda2000

Feedback Rating: ★★★★★ 5.0 out of 5.0	
Number of Ratings	5
Number of Canceled Bids	0

5 out of 5: "Fast, courteous service!"
Date: 10/05/2003   Rated by Buyer: maraf

5 out of 5: "Super fast shipping! Beautiful purse!"
Date: 09/20/2003   Rated by Buyer: vottas1

5 out of 5: "Good Buyer. Fast payment. A++++"
Date: 09/06/2003   Rated by Seller: carloslim888

5 out of 5: "Nice customer! Great asset to Amazon."
Date: 04/27/2003   Rated by Seller: enyaz

5 out of 5: "Great customer, will deal with again anytime. Highly recommended. AAA+"
Date: 04/24/2001   Rated by Seller: the-cat

Last Updated: October 5, 2003 02:19:51 PM PDT
Text Only   Top of Page

Giving feedback on your feedback

You should know that after feedback is submitted, it can't be changed. So you really only get one chance with each customer. You might have ten perfect fives on your record, but screw up once, and your stars reflect it.

However, things happen, and sometimes a sale goes south. Maybe you have a disagreement with a customer. Maybe you're just having a bad month. You can't remove feedback, but you can comment on the feedback you've been given. Here's how:

1. **Click on Your Account in the Shopping Tools menu.**

   The Shopping Tools menu is at the top of every page on the site.

2. **Click the Your Seller Account link.**

   You find this in the Auctions, zShops, and Marketplace box on the right side of the page.

3. **Click the View Your Member Profile link.**

   You need to scroll down a bit. It's below the fold, under the Your Storefront and Profile header.

4. **Click the Leave Feedback link.**

   This is in the first box of your Member Profile, just under your stars.

5. **Enter your comments in the field provided and then click Submit.**

Don't forget that all feedback — even feedback on your feedback — is permanent. So enter your comments thoughtfully. Also, you can't respond to individual ratings or comments, so you may want to refer to the comment you're addressing.

Hey Big Seller: Pro Merchant Subscriptions

Amazon says that the Pro Merchant subscription is for "frequent sellers." To me, that means anyone selling enough Marketplace items each month that they're paying more in flat fees than the $39.99 cost of the subscription. Because the Marketplace flat fee is about a buck per sale, you'd have to be selling more than 40 items a month to make the Pro Merchant subscription worth your while. (Pro Merchants also get their Auctions listing fees waived, but because that fee is only ten cents apiece, you'd have to be listing more than 400 items a month for it to matter and something tells me you're not doing that.)

Amazon only waives the flat fee with Pro Merchant subscriptions. You are still responsible for paying the commissions.

So what are the perks? These are the reasons to become a Pro Merchant at Amazon.com:

- ✔ **You are selling more than 40 items each month.** If you're a big seller, Pro Merchant can save you money.

- ✔ **You automatically get a zShops storefront.** Only Pro Merchants get storefronts. Having all your goods in one, easy-to-use place makes for good selling, especially if you have a way to point people to your store (say from your own Web site).

- ✔ **You get to use the Inventory Loader.** This is a bulk loading tool that can save you lots of time. It allows you enter all the items you're selling into one Excel spreadsheet and then upload it to the site at once!

- ✔ **You can list as many marketplace items as you want.** You have a limit of 40,000 items for zShops and Auctions, but you can list the day away in Marketplace.

✔ **You get to use Auction Pro.** If you are a big Auctions seller, Auction Pro can help you. It's an invitation-only program for Auctions sellers who sell a lot and have a high rating. Auction Pros get an icon by their display name, marketing incentives, and other perks. You have to be a Pro Merchant to apply.

How to sign up

In order to be a Pro Merchant, you need to have an Amazon account and you need to be set up for Amazon Payments. If you're not, Amazon walks you through the process as a part of Pro Merchant sign-up. In fact, if you don't already have an Amazon account, the Pro Merchant sign-up process is virtually the same as the Amazon Payments sign-up process, with the key difference being you have to start from the Pro Merchant subscription page.

Here's how to sign up for a Pro Merchant subscription if you *don't* already have an Amazon account:

1. **Click Help in the Shopping Tools menu.**

   This is at the top of every page on the site.

2. **Enter Pro Merchant in the Search field and then click Go.**

   You find the Search box at the top of the page. The very first search result you see is for the Pro Merchant subscription.

3. **Click the Pro Merchant Subscription link.**

4. **Click the Review the Terms and Subscribe link.**

   This lives in the first paragraph of text on the page. For the record, the terms on the next page are the same as the terms on the first Pro Merchant subscription page.

5. **In the new page that appears, click the Click Here To Start Your Subscription button.**

   You're taken to a Sign In screen.

6. **Enter your e-mail address in the field provided, click the circle that says that you don't have a password and then click the Continue button.**

   You come to a screen that asks you to create a password. Be sure to pick something easy for you to remember and very hard for someone else to guess.

7. **Enter your first and last names in the fields provided, enter your password twice, and then click Continue.**

8. **Enter your credit-card number and cardholder name in the fields provided.**

   In order to be a Pro Merchant, you have to give Amazon your credit-card info.

9. **Use the drop-down menus to choose card type and expiration date and then click Continue.**

   You need to supply the billing address associated with the card you gave.

10. **Enter your name, billing address, and phone number in the fields provided and then click Continue.**

11. **Check the box that indicates that you've read and agree to the Participation Agreement and then click Continue.**

You are now officially a Pro Merchant. Start selling!

To become a Pro Merchant if you *do* already have an Amazon account, complete the following abridged version:

1. **Click Help in the Shopping Tools menu.**

   This is at the top of every page on the site.

2. **Enter "pro merchant" in the search field and click "Go."**

   You find the search box at the top of the page. The very first search result you see is for the Pro Merchant subscription.

3. **Click the Pro Merchant Subscription link.**

4. **Click the Review the Terms and Subscribe link.**

   This lives in the first paragraph of text on the page. For the record, the terms on the next page are the same as the terms on the first Pro Merchant subscription page.

5. **Click the Click Here To Start Your Subscription button.**

   You're taken to a Sign In screen.

6. **Enter your password in the field provided and then click the Continue button.**

   You come to the registration form.

7. **Enter your daytime phone number in the field provided and then click Continue.**

   You may also want to change your nickname. Amazon supplies one, but if you don't like it, feel free to change it.

8. **Check the box that indicates that you've read and agree to the Participation Agreement and then click Continue.**

Closing up shop

You may find that you're just not selling enough to make a Pro Merchant account worth your while. No problem. You can cancel your account at any time and you won't be charged for the upcoming month.

Here's how to cancel your account:

1. **Click Your Account in the Shopping Tools menu.**

   This is at the top of every page on the site.

2. **Click the Your Seller Account link.**

   You find this in the Auctions, zShops, and Marketplace box on the right side of the page.

3. **Click Edit Your Buyer and Seller Settings.**

   This link is below the fold under the Your Account Settings header.

4. **Click the Cancel Subscription link next to the Pro Merchant Subscription header.**

5. **Click the Click Here To Cancel Your Pro Merchant Subscription button.**

Your subscription is cancelled! So you know, your subscription runs on a month to month schedule based on the day you signed up. If you signed up on the 15th of the month and cancel on the 25th, technically you're a member until the 15th of the following month but your subscription won't renew. In other words, Amazon doesn't prorate your account.

For the Not-So-Dumb Dummies: Web Services

According to Amazon.com, Web Services are "self-contained applications that can be published and invoked across the Web using XML-based protocols." I'm going to decipher that in a minute, but first let me tell you that you only need to read this if you have a Web site and/or are a software developer. Amazon's Web services are for people who want to enhance their own Web sites, develop applications for other people who have Web sites, or develop applications to help people sell products through Marketplace (things like pricing software and inventory loading tools). If that doesn't describe you, move on. I beg of you . . . spare yourself!

The Dummies definition

First of all, Web services are not just an Amazon thing. They're a Web thing and lots of people are excited about them. There are books on it. (In fact, one of them is called *.NET Web Services For Dummies*.) Still, for most of us, they're a mystery. We might interact with them regularly, but we don't know it.

The Amazon definition of Web services is a chunky one. (I'm a Web savvy person and when I read it my eyes began to cross a little.) My "Dummies" definition is decidedly less chunky, but probably loses some of the meaning. So all you developers out there, forgive me.

Web services are modular applications that can talk to each other. And because they can talk to each other, they can share information in a symbiotic way. But it's easier for us laymen to understand Web services in terms of what they do.

Here's a non-Amazon example: someone with a travel log Web site includes a Web services application from an online travel company so that their visitors can buy tickets without leaving their site. They're happy because they've provided a good service and kept their visitor there, and the online travel company is happy because they've made a sale.

Amazon's Web services foster the same kind of symbiosis. A developer might use Amazon's Web services to show Amazon search results on his or her own Web site. You can also use Amazon's Web services to let your customers add items to their shopping cart without leaving your site. Conceptually, Amazon's Web services are a souped-up version of the Associates Program. Functionally, they work in tandem because if you want to earn money using Amazon Web services, you must also be an Associate.

Where to go to find out more about it

If you are interested in using Amazon's Web services, you can find out more about the whole process and even download a developer's kit for free from the Amazon site. Your door to Web services development is just three quick steps (and a degree in computer science) away:

1. **Go to www.amazon.com.**

   If you're already at Amazon, that means you should click the Welcome tab.

2. **Click Sell Your Stuff in the subnav.**

   You're in the Make Money area of the site. Notice that all tabs have gone away except the Make Money tab and the Welcome tab.

3. **Click Web Services in the subnav.**

   You'll find yourself at the Web Services page — lots of good resources in the left nav!

You'll find all kinds of goodies in the Web Services section: discussion boards, tutorials, sample sites, "developer chat" (ooh la la). This is where you should go not only to find out about the program, but also to download the tools you'll need to start using the program.

If you want to check out a few sites that are using Web services, try www.nba.com, www.ipilot.net, or www.sellerengine.com.

The Fine Print: Rules and Policies

If you started your own business selling items on the Web, you'd have a lot of paperwork to do — lawyer stuff, IRS stuff, and insurance stuff. When you sell things at Amazon, they've done a lot of that work for you. Still, you can't escape the fine print.

There are rules and policies for each of the selling opportunities at Amazon.com. Before you embark on your first sale, you should familiarize yourself with them. Don't forget that when you post an item on their site, you're entering into a business agreement. So make sure you know what that means.

Here are some of the important rules and policies for selling with Marketplace, Auctions, or zShops:

- ✔ **No naughty content.** Nine out of ten times you can use common sense to determine what you can and can't sell on Amazon.com. But for that tenth time, read the prohibited content list in Chapter 1.

- ✔ **Describe your product accurately.** Amazon has specific guidelines about how to list the condition of your items. For example, "new" means brand new, unopened, in perfect condition. Also, be as straightforward as you can be. Neglecting to mention something about your item is no better than outright misrepresentation.

- ✔ **Don't abuse the ratings forum.** Don't post ratings to your own account. Don't take out a personal vendetta on someone else's. The ratings are the only way buyers have of evaluating sellers. So keep it clean and honest.

- ✔ **Only contact your buyer as it relates to your transaction.** I once bought a pair of cycling shorts on eBay and the seller proceeded to bombard me with spam. Don't do that. And definitely don't contact your seller in any kind of social way. This is business, man!

- ✔ **Don't bid on your own auction to jack up the price.** This is called "shill bidding" and it's very taboo in the world of online auctions. I don't think I need to tell you why.

There are many other rules associated with these programs. You find them in the Help department, along with the condition guidelines, the prohibited content list, and a whole lot of other stuff. Here's how to find them:

1. **Click Help in the Shopping Tools menu.**

   Yes. It's still at the top of each page.

2. **Click Policies, Glossaries, and FAQs.**

   You find the link under the Selling at Amazon.com header.

3. **Click on Policy Information.**

   Everything here is important, particularly the Participation Agreement as that's the legal contract. The community rules — we're talking the Amazon community here, not your home community — are also very important.

Changed your mind?

What do you do if you list something on the site and then change your mind? You can delete a Marketplace or zShops listing at any time provided it hasn't already been purchased. You can delete an Auctions item only if it has no bids. Here's how to delete a Marketplace, zShops, or Auctions listing from the site:

1. **Click Your Account in the Shopping Tools menu.**

   This is at the top of every page on the site.

2. **Click the Your Seller Account link.**

   You find this in the Auctions, zShops, and Marketplace box on the right side of the page. Your Seller Account page looks something like Figure 14-6.

3. **Click the appropriate Open or Opening Soon link.**

   Click one of the Open or Opening Soon links depending on when and where you listed your item. If your item hasn't posted to the site yet, choose Opening Soon for either Marketplace and zShops or for Auctions. If your item is already up on the site, choose the appropriate Open link.

4. **Click the Modify This Listing link.**

   Don't click the title of your item. That leads to your listing page. You want the link beneath the item you want to cancel.

5. **Click the Close This Listing Now button.**

   On the next screen, you're asked to give a reason for why you're closing the listing. This reason shows up on the listing page, so be professional but honest.

6. **Enter your reason for closing and click the Close This Listing Now button.**

   That's all it takes. You receive an e-mail confirming your cancellation almost immediately.

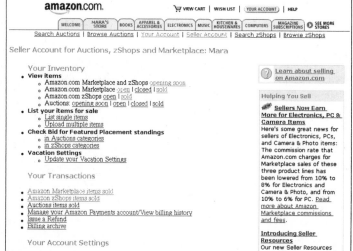

Figure 14-6: Manage your Amazon selling from your seller account page.

Returns

As part of doing business with Amazon, you are required to accept returns — even if the item is exactly as you said it was. If you do have a buyer who wants to return an item, you need to work out the logistics between the two of you. Your buyer can't return the item using the site the way they would with an item bought *from* Amazon.com.

A few things to note:

- ✔ All returns must happen within 60 days of the transaction.

- ✔ If the return is *not* due to your error, feel no obligation to refund the buyer's shipping costs.

- ✔ If you are at fault, you should reimburse all shipping costs.

- ✔ If you did not use Amazon Payments for the transaction, you need to administer the refund on your own — the steps below won't help you.

- ✔ If you are in no way at fault and you feel that the item has lost some of it's salability, you may decide to issue a partial refund. This is something you should work with your buyer, though, before you initiate it.

My Stupid Fight Club Story:
A Lesson in Haste and Forgiveness

I have actually committed an Amazon cardinal sin. I have neglected to ship an item that I sold on Marketplace. Here's what happened:

About a year or two ago I wanted to try out Marketplace. I grabbed a book off of my bookshelf — one that I'd read and was willing to part with — and posted it on the site. I chose a hardback book because I felt like it wouldn't be worth my while to post a paperback.

It was so easy. So fast. I entered the ISBN, entered Amazon's recommended price, and voila! I couldn't wait to go look at my used *Fight Club* listing. Imagine my horror when I found that my book was the cheapest used one listed — by about $110. Turns out I had a first run edition worth at least $120 bucks. I'd listed mine for $16.

I scrambled to cancel the item, but it was snapped up immediately. Some unsuspecting person had just scored big. I was beside myself. How could I have been so stupid? Why didn't I do my research? It would've taken me about 60 seconds.

And then I did the unthinkable. I wrote my buyer an e-mail explaining my ignorant foible and asked her if I could credit her account and sell the book for something closer to its actual value. She was a truly kind person and took pity on me (so I sent her a nice Amazon gift certificate) but she shouldn't have. I was in clear violation of the rules. If I had it to do again, I'd sell it to her for $16 and take the loss like a champ. Instead I behaved like a rookie. Granted I ended up selling the book for $120 (hey, that's a cashmere sweater!) but in the eyes of the Marketplace community, I was a cur.

So the lesson . . . well there were actually two. The first, and most obvious, is do your research. The second is that you run into some very nice people in your dealings on Amazon and it behooves you to be equally as kind.

When a buyer returns an item, you *have* to refund at least some of their money and it's your responsibility to initiate the refund. Again, they can't go to the site and return the item themselves. Here's how to refund a buyer's money — assuming that you used Amazon Payments for the initial transaction:

1. **Click Your Account in the Shopping Tools menu.**

   This is at the top of every page on the site.

2. **Click the Your Seller Account link.**

   You find this in the Auctions, zShops, and Marketplace box on the right side of the page.

3. **Click the Manage Your Amazon Payments Account/View Billing History link.**

4. **Click the Search Your Payments Transactions link.**

5. **Enter your password in the field provided and click the Sign In Using Our Secure Server button.**

   Notice that this is an unusual Sign In screen. It's the same drill, though.

6. **Use the drop-down menus to enter the date range for the transaction, click the appropriate circle, and then click Search.**

   You can also choose to narrow your search by title, transaction type, or status. You come to a page that looks like Figure 14-7.

7. **Click the transaction ID for the appropriate item.**

8. **Click the Refund link.**

9. **Enter the amount of the refund in the field provided and click the Refund button.**

   Amazon sets the default amount at a full refund. If you are giving a partial refund, change the amount accordingly. You can also enter a comment in the field provided. Use the drop-down menu to enter a reason for your refund.

Amazon refunds the buyer's credit card, deducts the refund amount from your Payments account, and credits you their fees and commissions.

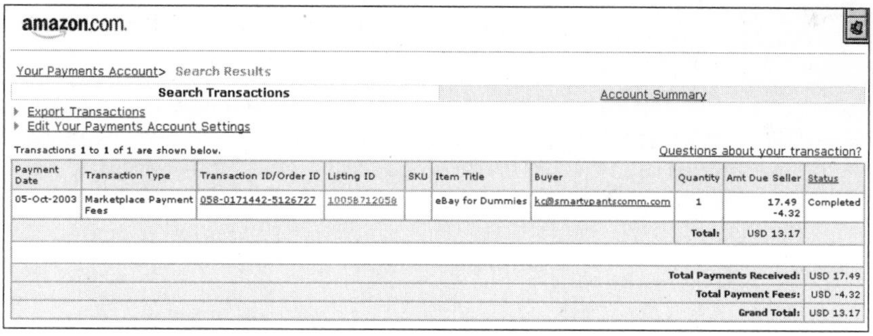

Figure 14-7: Click the transaction number of the item being returned.

What if it gets broken on the way

It's a bummer, but it happens. Even if you pack it precisely to Amazon's standards, sometimes bad things occur in transit. If an item breaks en route, you should give the buyer a complete refund and swallow the cost in the name of your feedback rating. But if it was an expensive item, that's gonna sting.

Amazon is set up to protect buyers with the A-to-Z Guarantee. Some buyers also ask you to get an escrow account. To protect yourself, you may want to insure your package. You can insure packages at the U.S. Post Office, FedEx, and UPS. It's worth the extra cost.

Other potential pitfalls

Let's face it. We live in an imperfect world. If you sell on Amazon long enough, something is bound to go wrong. Here's a short list of potential pitfalls and a few words about what you can do:

- ✔ **You shipped it and it came back to you.** First off, make sure you shipped it to the right address. If you didn't, e-mail your buyer immediately, beg forgiveness, and get it back out the door (with the right address) ASAP. Most normal buyers understand. If the address is correct, e-mail your buyer and get the scoop. Maybe they can supply you with another address. If all else fails, refund the buyer.

- ✔ **You shipped it and it got lost.** If you didn't insure the item, you just have to eat the cost. Don't accuse the buyer of trickery, even if you suspect them. This could do nasty things to your rating. If, though, you notice that the buyer has lots of bad feedback, you might report them to Amazon by e-mailing reports@amazon.com.

- ✔ **A buyer files an A-to-Z Guarantee claim against you.** This means that you and your buyer came to an impasse. If you really feel you shouldn't have to refund their purchase and they really feel you should, they may file a claim against you. Amazon sends you an e-mail to inform you of the claim, asking you to tell them when the item was shipped. And that's pretty much it (although you can also expect to get a nasty rating from that buyer).

If you have a "large" number of claims filed against you, Amazon terminates your account. I don't know how many "large" is, but if you have more than two or three filed against you, I'm thinking you should give up selling online.

Chapter 15

The Buying/Selling Circle: Amazon.com Marketplace

Amazon.com is its own little shopping ecosystem. You buy things. You use them. And then you can sell them to someone else who buys them, uses them, and maybe sells them to yet another person, and so on. It's the buying/selling circle of life.

In this chapter I show you how to use Marketplace to sell the things you've purchased at Amazon.com — and maybe things you didn't buy there, but that they sell. I tell you where to go to list your items, what items to list, and how to describe them. I cover pricing, shipping, and communicating with your buyer. I show you how to maximize this selling program so you can play your role in the shopping circle of life.

Marketplace Basics

Amazon Marketplace is the backbone of selling on Amazon.com. It's a simple but brilliant idea: Let people sell the items they bought at Amazon to other Amazon customers. After all, lots of people don't care if their book or CD is used. They'd rather save a few bucks.

But Marketplace came from humble beginnings. Originally, the idea was to compete with eBay, and Amazon Auctions was the way to sell on Amazon.com. Then zShops was born — to give customers their own little space on the site where they could sell fixed-price items that you couldn't already find at Amazon.com. But not every person wants a whole storefront, and not everyone has something exotic to sell. So, with relatively little fanfare, Marketplace came to be — and unlike Auctions and zShops, it's flourishing.

Anyone can sell with Marketplace. They've made it incredibly simple to use. But before you get started, there are a few things you need to know. Here are the Marketplace basics:

- **You can sell any item in Amazon's catalog.** And it doesn't actually matter where you bought it.

- **Your item is featured on the detail page of the same item that Amazon is selling new.** In my opinion, Marketplace has been successful because of this arrangement. It's basically free advertising. Every time someone searches for that new book or video or other product, they're inadvertently searching for your used version.

- **There are four classifications of used items on Amazon.com.** They are "new" as in brand, spanking new, "collectible," "refurbished," which means "good as new" still in its original box with an original manufacturer's warranty, and regular, old "used."

- **You handle the shipping.** You ship your item directly to your buyer. Amazon supplies a shipping credit.

- **All payments are run through Amazon.com.** This makes it easy. Buyers can use their regular accounts to make their Marketplace purchases, and you are paid through a program called Amazon Payments.

What you can and can't sell using Marketplace

The short answer is that you can sell anything in their catalog. But, like all good things, there are a few "buts." Here are the things you can't sell through Marketplace:

- **Promotional books, music, videos or DVDs.** These are items that are released early, usually to industry people for promotional purposes (Amazon itself gets tons of them!). You can't sell them on the site, as *they are not authorized for retail distribution or sale.*

- **Unauthorized and unlicensed merchandise.** This applies to books, music, videos, DVDs, and especially software. Here's what Amazon has to say about it: "All items sold through Amazon Marketplace must be commercially produced and authorized or licensed as a retail product."

> ✔ **Recopied media.** It may be obvious to you, but I'll say it anyway. You can't make a bunch of copies of your favorite Elton John CD and sell them on Amazon.com. If you did, you'd be infringing on all kinds of copyrights and trademarks. Whole industries get upset about that, and people have been sued and worse. (But you knew that.)

Where to go to start selling

Before you go anywhere, go to your garage. Got a pile of stuff that is waiting for a garage sale? There may be goodies in there that you can sell at Amazon instead. Remember, it just has to be something in Amazon's catalog — it doesn't matter if you didn't buy it there. So cull through your giveaway pile, your bookshelf, your CD collection. You'll probably find tons of things to sell.

The next stop on the selling train is the site. Go to Amazon and see if your items are there. Also, check out the More Buying Options box to see how many (if any) are already being sold through Marketplace. It may be that none are being sold used but that buyers are waiting. (If this is the case there will be a "buyers waiting" message in the box.) That makes for some good selling for you!

When you've found some stuff to sell and you've done your research, there are two easy places you can go to list items through Marketplace: the detail page and the Sell Your Stuff area.

To access the detail page of the item you want to sell, simply do a search for that item and click the appropriate search result. (Need help searching? Read Chapter 8.) You also need to do a search to ensure that the item is, in fact, in Amazon's catalog.

To access Marketplace listing pages from the Sell your Stuff area, do the following:

1. **Go to www.amazon.com.**

   If you're already on the site, but not at the Welcome page, click the Welcome tab. Just so you know, you can only find Sell Your Stuff in the subnav when you're on the Welcome page.

2. **Click Sell Your Stuff in the Subnav.**

   You come to a page that look likes Figure 15-1. This is the Marketplace home base; you can search for your item from here by keyword or by ISBN (for books only), ASIN, or UPC. Notice how both the tab and the subnav have changed. You can access three of the six selling/partnering opportunities from the Make Money subnav.

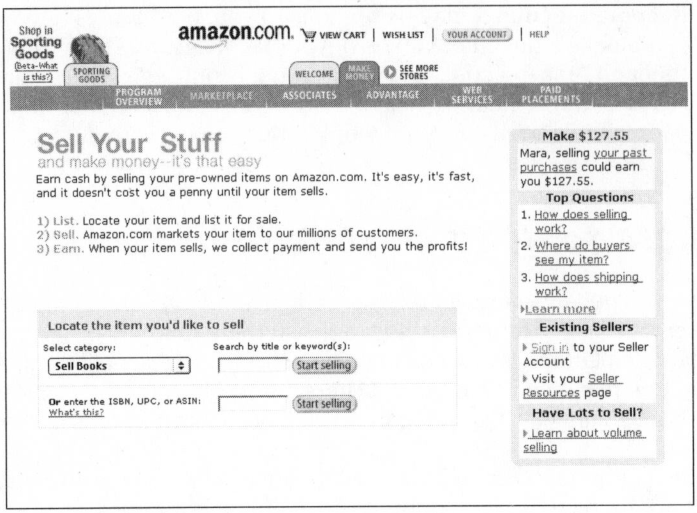

Figure 15-1:
The Marketplace page in the Make Money area.

(screenshot showing Amazon.com Sell Your Stuff page)

Listing Your Item

Listing your items is actually a surprisingly simple process. You can do it most easily from the detail page or from the Marketplace page in the Sell Your Stuff (also known as Make Money) section of the site. I outline both processes here, and then give you some more detailed tips and info on describing the condition and setting your price later in this chapter.

In order to sell at Amazon.com, you need to have an Amazon account. If you don't, you're walked through the process as a part of listing your item. You can also read Chapter 3 to find out how to set up an Amazon account. But just so you know, the instructions below assume that you already have an Amazon.com account.

Here's how to list an item from the detail page:

1. **Go to the item's detail page.**

   Do this by searching for the item and clicking the appropriate search result.

2. **Click the Sell Yours Here button.**

   You find it in the More Buying Choices box, just below the Ready to Buy? box on the right side of the page. (See Figure 15-2.)

Figure 15-2:
Click the
Sell Yours
Here button
to start the
selling
process.

3. **Verify your item.**

The new page that appears (see Figure 15-3) asks you to verify that this is
the exact item you want to sell. This is actually a very important step —
especially if you're selling a book. The classic pitfall is to accidentally
sell a paperback as a hardcover or vice versa. So do be sure to check!

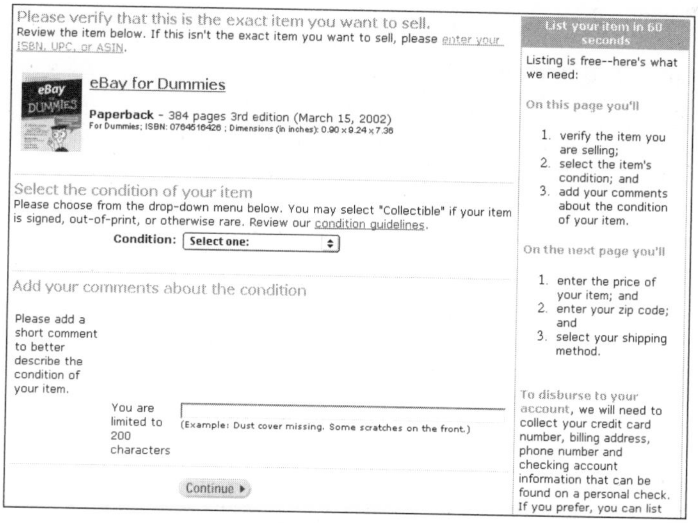

Figure 15-3:
You verify
your item,
describe its
condition,
and select
shipping
options all
on this
page.

Please verify that this is the exact item you want to sell.
Review the item below. If this isn't the exact item you want to sell, please enter your
ISBN, UPC, or ASIN.

eBay for Dummies

Paperback - 384 pages 3rd edition (March 15, 2002)
For Dummies; ISBN: 0764516426 ; Dimensions (in inches): 0.90 x 9.24 x 7.36

Select the condition of your item
Please choose from the drop-down menu below. You may select "Collectible" if your item
is signed, out-of-print, or otherwise rare. Review our condition guidelines.

Condition: [Select one: ‡]

Add your comments about the condition

Please add a
short comment
to better
describe the
condition of
your item.

You are
limited to
200
characters

[   ]
(Example: Dust cover missing. Some scratches on the front.)

[Continue ▶]

List your item in 60
seconds

Listing is free--here's what
we need:

On this page you'll

1. verify the item you
   are selling;
2. select the item's
   condition; and
3. add your comments
   about the condition
   of your item.

On the next page you'll

1. enter the price of
   your item; and
2. enter your zip code;
   and
3. select your shipping
   method.

To disburse to your
account, we will need to
collect your credit card
number, billing address,
phone number and
checking account
information that can be
found on a personal check.
If you prefer, you can list

4. **Use the drop-down menu to describe the condition of your item.**

You have several choices that range from new to collectible to used-
acceptable. More details on this later in the chapter.

5. **Add your comments about the item in the field provided and click Continue.**

   If you chose anything other than "new," you may want to add comments that give more details on the item's condition. It's not mandatory, but it's a good practice — an informed buyer is a happier buyer.

6. **Enter your price in the field provided.**

   Amazon advises you of both the highest price you can enter and their recommended price based on the condition you chose. More on this later in the chapter.

7. **Enter your zip code in the field provided.**

   This is the zip code for your Ship From location.

8. **Select your shipping options by clicking the appropriate boxes and click Continue.**

   You are required to offer standard shipping and you can choose to also offer international and expedited shipping.

   Offering international shipping increases the number of potential buyers, but it also slightly increases the hassle factor, because you need to figure out how to get it to, say, Eritrea. With expedited shipping you get a larger shipping credit, but, of course, faster shipping costs more. Still, it's a good option to offer around the holidays, when all the procrastinators (like moi) are desperate!

9. **Confirm and click List Item For Sale.**

   You come to a page that looks like Figure 15-4. Notice that Amazon outlines all the money-related info associated with your items. You'll find things like how much you're charging, what their fees are, and your shipping credit — the amount Amazon tacks on to your payment to cover shipping costs. Make sure that all the information is correct.

Once you click the list button, your listing is official. You can change the price or cancel the listing at any time until someone purchases your item. For instructions on how to cancel a listing, read Chapter 14. Here's how to change the price of your listing:

1. **Click on Your Account in the Shopping Tools menu.**

   You'll find this at the top of most pages on the site.

2. **Click on Your Seller Account in the Auctions, zShops, and Marketplace box.**

   This is on the right side of the page. When you click, it takes you to the Your Seller Account page.

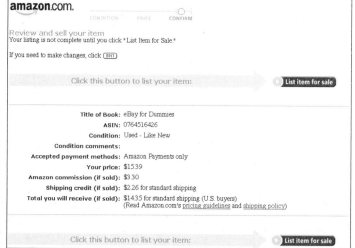

amazon.com.

CONDITION   PRICE   CONFIRM

Review and sell your item
Your listing is not complete until you click "List Item for Sale."

If you need to make changes, click ⌐EDIT⌐

Click this button to list your item: ▶ List item for sale

Title of Book:	eBay for Dummies
ASIN:	0764516426
Condition:	Used - Like New
Condition comments:	
Accepted payment methods:	Amazon Payments only
Your price:	$15.39
Amazon commission (if sold):	$3.30
Shipping credit (if sold):	$2.26 for standard shipping
Total you will receive (if sold):	$14.35 for standard shipping (U.S. buyers) (Read Amazon.com's pricing guidelines and shipping policy)

Click this button to list your item: ▶ List item for sale

Figure 15-4:
Double-check your information before you take the plunge!

3. **Click on the appropriate link under the View Items heading.**

   You'll find this in the Your Inventory section. If you've just listed the item (as in, ten minutes ago) and want to change the price, click the Opening Soon link next to Amazon.com Marketplace and zShops. If the listing is already open, click the Open link next to Amazon.com Marketplace.

4. **Click Modify This Listing under the appropriate item.**

   This will take you to that item's information page where you can edit the price.

5. **Enter the new price in the field provided and click Continue.**

   You'll have to scroll down to find Continue — way at the bottom of the page. Next you'll come to a Confirmation page.

6. **Review your listing and click the Submit Your Listing button.**

   That's all she wrote. You'll come to a page acknowledging your change.

Here's how to list items from the Marketplace page (within the Sell Your Stuff/Make Money area):

1. **Click Sell Your Stuff.**

   It's in the Welcome page subnav.

2. **Enter search information in the fields provided and click Start Selling.**

   You can search by keyword or ISBN, ASIN, or UPC. You come to a Search Results page that looks like Figure 15-5.

Figure 15-5:
Search
results
when selling
through
Marketplace
are different
than your
usual
Amazon
search
results.

3. **Click the Sell Yours Here button.**

4. **Complete Steps 3 through 9 given earlier.**

Describing the condition

I can't stress enough how important it is to list your item accurately! Amazon.com has very specific guidelines for describing the condition of the items you sell on Marketplace. Make sure you follow them to the letter. You don't want to be that seller who fibbed (even unintentionally) about their item. That makes for some stinky ratings (ratings being the public feedback that your buyers give you).

The classifications for item condition include both the status of the item and — for a used item — its physical condition. An item can be one of four statuses — or is that statii?:

✔ **New.** This means brand new, never used, still in the packaging and in perfect shape.

✔ **Used.** This is anything that's not "new."

✔ **Refurbished.** These are nonmedia used items that are "good as new" with a manufacturer's warrantee.

✔ **Collectible.** This applies only to media items — books, music, videos, and DVDs. In order for an item to be collectible it needs to be empirically unique (as opposed to just special to you). Signed items, out-of-print items, and rare items are all collectible.

Here's an overview of the four different physical condition classifications:

- ✔ **Like New.** New enough that you'd feel comfortable giving it as a gift. It doesn't have to be in its original packaging, but it has to be otherwise perfect.

- ✔ **Very Good.** This means you've taken very good care of it, but it wouldn't be mistaken for new. There might be some small signs of cosmetic wear.

- ✔ **Good.** Definitely showing signs of wear, but still functions perfectly.

- ✔ **Acceptable.** This can show significant signs of cosmetic wear, but it still has to work. That means if it's a mixer, it mixes — on all settings. If it's a book, it's got all its pages and they're all readable.

So an item might be used-like new, or collectible-acceptable. These classifications give more detail, so the buyer has a better idea of what they're getting. Amazon's guidelines are actually more specific than the overview I just gave. If you need more information, you can access the Help department by clicking Selling at Amazon.com, then Listing Your Item, and then Conditions Guidelines.

How to set your price

Amazon makes a recommendation for how you should price your item within the listing process, but you shouldn't rely solely on that. Before you list any item, make sure that you know for sure what you've got and what it's worth. You can do that by searching around on the Web a bit, or just by looking at the item's detail page on Amazon.com. Either way, it's worth the extra time. (Read my *Fight Club* tale in Chapter 14 if you need convincing.)

Also, Amazon lists products in lowest-to-highest price order, and, of course, the item at the top often sells first. So you might pull a Price is Right maneuver and list your item at one cent less than the current lowest price (assuming it's in a comparable condition). That way it'll show up first on the list.

Amazon has several rules regarding pricing. If you break them within the listing process, they let you know by keeping you from finalizing your listing. They send you back to the pricing page with some text that explains your mistake. (See Figure 15-6.) It makes it easier to know what those rules are ahead of time. Here they are in a nutshell:

- ✔ **New.** For books, music, videos, DVDs, software, and computer games, you have to set your price at or below the Amazon.com price. For all other items, you can set any price, but I think it's unlikely that anyone will buy yours if it's more expensive than the Amazon price.

- ✔ **Refurbished.** You have to set the price at or below the latest Amazon.com price. If you want to sell it, though, you price it lower than Amazon's price.

✔ **Used.** Again, at or below Amazon.com's price for the same item new.

✔ **Collectible.** You can set the price at whatever you want. This is one that requires some knowledge and/or research to get a sense of market value. Also, make sure you let buyers know *why* your item is collectible by filling out the comment section in the listing process.

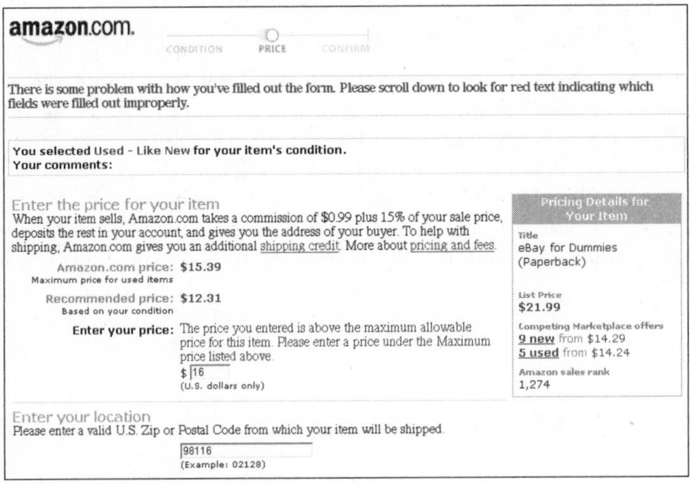

Figure 15-6:
Break the price rules and Amazon sends you back to try again.

Even if Amazon's price changes, your price stays wherever you set it. You have to change it manually and you can do that from your Seller Account. To access your Seller Account, click Your Account in the Shopping Tools menu at the top of the page to go to the Your Account page and then click the Seller Account link in the Auctions, zShops, and Marketplace box on the right side of the page. Use the inventory links to find the item you want to change. (For more detailed instructions look at the Listing Your Item section of this chapter.)

Communicating with Your Buyer

When your item sells, you'll get an e-mail from Amazon notifying you of that fact. You don't have to worry about getting paid. With Marketplace, that happens automatically. All you have to do now is ship the item.

You will need to communicate with your buyer once they purchase your item. But don't become overzealous and bombard your buyer with e-mail. Keep it professional, courteous, and brief. Remember what happened to Bridget Fonda in *Single White Female*? This isn't a friendship you're starting. It's a business transaction.

As far as I'm concerned, there are only three times that you should e-mail your buyer:

✔ **When they make the purchase.** This is optional. Amazon sends you an e-mail with the buyer's shipping address and e-mail address. Some people send an e-mail just to make contact and acknowledge the purchase. I've gotten these e-mails and I appreciate them.

✔ **When you ship the item.** This is not optional. You should send an e-mail to your buyer on the day you ship the item. They know when to expect its arrival — and if it doesn't show up, they can act quickly.

✔ **When something goes wrong.** Mishaps occur, and when they do it's best to keep your buyer in the loop.

Pack It Up. Ship It Off.

Here's what you should do to ensure a good shipping experience for you and your buyer:

✔ **Carefully read your Sold — Ship now! e-mail.** When your item sells, Amazon sends you an e-mail that looks like Figure 15-7. You can find all the information you need to complete the transaction — your buyer's shipping address, their e-mail address, a link to the shipping guidelines, your packing slip, and more.

✔ **Print out your packing slip and include it in your package.** This is part of the body of your Sold — Ship now! e-mail (as shown in Figure 15-7). You can print the whole e-mail and cut out the packing-slip part, or cut and paste the packing-slip part into a new document and print that. If all else fails, you can handwrite the information and include *that* in your package.

✔ **Pack your item carefully.** Refer to Amazon's shipping guidelines. You can get to them by clicking the link in your e-mail, or by going to the Help Department. You'll find the guidelines under Shipping and Packaging in the Fulfillment, Getting Paid and Feedback section of the Selling at Amazon.com area.

✔ **Label your package clearly.** Make sure you put *Your Amazon.com Marketplace Order* prominently on the outside of the package.

✔ **Ship your package.** You know that Amazon gives you a shipping credit for Marketplace orders. (If you're not sure how much of a credit, check out Chapter 14.) There is no negotiating that credit. If the credit covers your shipping costs, great. If it doesn't — sometimes giant, heavy items or strangely shaped items or items going to crazy places cost more than the credit — you are still required to ship the item. On the other hand, sometimes the credit more than covers it. When this happens, one great way to improve your feedback rating is to upgrade your buyer's shipping to First-Class Priority Mail. It doesn't cost much more, but it fills buyers with glee.

✔ **E-mail your buyer.** Let them know that you've shipped, when to expect the item, and what method you used for shipping.

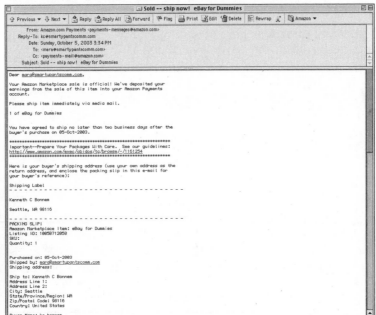

Figure 15-7:
The Sold — Ship now! e-mail has all the information you need.

Chapter 16

Where on Earth Did You Find That? Auctions and zShops

*A*uctions and zShops are the Cinderellas of Amazon.com. They're such great programs, I feel everyone should be talking about them. Don't the masses know that walking arm in arm with Amazon.com means walking arm in arm with *37 million customers?* Alas, they don't. But now you do.

You can actually make a lot of money selling with Auctions and zShops. You just need the three *S*s: the stuff, the show, and the service. (Those are my three *S*s, by the way.) In this chapter I talk about all three. I give you a quick overview of what you can and can't, and what you should and shouldn't sell at Amazon.com. I show you how to create an Auctions listing that gives your buyers all the information they could ever want. I help you list single and multiple items with zShops and tell you how to make the most of your storefront. I explain the supplementary selling services Amazon offers and give you pointers on how to best deal with your buyers — the good, the bad and the ugly.

That said, this is really a "basics of . . . " kind of chapter — it would take a separate book to hold everything there is to know about using Auctions and zShops. So I encourage you to spend some time reading the Auctions and zShops sections of Amazon's Help department — you know, that department that pops up when you click Help in the Shopping Tools menu of any page on the site. The Auctions and zShops sections hang out under the Selling at Amazon.com heading and they are absolutely packed with the information you need to be a selling pro.

The Differences between Auctions and zShops

There are two main things that Auctions and zShops have in common and two main things that differentiate them.

Here's what they share:

- ✔ **They're both selling opportunities at Amazon.com.** That's right. You can use either program to sell stuff and make some money.

- ✔ **Both programs allow you to sell items that are not already in Amazon's catalog.** That's not to say you have carte blanche, just that you are not restricted to items they already sell as you are with Marketplace. (For more on Marketplace, see Chapter 15.) When you sell with either Auctions or zShops, your items will get detail pages of their own.

And here's what makes them different:

- ✔ **The price.** Auctions items go to the highest bidder, while zShops is a fixed-price selling venue.

- ✔ **The quantity.** You can use Auctions to sell just one item or to sell hundreds of items. zShops, however, is only for volume sellers.

- ✔ **The Pro Merchant Subscription.** zShops requires you to have a Pro Merchant subscription.

There are other differences — different fees and commissions, to name two — but these three are the biggies that can help you figure out where you should be selling.

If you've read Chapter 15 on Amazon's Marketplace feature and spent a little time considering the three selling venues, you may have spotted the hole in the system: As of this moment, there is no good venue for selling single items that are *not* in Amazon's catalog at a fixed price. You can sell a single, fixed-price item through zShops, but it has to be a spendy number to warrant paying the $39.99 monthly subscription fee. (You can also set a reserve price in your auction to ensure you get the amount you want, but that's not really the same. You still have to auction it off.)

What You Can, Can't, Should, and Shouldn't Sell

First things first: Amazon.com isn't a virtual red-light district. So if you were thinking of setting up an online shop to sell merchandise that would require the use of "Adult" as a descriptor, think again. (For example, toys are fine. Adult toys are not.) On the site, Amazon says it subscribes to a "community standard" and that all sellers must subscribe to this standard as well (and next up is an outline of the Don'ts in this standard).

You probably won't feel compelled to buck the system here. If you do, you should know that Amazon reserves the right to determine what is appropriate for their site. You should also know that if they determine your item (or items) to be inappropriate, they remove the offending stuff from the site without refunding any of their listing fees.

So what you *can* sell is anything that's both legal and appropriate. Here's a list that gives a better idea of what that means:

✔ **No pornography.** This includes hard-core stuff, "toys," and bizarre things like "soiled undergarments" (eewww). You *can* sell condoms, "unrated erotic videos," and artsy erotica, but you have to put censor strips over all nudity and any graphic text that might show up in the photo. The differentiation they make here is that if you'd find it in an independent bookstore, it's probably okay. If you'd find it in an adult entertainment store, it probably isn't. As for the overlap, use your common sense and remember that people under 18 also shop at Amazon.com.

✔ **No offensive material.** The things that Amazon lists as examples of offensive material are "crime-scene photos or human organs and body parts." So if you're selling stolen organs on the black market, Amazon.com isn't for you. Perhaps a more relevant reading of this rule would include things that are blatantly racist, things that encourage acts of violence, and so on. They do encourage sellers to be mindful of other cultures and remember that the audience is "our global community."

✔ **No illegal items.** This isn't just the obvious stuff — narcotics, Cuban cigars, and so on. It also includes anything that would encourage or abet an illegal act — like those cable descramblers or lock-picking devices you might have in the back of the garage (but probably don't, right?). They make a point of noting that you can sell packaged food as long as it "meets all applicable federal, state, and local standards for sale to consumers." That's right — Spam is not an illegal item, as long as it's the kind you can actually put in a sandwich.

✔ **Stolen goods.** If this is the rule that keeps you from selling at Amazon.com, I'm going to hazard a guess that not being able to list your Auction item is the least of your worries.

✔ **No items that overtly infringe upon an individual's privacy.** No videos you took of your celebrity (or noncelebrity) neighbor. No photos that the subject might not want on the Internet. Nothing that would reveal someone else's personal information. Use yourself as the benchmark here. If you're someone with few or no inhibitions, then use a more private friend as the benchmark. Also, telemarketers be warned! This prohibition includes marketing lists.

✔ **No recopied or bootlegged media.** You are not allowed to copy books, music, videos, images, and so on, and sell them at Amazon.com. You can't even make an awesome mix tape and sell it at Amazon.com. It's not because Amazon is persnickety. This is now an industry standard, and it includes things like tapes of concerts you've been to, pay-per-view events you recorded on TV, movies you've taped, and so on.

✔ **No promotional media.** These prerelease items are usually given to industry people and marked *Promotional Use Only* (or words to that effect). This includes advanced copies of books.

✔ **No copied or bootlegged video games.** If you're going to sell a video game at Amazon, it has to be the full retail version — just like one you'd buy at the mall.

✔ **No copied software.** Same deal here. It has to be the retail version that you'd buy at the mall.

✔ **No satellite technology.** Amazon says, "Any item that enables unauthorized transmission/reception of a satellite broadcast/signal is prohibited." So, for example, you can't sell the smart card out of your cell phone.

✔ **No replicas of trademarked items.** In other words, no fakes allowed. So if you were thinking about selling that so-close-even-Kate-herself-wouldn't-know Kate Spade knockoff, don't. You'd be playing with fire.

✔ **No unauthorized celebrity stuff.** If you're going to create your own set of Madonna coasters, you need to get her permission. If you already own a set of authorized Madonna coasters, you can resell those.

✔ **No domain names.** I don't know that anyone would come to Amazon. com to buy a domain name, but it doesn't matter, because sale of them is prohibited!

✔ **No firearms, ammunition, or weapons.** The only kind of gun you can sell at Amazon.com is one that shoots rubber pellets or foam darts. This rule also applies to other weapons like martial-arts throwing stars and stun guns. Also, no fireworks. The idea here is that you can't sell anything that is designed to be used as an implement to harm someone.

✔ **No phony "come to my Web site" listings.** If you're going to sell at Amazon, you actually have to sell *at* Amazon. Don't use Auctions as a vehicle to get people to your own online store by creating a listing that gives people instructions on how to get there. That won't float with the powers that be.

✔ **No products that have been recalled by the Consumer Product Safety Commission (CPSC).** No recalls. Not even if you're Californian. For a list of recalled items, go the CPSC Web site at `www.cpsc.gov/cpscpub/prerel/prerel.html`.

✔ **No living creatures and unauthorized/illegal wildlife products.** To clarify, you definitely can't sell 99 percent of the live animals that come to mind. No dogs. No cats. No ferrets. The only ones you *can* sell are shellfish and crustaceans (as food), assuming you obey all applicable laws. Don't just think you can send a bucket of clams through the mail. You can't. And by "unauthorized wildlife products" they mean things like the skin of an endangered animal or an elephant tusk. You can sell authorized products like fur coats (assuming, of course, that they're not made of fur from an endangered species). Also, you can sell legal plants.

✔ **No real estate.** No auctioning off the Brooklyn Bridge or your summer home in Aspen (even if you really are the owner).

✔ **No wine and other alcoholic beverages.** This is not based on the "appropriate" rule. You can't sell alcoholic beverages at Amazon.com primarily because of the various governmental restrictions on the sale of those items. I wouldn't want you to think Amazon prudish.

So what *can* you sell? Anything else. What *should* you sell? That's another matter all together. I don't know, empirically, what you should sell on Auctions and zShops. Nobody does — so much of it has to do with taste. As an example, the year zShops launched, one of the hot items being sold was the Turducken — a chicken stuffed in a duck stuffed in a turkey. (Not live, of course, because that would be against the rules.) Who could've predicted it? Not me. Who'd *eat* it? Anyone craving a poultry medley, I guess.

I'm making a disclaimer — I'm no Auctions/zShops clairvoyant. But I have spent a lot of time with the site and I do feel I can give you some pointers. Here are a few Dos and Don'ts for selling at Auctions and zShops:

✔ **Don't sell inexpensive single items that are in the catalog.** First of all, any item you list in Marketplace will also show up in zShops. So there's no reason to pay the subscription fee if you don't have to. Also, your items will get more exposure through Marketplace because they're shown on the detail page of the new item that Amazon is selling. If you're creating a zShop, you could create one that sold items in the catalog — but only if it made sense (see the next bullet).

✔ **Do sell items that go together.** When you're creating a zShop, sell items that make sense together. This is how you make additional sales. For example, if someone is buying a fishing rod, they might also be looking for a reel.

✔ **Don't sell what everyone else is selling.** Be sure to visit the site and do some research before you list your item. Find out if your item is already being sold. Is the market flooded? Are like items selling? Do a little digging and find out whether you're offering unique merchandise. If you are, you have a better chance of selling it.

✔ **Do sell items that are "hot."** Popular, that is (not stolen). The key here is to know what's hot. One good way to do research on this is to check out Amazon's Top Sellers and then do a little extrapolating. In other words, if an artist's new CD is a top seller, then maybe items related to that artist would be hot sellers. Admittedly, there's a fine line between selling an item that's hot and selling something that everyone else is already selling. So you really have to do your research.

✔ **Don't sell things that are inexpensive and easily accessible when new.** This may seem obvious, but every now and then I come across something on the site and think, "Who on earth would buy that and why?" If you're selling something that I can buy at the drugstore down the street for two dollars more, I'll buy it at the drugstore and eat the two bucks.

✔ **Do sell one-of-kind or rare items.** To me, this is what Auctions and zShops are all about. That's not to say that you have to sell handmade things or collectibles there. You can sell *just about* anything, but originally these two stores were billed as the places to find special, unusual items. So listen up, all you crafty people out there! Auctions and zShops are a great place to sell your wares.

Creating a Good Auctions Listing

I'm going to get into the nitty-gritty of Auctions here. But don't dismay. zShops is next in line, later in the chapter.

Creating a good Auctions listing is a craft (and you can acquire the tools you need to master it right here). All the thinking and planning and researching in the world won't help you sell if you don't have a good listing. So what makes a listing good? The right kind of information. Here are the essentials for any good listing:

✔ **A precise title.** You have a total of 80 characters at your disposal. Use them wisely. Describe the item you're selling as accurately as you can in as few words as is possible. For example, if you're selling a set of stationery, you're better off with a title that says, "Set of five hand-printed "Year of the Sheep" cards with envelopes" (65 characters) than just "Set of hand-printed cards" (27 characters). Be brief, but not at the expense of being precise.

✔ **A good photo.** As far as I'm concerned, you have to have a photo (unless you're selling something for which a photo wouldn't be relevant — like a date with Brad Pitt). And not just any old photo. You need a good photo. More on this later in the chapter.

✔ **An accurate description.** You have a lot of room here — 4,000 characters, including spaces. Use it to give your buyer every piece of information you can envision them wanting. Amazon suggests that you put yourself in the buyer's shoes. That's good advice. Better yet, look at a few similar auctions and take note of the information (or lack of information) given. Did you walk away from the listing with unanswered questions? Write them down and be sure to answer them in your description. Think about what makes your item unique and include that information. And most important, remember that honesty is the best policy, so be as truthful and as accurate as you can be.

✔ **Precalculated shipping costs.** You can put something in your description that states that the buyer pays for shipping costs, but it's better to actually calculate them and include them as a line item in the auction form itself. That way buyers know what to expect and aren't at risk for getting shipping fee sticker shock. What some people do is figure out the most expensive possible shipping price within the areas that they're willing to ship to and list that. Other people find a range and list that (and I prefer this as a buyer). Or, for example, if they're shipping from the Midwest and they are only willing to ship to the continental U.S., they might list the amount they'll charge to ship to the West Coast and the amount they'll charge to ship to the East Coast.

✔ **The right categorization.** This is not important for the detail page itself, but for getting people there. Putting your item in the right categories means that it shows up in the appropriate search results. If you're uncertain about where your item belongs, do some browsing for similar items (within Auctions) and see where they show up.

I'm a firm believer that the success of any auction lies in the prep work. The actual listing process is much simpler.

As with any other Amazon transaction, you must have an Amazon account to list an item on Auctions. If you don't, you're walked through the sign-up as a part of the listing process. You can also set an account up ahead of time (see Chapter 3 for instructions). All sellers must also be signed up for Amazon Payments. You won't be able to sell if you aren't. Again, you do it either as a part of the listing process or separately. For instructions on how to sign up for Amazon Payments, see Chapter 14.

These instructions assume that you already have an account and that you're set up to pay using Amazon Payments:

1. **Click Your Account in the Shopping Tools menu.**

   The Shopping Tools menu sits at the top of just about every page on the site.

2. **Click the Your Seller Account link.**

   This is in the Auctions, zShops, and Marketplace box on the right side of the page.

3. **Click the List Single Items link.**

   You'll find this under the List Your Items For Sale heading in the Your Inventory section.

4. **Click Amazon Auctions.**

   You come to a page that looks like Figure 16-1. This is where you will enter your item information. (If you're not already set up with Amazon Payments, you'll be taken to a Sign In screen and then a screen where you'll enter your credit-card info and check that you've read and agree to the terms of the participation agreement.)

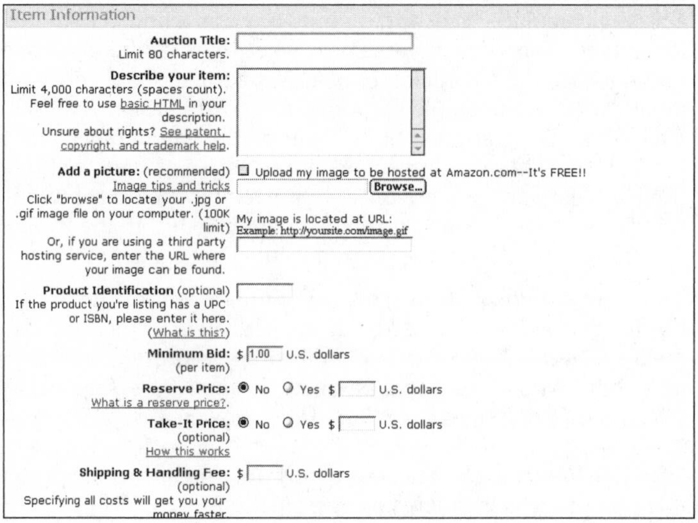

Figure 16-1: The Item Information section of the Auctions listing page.

5. **Enter your auction title and description in the fields provided.**

   Remember to be descriptive and straightforward. Also, check for spelling errors.

6. **Click the Upload My Image box and then either click Browse or enter the URL for your image in the field provided.**

   The first thing you need to know is that all images must either be GIFs or JPEGs. (For more file information, click the Image Tips and Tricks link.) If you are technically savvy enough to have your image hosted on the Web somewhere, then you probably don't need an explanation of how to enter the URL in the field. Everyone else should choose the first image option. When you click Browse, you get a chance to comb through the folders on your computer's hard drive in search of your image. To make this process easier, make sure beforehand that you've stored the image somewhere obvious (say, in a folder on your desktop). When you locate the image, simply double-click it and you're taken back to the Auctions listing page, where the name of the image appears automatically in the field. What happens here is that because you and your hard drive are connected to the Internet, Amazon's technology can make a copy of your image and store it on their server.

7. **If applicable, enter the UPC or ISBN number of the item you're selling in the Product Identification field.**

These two numbers are standard identification numbers (ISBNs are for books, UPCs are for most other things). If there is one, you may as well add it. It gives the user more information — they can use the numbers to look up the product and see it new either on Amazon or somewhere else.

8. **Enter a minimum bid in the field provided.**

Amazon puts $1.00 in that field as a default. You can change that number as you like. Just keep in mind that your minimum bid should allow some "bidding up." In other words, if you're hoping to sell an item for $30.00, don't set the minimum bid *at* $30.00. Set it a little bit lower to attract bargain hunters and to allow a little competitive bidding to occur. But don't set it so low that you're giving something away if you have a lack of bidders. If you're not going to have a reserve price — the minimum amount of money you're willing to take for the item — set your minimum bid somewhere close to the lowest amount you're willing to accept for the item.

9. **In the Reserve Price section of the page, either click the No radio button or click Yes and then enter your reserve price in the field provided.**

You don't have to enter a reserve price. If you choose to, however, I recommend that you don't make it wildly different from your minimum bid. When you set a reserve price, highest bids won't count as *winning* bids until they match or exceed it — and remember, bidders don't know what the reserve is. So it's possible for a bidder to have a maximum bid that is *lower* than your reserve price but *higher* than your minimum bid. That means the bidder is bidding on your auction without any chance of winning — which is frustrating and not a good way to attract customers. Please note that once you set a reserve price and list your auction, you can't change the reserve price later.

10. **In the Take It Price section, either click the No radio button or click Yes and then enter your Take-It Price in the field provided.**

This is the amount of money that you'd be willing to accept for the item — much like eBay's Buy it Now option. It's a cool feature as it allows shoppers to buy your items with 1-Click. If someone does buy your item using the Take-It price, the auction automatically ends. Take-It Prices are listed on the auction detail page.

11. **Enter your shipping and handling fees in the field provided.**

This is optional, but I highly recommend it. If you need help calculating fees, visit the Web site of the carrier you plan to use. And remember, shipping sticker shock makes for unhappy buyers (and bad ratings). So don't use the shipping and handling as a way to make more money. Keep it realistic and your buyers will be happy.

12. **Use the drop-down menus to enter your item in the appropriate category.**

    There are just shy of 20 drop-downs here (as shown in Figure 16-2) — and you can pick only one! Be mindful and put your stuff in the right category so it'll show up in the right search results and in the right browse nodes. If you're uncertain about where your item belongs, do some browsing for similar items (within Auctions) and see where they show up.

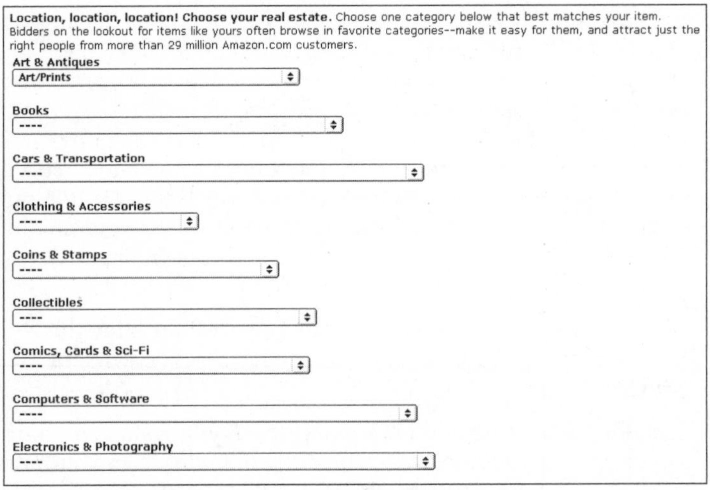

Location, location, location! Choose your real estate. Choose one category below that best matches your item. Bidders on the lookout for items like yours often browse in favorite categories--make it easy for them, and attract just the right people from more than 29 million Amazon.com customers.

Art & Antiques
Art/Prints

Books

Cars & Transportation

Clothing & Accessories

Coins & Stamps

Collectibles

Comics, Cards & Sci-Fi

Computers & Software

Electronics & Photography

Figure 16-2: Drop-down central! This is where you'll categorize your auction.

13. **Enter your listing information.**

    Figure 16-3 shows the listing information section of the form. Use the drop-down menu to choose the duration of your auction (default is at 7 days). Click the appropriate circles to choose the type — standard, Dutch, or private (see the "Standard, Dutch, or Private?" sidebar for more info on these) — and whether or not to relist (you get one freebie here). You can also check the box if you want to carry over merchandising features and fees.

14. **Enter your selling preferences.**

    Figure 16-4 shows the Selling Preferences area of the form. This is where you enter the critical payment and shipping information. Click the boxes and circles as appropriate. Remember that you are required to accept Amazon Payments; any other method of payment is optional. Also, although the Returns section of the form is optional, *accepting* returns is not — that's something you have to be prepared to do if you want to do business. In effect, what you're really entering here is your policy on refunds.

15. Choose optional features.

These are additional merchandising tools that you can use to promote your auction. Most of them cost money. (More on these later in the chapter.)

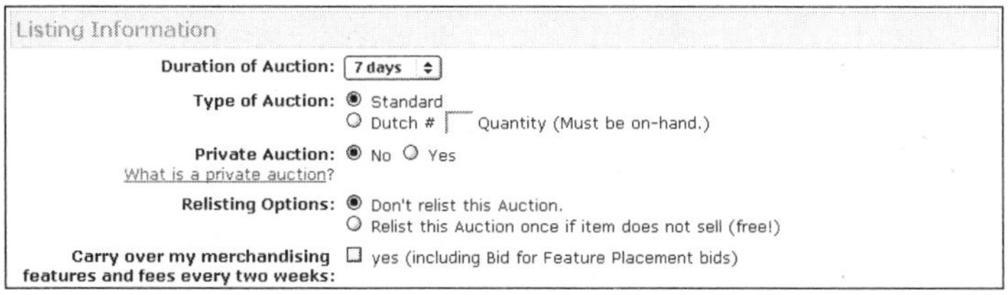

Figure 16-3:
Your listing
information
goes here.

Listing Information

Duration of Auction:	7 days ⬍
Type of Auction:	⦿ Standard
	○ Dutch # ☐ Quantity (Must be on-hand.)
Private Auction:	⦿ No ○ Yes
What is a private auction?	
Relisting Options:	⦿ Don't relist this Auction.
	○ Relist this Auction once if item does not sell (free!)
Carry over my merchandising features and fees every two weeks:	☐ yes (including Bid for Feature Placement bids)

16. Click the Preview Your Auction button.

You're taken to a page where you can review your information. If you need to make changes, click the Edit button to return to the listing form.

17. Click the Submit Your Auction button.

Once you do this, your auction is live! You come to a confirmation page that includes a link to your auction's detail page.

Standard, Dutch, or Private?

A standard auction is exactly that — any plain, old auction where you offer up an item and people bid on it. The highest bidder wins and everyone else goes home empty handed.

In a Dutch auction, the seller has more than one of the same item to sell and auctions them all off at the same time. Bidders commit to both the number of the items they want to buy and how much they want to bid per item. The final per-item price in a Dutch auction is determined by the lowest winning bids. Then the items are distributed based on bid amount and quantity requested with highest winning bidder getting dibs. Amazon's own example spells it out more clearly. "Joe and Sue are the individual high bidders in a Dutch auction for lamps. Joe placed a bid for 30 lamps at $20 each. In a subsequent bid, Sue offered to buy 10 lamps at $65 each. Because Sue's high bid ($65) is greater than Joe's high bid ($20), Sue is entitled to all 10 lamps she requested at the $20 price (the lowest winning bid). Joe is entitled to the remaining 20 lamps at $20 each, even though his original bid was for a quantity of 30."

Private auctions are much simpler, though they're pretty rare and usually for high-ticket items. During a private auction, bids are public on the site as usual, but bidders are not identified. When the auction ends, both the seller and the highest bidder are notified via e-mail.

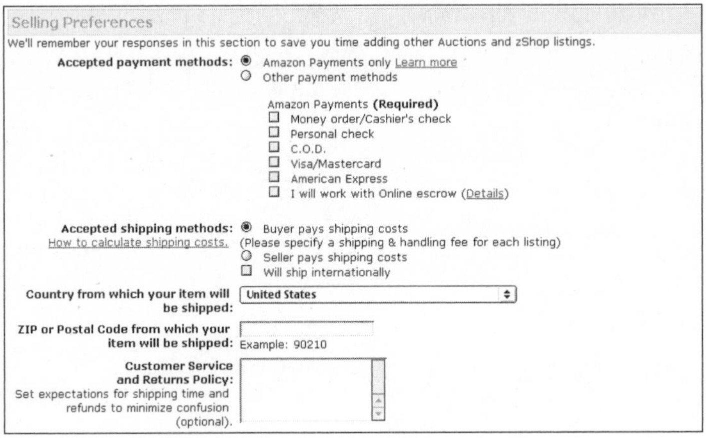

Figure 16-4:
Your Seller
Preferences
outline your
policies on
payment
and
shipping.

Editing or Canceling an Auction

When you've successfully posted an auction, you can edit it as necessary.
Here's how to do that:

1. **Click Your Account in the Shopping Tools menu.**

   Look for this at the top of just about every page on the site.

2. **Click the Your Seller Account link.**

   This is in the Auctions, zShops, and Marketplace box on the right side of
   the page.

3. **Click the Open link in the Auctions section.**

   You'll find the link in the View Items section of Your Inventory. This link
   will take you to a page that lists all your open items.

4. **Click the Modify Listing link for the item you want to edit.**

   This takes you to the auctions-listing form for that item. From here, the
   editing process is exactly like the original listing process. Make the necessary changes, but remember that you can't change a reserve price
   once it's set.

5. **Click the Preview Your Auction button.**

   Review your new information and click the Edit button to return to the
   listing form.

6. **Click the Submit Your Auction button.**

   You should see your edits on-screen immediately. Click the link to your
   auction to confirm that it works.

It is really important that you not change the description of your item in such a way that existing bidders will be disappointed. If you must do this, just know that they can cancel their bids and that it's a pretty good way to get some bad feedback.

Also, you may have noticed that an End This Auction Now button appears on the listing form after you complete Step 4 in this process (as shown in Figure 16-5). You can end an auction before it closes, but if there are bidders, it's strongly discouraged. (This recently happened to me and I was so annoyed! I wanted that little key chain and was anxiously awaiting the end of the auction to see if I'd won.) If you absolutely have to do that, here's how to do it:

1. **Click Your Account in the Shopping Tools menu.**

   It's at the top of just about every page on the site.

2. **Click the Your Seller Account link.**

   This is in the Auctions, zShops, and Marketplace box on the right side of the page.

3. **Click the Open link in the Auctions section.**

   The link, which lives in the View Items section of Your Inventory, takes you to a page that lists all your open items.

4. **Click the Modify Listing link for the item you want to edit.**

   You should be at the listing form for the auction you want to cancel. At the top of the page (which looks like Figure 16-5), you'll see the End This Auction Now button.

Figure 16-5:
The End This Auction Now (cancellation) button is at the top of every live listing form.

5. **Click the End This Auction Now button.**

   You come to a page that looks like Figure 16-6.

amazon.com.   VIEW CART | WISH LIST | YOUR ACCOUNT | HELP

WELCOME | MARA'S STORE | BOOKS | APPAREL & ACCESSORIES | ELECTRONICS | MUSIC | KITCHEN & HOUSEWARES | COMPUTERS | HOME & GARDEN | SEE MORE STORES

Search Auctions | Browse Auctions | Your Account | Seller Account | Search zShops | Browse zShops

Seller Account: Mara > Open Auctions

Hand-printed "Year of the Sheep" cards with envelopes

Current high bid: $0.00
Auction ends: 6 days, 12:39:59

Ending an auction early is not encouraged, as it is disruptive to the auction process. Please close auctions early only when it is absolutely necessary and be sure to contact any winning bidders immediately.

Reason for ending this auction early:
[   ] End this auction now

6. **Enter your reason for ending the auction in the field provided and click End This Auction Now.**

   That's it. Your auction is cancelled and you'll receive an e-mail confirming cancellation shortly thereafter. Any existing bidders will also receive an e-mail that the auction has been cancelled.

Selling with zShops

When you use zShops to sell your merchandise, you have to meet three requirements:

- ✔ **You must have an Amazon account.** If you need instructions on how to set one up, read Chapter 3.

- ✔ **You must be signed up to accept Amazon Payments.** All Amazon sellers have to accept Amazon Payments. With zShops, you can also accept other forms of payment. To find out how to sign up, read Chapter 14.

- ✔ **You must have a Pro Merchant account.** All Amazon sellers can make use of a Pro Merchant account, but only zShops requires it. To find out how to sign up, read Chapter 14.

Once you've signed up for all three, you're ready to sell! And don't forget, you can also use your Pro Merchant subscription to sell in volume, both on Auctions and with Marketplace.

Listing a single item

I know I said that zShops is for volume sellers — and nine times out of ten, it is. But sometimes people list single items with zShops. These are usually high-ticket items that warrant spending the $39.99 monthly Pro Merchant subscription fee. (Recently I found a $2,500 dirt bike on zShops — that's a good example of a single item worth listing.) If you have a high-ticket item you'd like to sell, here's how to do it (note that these instructions assume that you've already met the three requirements just described — that you have an Amazon account, that you're signed up for Payments, and that you have a Pro Merchant account):

1. **Click Your Account in the Shopping Tools menu.**

   It's at the top of just about every page on the site.

2. **Click the Your Seller Account link.**

   This is in the Auctions, zShops, and Marketplace box on the right side of the page.

3. **Click the List Single Items link.**

   You'll find this under the List Your Items For Sale heading in the Your Inventory section.

4. **Click Amazon zShops.**

   Note that if you're not already set up with Amazon Payments, you'll be taken to a sign-in screen and then a screen where you'll enter your credit-card info. If you are signed up, you come to a page that looks like Figure 16-7. Scroll down a bit and you'll see that this is the zShops single-listing form (almost identical to the Auctions single-listing form). But before you scroll, notice that you have the option to list with Marketplace — but only (of course) if the item you're selling is in Amazon's catalog. All Marketplace items also show up in zShops, but not vice versa. Here I'm assuming that you're listing an item that *isn't* in the catalog. For those few times when it might be, you'd list it in zShops anyway. (I tell you about those times in the "Scary math — better to sell with zShops or Marketplace?" sidebar later in the chapter.)

5. **Enter your title and description in the fields provided.**

   Remember to be descriptive and straightforward. Also, check for spelling errors.

6. **Click the Upload My Image . . . box and then either click Browse or enter the URL for your image in the field provided.**

   As with Auctions, all images must either be GIFs or JPEGs. (For more file information click the Image Tips and Tricks link.) If you have your image hosted on the Web somewhere, enter the URL in the field provided. For everyone else, click Browse and search through the folders on your computer's hard drive to find your image. To make things easier for yourself, store the image somewhere obvious, like in a folder on your desktop. When you locate the image, simply double-click it and you're taken back to the zShops listing page, where the name of the image appears automatically in the field. (Because you and your hard drive are connected to the Internet, Amazon's technology can make a copy of your image and store it on their server.)

Figure 16-7:
The zShops single-listing form offers the option of listing with Marketplace as well.

7. **Enter the price in the field provided.**

    Just to remind you, this is a fixed price. Also, don't forget that Amazon takes a percentage of the closing fee; take that into account when you're banking on your profits.

8. **Enter your quantity-on-hand in the field provided.**

    Even though this is a single listing, you can still have more than one on hand. You have to have *at least* one on hand.

9. **Enter your shipping and handling fees in the field provided.**

    Again, optional but highly recommended. If you need help calculating fees, visit the Web site of the carrier you plan to use.

10. **Use the drop-down menus to enter your item in the appropriate category.**

    Remember that you can pick only one; make sure you put your stuff in the right category.

11. **Check the Yes box if you want to carry over your merchandising features and fees.**

    I actually think this belongs below the optional features (it would definitely make more sense there). What this means is that if you're going to sign up for some of Amazon's optional features for the item you're list-ing, you can carry them over (or automatically renew them) for as long as the item is listed. So, for example, if you decide to pay $2.00 for a boldfaced title, and you check the box, you'll be paying $2.00 every two weeks to keep the title boldfaced.

12. **Enter your selling preferences.**

This is where you enter critical payment and shipping information. Click the boxes and circles as appropriate.

It bears repeating: You are required to accept Amazon Payments; any other method of payment is optional. Also, what you're really entering here is your policy on refunds; although the Returns section if the form is optional, actually accepting returns is not.

13. **Choose optional features.**

Optional features are the same for Auctions and zShops. They are addi-tional merchandising tools you can use to promote your listings. You can find out more about these by reading the "Snazzing It Up for Better Selling" section, later in this chapter.

14. **Click the Preview Your Listing button.**

You're taken to a page where you can review your information. If you need to make changes, click the Edit button to return to the listing form.

Scary math — better to sell with zShops or Marketplace?

If you're selling a particularly spendy (that's the optimistic word for *pricey*) item, even if it *is* in Amazon's catalog, it might be better to list it *only* in zShops and pay the $39.99 monthly fee. So how spendy *is* spendy?

Remember, when you list with Marketplace you pay a $.99 listing fee and a percentage of the total price of the item. That's 6 percent of sales price on computers, 8 percent on camera, photo, and electronics, and 15 percent on all other products. When you list with zShops, you pay your Pro Merchant subscription monthly fee of $39.99 plus a 5 percent closing fee on items that sell for $0.01 to $25.00, a $1.25 addi-tional flat fee plus 2.5 percent closing fee on

items that sell for $25.01 to $1,000.00, and a $25.63 additional flat fee plus 1.25 percent clos-ing fee on items that sell for more than $1,000.

Consider this: If you're selling a plasma TV for $950, you give Amazon roughly $77 if you sell through Marketplace. If you sell it through zShops and it only takes one month to get that sale, you only give Amazon about $65. The more expensive the item, the greater the gap between those two numbers. So when you're selling an expensive item, do the math. Then decide whether the numbers warrant selling on zShops instead of Marketplace, keeping in mind that Marketplace gives you more exposure.

15. **Click the Submit Your Listing button.**

You're done! You can edit any zShops listing from your Seller Account page in the same way that you'd edit an Auctions or Marketplace listing.

Listing multiple items

You *can* list items in zShops one by one, but if you have several items to list, you can save time by using the Inventory Loader. The Inventory Loader is the Marketplace and zShops multiple-listing tool (in Auctions it's the Auctions Bulk Uploader). Using the Inventory Loader is simple. Preparing to use it is not as simple.

In order to use the Inventory Loader, you need to put your items into a single Excel spreadsheet according to Amazon's guidelines (booksellers can also use a Universal Information Exchange Environment document). You can find detailed instructions on how to prepare your spreadsheet in the Selling at Amazon.com section of the Help department. Click zShops, then zShops Volume Listing Tools, and then Building Your Spreadsheet.

You have the option of having Amazon send you a prepared Excel spreadsheet. If you're at all uncomfortable with Excel, I recommend you take advantage of this offer. Just click the Click Here link in the second paragraph of the Build Your Spreadsheet page and your e-mail client program generates an e-mail. You don't need to write anything in the subject line or body of the e-mail. Just click the Send button. You'll receive the spreadsheet template via e-mail almost immediately. It comes ready for either Marketplace or zShops. If you're using it for zShops, just ignore or delete the Marketplace-specific columns.

Once you've completed your spreadsheet, you're ready to upload your items. Here's how:

1. **Click Your Account in the Shopping Tools menu.**

   It's at the top of just about every page on the site.

2. **Click the Your Seller Account link.**

   This is in the Auctions, zShops, and Marketplace box on the right side of the page.

3. **Click the Upload Multiple Items link.**

   This link lives under the List Your Items For Sale heading in the Your Inventory section.

4. **Click the Tab Delimited link.**

   Unless you're using UIEE software, this is the link for you. You'll come to a Sign In screen.

5. **Enter your password in the field provided and click the Sign In Using Our Secure Server button.**

   You come to a page that looks like Figure 16-8.

6. **Use the drop-down menus to choose your selling venue and upload option.**

   Choose zShops Only for the selling program and Add/Modify/Delete for your upload option.

7. **Click Browse to find the file you want to upload.**

   Clicking Browse sends you combing through the folders on your computer's hard drive in search of your file. To make that easier, store the file somewhere obvious (such as a folder on your desktop). When you locate it, simply double-click it (or click the Open button). Amazon makes a copy of your document and stores it on their server. You'll be taken back to the upload page where you should see the name of the file automatically placed in the appropriate field.

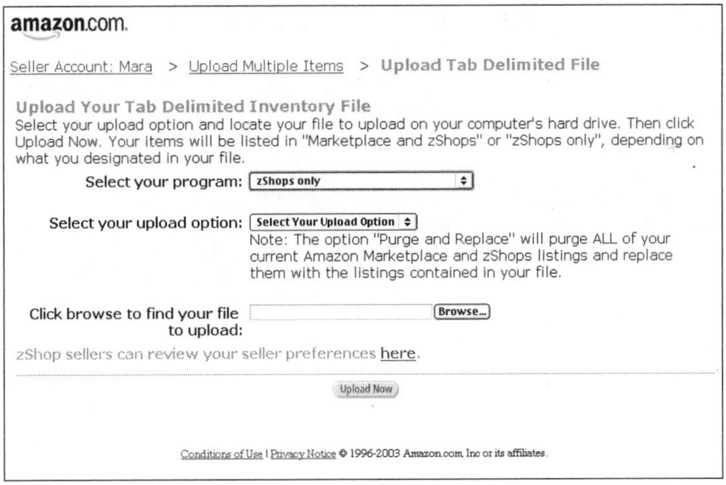

WARNING!

---

amazon.com.

Seller Account: Mara > Upload Multiple Items > Upload Tab Delimited File

Upload Your Tab Delimited Inventory File
Select your upload option and locate your file to upload on your computer's hard drive. Then click Upload Now. Your items will be listed in "Marketplace and zShops" or "zShops only", depending on what you designated in your file.

Select your program: [zShops only ▾]

Select your upload option: [Select Your Upload Option ▾]
Note: The option "Purge and Replace" will purge ALL of your current Amazon Marketplace and zShops listings and replace them with the listings contained in your file.

Click browse to find your file to upload: [   ] [Browse...]

zShop sellers can review your seller preferences here.

[Upload Now]

Conditions of Use | Privacy Notice © 1996-2003 Amazon.com, Inc or its affiliates.

Figure 16-8: The Upload Multiple-Listings page.

---

8. **Click the Upload Now button.**

   That's all it takes. You come to a page that looks like Figure 16-9. You can check the status of your upload to make sure that everything went okay by clicking the Review Inventory Upload Status button. If it didn't go right, Amazon sends you an e-mail with a link to a detailed error log that explains what went wrong.

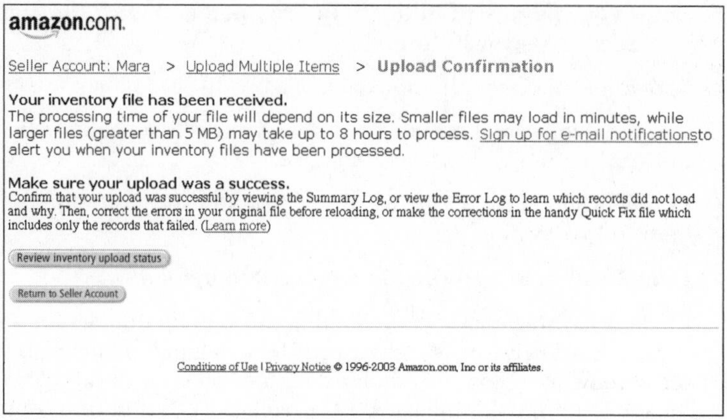

amazon.com.

Seller Account: Mara > Upload Multiple Items > **Upload Confirmation**

Your inventory file has been received.
The processing time of your file will depend on its size. Smaller files may load in minutes, while larger files (greater than 5 MB) may take up to 8 hours to process. Sign up for e-mail notifications to alert you when your inventory files have been processed.

Make sure your upload was a success.
Confirm that your upload was successful by viewing the Summary Log, or view the Error Log to learn which records did not load and why. Then, correct the errors in your original file before reloading, or make the corrections in the handy Quick Fix file which includes only the records that failed. (Learn more)

[Review inventory upload status]

[Return to Seller Account]

Conditions of Use | Privacy Notice © 1996-2003 Amazon.com, Inc or its affiliates.

Figure 16-9:
This is the Multiple Item Upload Confirmation page.

Snazzing It Up for Better Selling: Good Photos and Optional Features

There are several things you can do to your auctions and zShops listings to give them some oomph. Some of them are free and some cost money. All of them are available from the auctions or zShops listing forms.

The first, and as far as I'm concerned the most important, is the photo. I've already mentioned the photo and sung its praises, but let me say it again: You have to have a good photo! Maybe you'll sell something without a photo. I'm sure it happens every now and then. But ask yourself this: Would you buy something online from a stranger if you couldn't look at it first?

Amazon has a wealth of good photo tips on its site and you can access them from the listing form itself. Just click the Image Tips and Tricks link from the Item Information section of the listing form. You'll find instructions on how to capture your image, convert it to digital, size it, and upload it to the site. Also, when you take your photo, make sure it's a good one. Here are a few more tips:

✔ **Use a solid background.** Don't distract buyers with background mumbo jumbo. Try laying your item on a piece of white poster board.

✔ **Make sure you have enough light.** A dark photo is not a flattering photo. If you are taking the photo in a room that's not well lit, use a flash and bring in an extra lamp for more light.

✔ **Take several shots.** And then pick the best one.

✔ **Put a few photos in your image.** This is for those of you who are comfortable using photo-manipulation programs. Amazon allows you to upload one *image* per detail page, but that doesn't mean the image has to contain only one *photo*. If you want, take a general shot of your item and then a couple of detail shots. Make the general shot the largest and use the detail shots smaller and on the side. You can then save it as one image and upload it to the site. It will be hard to discern details in the thumbnail, but much more detail will be available in the full-size photo farther down the page.

The other ways to spice up your listings are to make use of the optional features that Amazon offers. The Optional Features section is that last section on the listing form (see Figure 16-10) and you can activate these features from the form. Here's a quick review of what each one is:

✔ **Boldface title.** This is exactly like the yellow pages. For $2.00 you can have your title bolded in the search results and on browse pages. According to Amazon, there is a 30 percent increase in sales for titles that choose the boldface title.

✔ **First bidder discount.** You have the option of giving the first bidder on your item a 10 percent discount. It costs you 10 percent of the final price, but you have a better chance of selling it. The sell-through increase is 15 percent.

✔ **Crosslinks.** This is a way to cross-merchandise your item by surfacing it on other relevant pages on the site. Happily, crosslinks are free. To use them, you just have to find three items in the Books, Music, Video, or DVD stores that you feel are related to your item and put their ASINs or ISBNs in the fields provided. (ASINs and ISBNs are product identification numbers. You can find them in the product information on an item's detail page.) Crosslinks increase sell-through by 20 percent.

✔ **Bid for featured placement.** You can use this to get yourself featured higher up on search results and browse pages. In effect, it's an auction for placement; you are bidding against other sellers. Why? Simple: Featured placement increases sell-through by 60 percent. To find out more about this program, click the <u>Learn More</u> link in the Increase Your Bids for Featured Placement section of the listing form. You can also access this information from the Auctions and zShops sections of the Selling at Amazon.com area in the Help department.

There are other ways to promote your listings. You can find out about them in the Help department by going to the Selling at Amazon.com section, clicking on either the Auctions link or the zShops link and then on Promoting Your Auctions/zShops Listing.

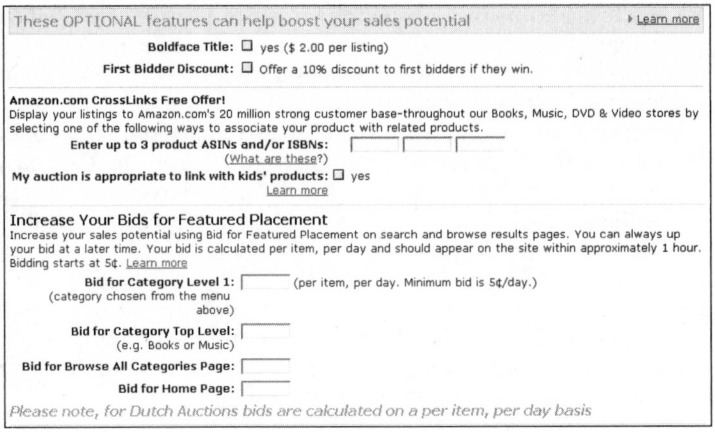
These OPTIONAL features can help boost your sales potential ▸ Learn more

Boldface Title: ☐ yes ($ 2.00 per listing)

First Bidder Discount: ☐ Offer a 10% discount to first bidders if they win.

Amazon.com CrossLinks Free Offer!
Display your listings to Amazon.com's 20 million strong customer base-throughout our Books, Music, DVD & Video stores by selecting one of the following ways to associate your product with related products.

Enter up to 3 product ASINs and/or ISBNs: [ ] [ ] [ ]
(What are these?)

My auction is appropriate to link with kids' products: ☐ yes
Learn more

Increase Your Bids for Featured Placement
Increase your sales potential using Bid for Featured Placement on search and browse results pages. You can always up your bid at a later time. Your bid is calculated per item, per day and should appear on the site within approximately 1 hour. Bidding starts at 5¢. Learn more

Bid for Category Level 1: [ ] (per item, per day. Minimum bid is 5¢/day.)
(category chosen from the menu above)

Bid for Category Top Level: [ ]
(e.g. Books or Music)

Bid for Browse All Categories Page: [ ]

Bid for Home Page: [ ]

Please note, for Dutch Auctions bids are calculated on a per item, per day basis

Figure 16-10: Optional features help you advertise your auction.

Your zShops Storefront

When you become a Pro Merchant, you also get your own zShops storefront. These are accessible from item detail pages, and they are your own for "decorating" as you please.

You don't *have* to spruce up your storefront. If you want, you can just rely on your items surfacing in search results and on browse pages. But if you want to direct people to your zShop — say, from your own Web site — you should make it look good.

Here are the things you can do to make a more professional-looking zShop:

- **Customize your brand bar.** The *brand bar* is the strip that surrounds your page and identifies your store. Amazon automatically puts your nickname there, followed by *zShop*, and sets the default color at gray. You can replace your nickname with another name or your company's logo, change the brand-bar color, and add your business' URL and e-mail address at the bottom of the page.
- **Beef up your Browse box.** When you upload several items to zShops and you enter each item in a category, Amazon will use those categories to create a default Browse box for your storefront. You can recategorize them yourself and create a custom browse box that'll make more sense in your store. You can do this as an edit or when you upload.
- **Create a Custom Search box.** The Custom Search box is in the upper-left corner of your store. You can give it its own label and fill it with links to prearranged search results — a quick way to highlight certain products in your store.

✔ **Include featured listings.** Featured listings show up on the right side of your page. They're just like the featured products on Amazon store pages. You can show as many as five featured listings on your page at one time. (You can choose to have more; Amazon rotates through them.) Make sure you choose items that have good photos and solid descriptions; they make good featured listings.

✔ **Include a description of your store and a photo.** Tell potential buyers a little bit about your store and include a photo. (It doesn't *have* to be of you — just something to give the page some life, See Figure 16-11.)

You can add these features to your zShop by clicking the Edit Your zShops Storefront link on your Seller Account page. If you need more information or instruction on how to add these features, visit the Help department. For detailed information in the zShops section of Selling at Amazon.com, just click zShops Storefront.

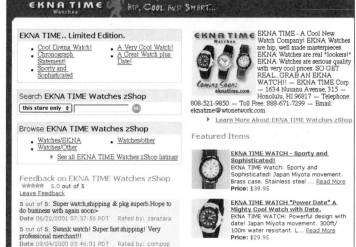

Figure 16-11:
Ekna Time has done a great job of personalizing their zShop!

Sold!

So what happens when your Auctions or zShops item sells? Three things. You make contact. You collect payment. You ship the item. Most of the time, sales go smoothly. But if you've spent any time at all looking at vendor feedback ratings at Auctions and zShops, you know that even great vendors can have rough sales. Here are a few pointers for keeping your sales running smoothly:

✔ **Stay in touch but don't stalk.** Contact your buyer only when necessary. My definition of "necessary" is when they make the purchase, when you ship, and if anything goes wrong.

✔ **Collect all non-Amazon-Payments payments.** If you're going to accept other methods of payment and a buyer chooses to pay that way, make sure you arrange payment as soon as the item sells.

✔ **Pack carefully and wisely.** *Carefully* means that you should use materials suited to the item you're sending so it arrives safe and sound. *Wisely* means you've been meticulous about labeling your package — be sure to write "Your Amazon.com zShops/Auctions Order" clearly on the package.

✔ **Ship promptly.** You will get a negative feedback rating if more than a few days pass. So ship as soon as is possible.

For more information on what to do after a sale (and some troubleshooting help) visit the Selling at Amazon.com section in the Help department. You'll find what you need in the Auctions and zShops sections under Making an Auctions/zShops Sale.

Chapter 17

Leveling the Playing Field: Amazon.com Advantage

. . . .

In This Chapter

▶ Finding whether Advantage is right for you

▶ Applying for Advantage

▶ Marketing your products

▶ Keeping your inventory stocked

▶ Getting paid

▶ Understanding the agreement

. . . .

Amazon.com Advantage started out as a little pet project — a way to give independent publishers a leg up in the world of book sales. Buying on the Internet was just starting to happen and Amazon.com was the pioneer. They thought, *Why not approach small publishers who have no good way to distribute their products and let them put stuff on the site?* They called it "leveling the playing field" because Advantage titles got the same detail page — thus had the same presence — as any title on the site.

The program was a success and the pet project grew to be a real business. Today Advantage includes music and video as well as original books. Today there are thousands of Advantage members, and hundreds of thousands of their titles on the site.

In this chapter, I cover all the Amazon.com Advantage essentials. I start by telling you who should sign up for the Advantage program, because it's not for everyone. I show you how to apply, and what to do after you're accepted into the program. I cover marketing, inventory management, and payment. And I tell you what you need to know about the rules so you don't get into trouble along the way.

Who Can Apply?

As I said, Amazon.com Advantage isn't for everyone. It isn't even for every independent publisher, label, or studio. If you're thinking of applying for the Advantage program, make sure you meet these criteria:

- ✔ **You have an e-mail account and Web access.** Amazon.com is a Web-based business and so is Advantage. You do all your account management — and 99 percent of your communicating — electronically. That means you have to have e-mail and Internet access.

- ✔ **You are located in North America.** Alas, as of right now, the only other Advantage program is Advantage for books in the U.K.

- ✔ **You have worldwide distribution rights.** You must have these for all titles that you enroll in the program.

- ✔ **Your titles have the appropriate codes.** Books have to have ISBNs printed on them. CDs, videos, and DVDs must have UPCs printed on them (on the sleeves for videos and DVDs). All titles must have bar codes printed on them; the bar codes must scan to match the ISBN or UPC of the title they accompany.

- ✔ **You actually have the title in hand.** Don't apply for the program using titles that haven't been released yet. Amazon asks that you have titles in hand, ready to ship.

- ✔ **Your titles are packaged appropriately.** CDs, videos, and DVDs should be shrink-wrapped, and CDs should be in a "protective case" (a jewel case is standard).

- ✔ **Your books list for at least $2.99.**

- ✔ **Your titles meet Amazon's suitability standards.** This doesn't just mean "no porn." This also relates to things like quality of production.

The Program Basics

Advantage is essentially a consignment program. You give Amazon your titles and they sell them and take a cut of the profits. Here are the program basics:

- ✔ **Getting accepted.** Not everyone can be an Advantage member. (See the "Who Can Apply?" section for details.) You fill out an application online and if you're accepted into the program, you receive a confirmation e-mail with a couple of weeks.

- ✔ **Getting your titles on the site.** You send the Advantage team a marketing package that includes information on how to categorize your titles (so they end up in the right place on the site), actual physical copies of the titles so they can scan the cover art, and any additional information to put on your titles' detail pages. The Advantage team uploads your titles to the site.

✓ **Shipping copies of your titles to Amazon.** After you're accepted, you receive an e-mail order from Amazon. You send the requested number of units directly to the specified Amazon distribution center. Every time your inventory is low, you receive an e-mail with a new order (assuming your sales are okay); you're responsible for replenishing the stock.

✓ **Getting your titles to consumers.** Here's the great part: Amazon takes care of all that. They take and process the order. They handle all the fulfillment. And they deal with any returns.

✓ **Getting paid.** Amazon automatically pays you for titles sold in the previous month. In other words, they pay monthly net every 30 days.

✓ **Getting the man paid.** Amazon takes a 45 percent cut of the listing price. That may sound like a lot, but it's actually based on a standard 55 percent purchase discount. They also charge a yearly membership fee of $29.95 that's automatically deducted from your account.

Sign on the Dotted Line

It's surprisingly easy to sign up for Advantage. So easy, in fact, that you might jump into it without giving it the proper forethought.

Remember, by signing up for Advantage, you're signing a legally binding business agreement with Amazon.com. So make sure you know what you're getting into.

The best way to find out exactly what you're getting into is to read the Advantage membership agreement. You can access it from the main Advantage info page. To get there, do the following:

1. **Click See More Stores.**

   You find this at the top of almost every page on the site, just to the right of the tabs.

2. **Click the Advantage link in the Make Money box.**

   This is on the right side of the store directory page. It takes you to what I call the "teaser" page — a screener to make sure that people don't confuse Advantage with Marketplace. It's also where you sign in once you're a member.

3. **Click either of the <u>Read More About the Advantage Program</u> links.**

   There's one in the first paragraph and one in the box on the left. Both take you to the *real* Advantage page (which looks like Figure 17-1).

Figure 17-1:
You can find
out about
the
Advantage
Program
from this
page.

All about the membership agreement

To access the membership agreement, just click the link under Additional Information on the Advantage info page. The membership agreement is exactly what it looks like: a legal document. You should read through it thoroughly and probably have a lawyer look at it, but here are some of the finer points:

- ✔ **Amazon holds the cards.** They can reject your application, even if you meet all the criteria. They don't typically do this, but they can.

- ✔ **No refunds.** They bill you $29.95 for the yearly membership fee each May. If for any reason your membership is terminated, they keep the dough.

- ✔ **Every title gets reviewed.** Getting accepted by virtue of a few titles does not mean that every title you ever submit will be accepted. Amazon screens every title you send them and, like the application process, they can reject any title at their sole discretion — even if it meets criteria.

- ✔ **You pay for shipping.** Not to individual customers, but to Amazon's distribution centers. This includes freight, insurance, and any customs duties.

- ✔ **Until it gets there, it's your baby.** Until your items arrive at the distribution center and are deemed acceptable, they are your responsibility. That means that if they get lost along the way or damaged en route, you bear the expense. And, if they show up but don't meet Amazon's standards (bar codes in the right place and so on), *you* pay the return shipping expense.

✔ **Speed counts.** The availability listing of your title on its detail page depends on your speed in refilling orders. When Amazon has your title in stock, they list its availability as "usually ships in 24 hours." When it's not in stock, availability changes to reflect your delivery history.

✔ **Amazon names their price.** You suggest a retail price for each title, but Amazon makes the ultimate decision and that's that.

✔ **You only get paid if your titles are bought.** Remember, this is a consignment program. Amazon places orders with you, but they're not actually buying the titles. You get paid when Amazon's customers buy the titles.

✔ **Use Mickey and you pay the price.** You really do have to have worldwide distribution rights and if your titles break any copyright laws, you are responsible for any expenses incurred. In other words, you pay for the lawyers and the settlement if Disney sues.

✔ **Zip the lip.** If Amazon sends you any confidential info as a part of your participation in the program, you agree that you will keep it confidential.

✔ **They can change the name of the game.** Amazon reserves the right to change the membership agreement at any time *without* telling you about it. If you continue with your membership, you are legally agreeing to the new terms.

✔ **The Dear John letter.** Both you and Amazon can end the agreement at any time and for any reason, but it has to be in writing. Also, if either of you end the agreement, Amazon has the right to buy any of your remaining title that it has in stock at the 45 percent price. This is actually a good thing. Here's something not as good: If they end the agreement after the first six months (or during the first six months because of something naughty that you did), you pay for the returns.

✔ **Just friends.** Just so you know, by signing up for Advantage, you're not "in business" with Amazon.com. Basically, they owe you nothing outside of the agreement.

✔ **They're not promising the moon.** Amazon's deep pockets are closed to you when it comes to litigation. If something were to happen that was their responsibility and that affected your sales, they would only be liable for the total amount of your previous year's Advantage profits (your 45 percent).

✔ **This applies to you and yours.** If you put someone else in charge or give that person ownership of your titles, then that person is beholden to the agreement. Also, you have to notify Amazon in writing when you make this designation.

Remember, by applying for the program, you're agreeing to the terms and conditions outlined in the membership agreement.

Instructions and rules

Because they are referred to so many times in the membership agreement, the instructions and rules are also part of the agreement. So you should get to know them.

I've outlined some of them earlier in this chapter (in the "Who Can Apply?" and "The Program Basics" sections), but you can access the instructions and rules in their entirety on the site (unlike the membership agreement, they're written in laymen's terms). Here's how:

1. **Click See More Stores.**

   You find this link at the top of almost every page on the site, just to the right of the tabs.

2. **Click Advantage in the Make Money box.**

   The Make Money box is on the right side of the store directory page.

3. **Click either of the Read More About the Advantage Program links.**

   There's one in the first paragraph and one in the box on the left.

4. **Click Instructions & Rules.**

   You find this link in the Browse box under Additional Information.

Get Ready to Apply Yourself

When you apply for Advantage, you're getting ready to participate in a real — legally binding — business relationship. Nothing too scary there, but it's worth keeping your eyes open.

You have to remember two things: By sending off your application you're agreeing to Amazon's terms and conditions should you be accepted, and not everyone gets accepted. Amazon reserves the right to deny membership at their sole discretion. If you don't meet the criteria I outlined in the "Who Can Apply?" section earlier in this chapter, you definitely won't be accepted, but the "sole discretion" part means they can deny your application for reasons other than those — say, because the guy you bullied in fifth grade is now the guy who approves applications at Amazon.com Advantage. (Okay, not really. But weirder stuff has happened.)

When you sit down to apply, make sure you've thoroughly read the membership agreement and the instructions and rules. Also, have your checkbook (business checkbook if you've got one) ready.

The application is meaty. You have to give them two types of information: your Advantage account information and your titles information. Steps 1 through 15 are Advantage account information — long but relatively painless. Steps 16 through 18 are title information — just three steps, but more work. Step 19 is a cinch — just double-checking your work.

Here's how to apply:

1. **Click See More Stores.**

   There it is at the top of almost every page on the site, just to the right of the tabs.

2. **Click Advantage in the Make Money box.**

   This is on the right side of the store-directory page.

3. **Click either of the Read More About the Advantage Program links.**

   There's one in the first paragraph and one in the box on the left.

4. **Click the Apply Now! button.**

   This takes you to a page that looks like Figure 17-2. As you work through this page, be sure to read it carefully.

5. **Check the boxes to show that you are eligible to be an Advantage member.**

   And really, don't apply unless you're positive that you're eligible.

6. **Check the box that indicates you've read — and agree to — the terms and conditions in the membership agreement.**

   I know I'm starting to sound like your mom, but I'll say it one more time: *Did you do your homework?* If not, read that agreement, make sure you understand it, and consider having a lawyer check it out for you. (That's the last time. I promise.)

7. **Enter a login name and password in the fields provided.**

   As always, pick a password that's easy for you to remember and hard for someone else to guess. Amazon suggests you write them both down and that's not a bad idea (as long as you have a *really* secure place to keep the piece of paper). Also, note that unlike your consumer Amazon login and password, these are case sensitive.

8. **Enter the name and URL for your own Web site in the fields provided.**

   This isn't mandatory, but it helps them in their application-review process.

9. **Use the drop-down menu and field provided to tell them how you discovered the program.**

   Again, not mandatory, but this helps them with their own marketing efforts — and they're the nice people who are helping out your business, so give 'em a hand.

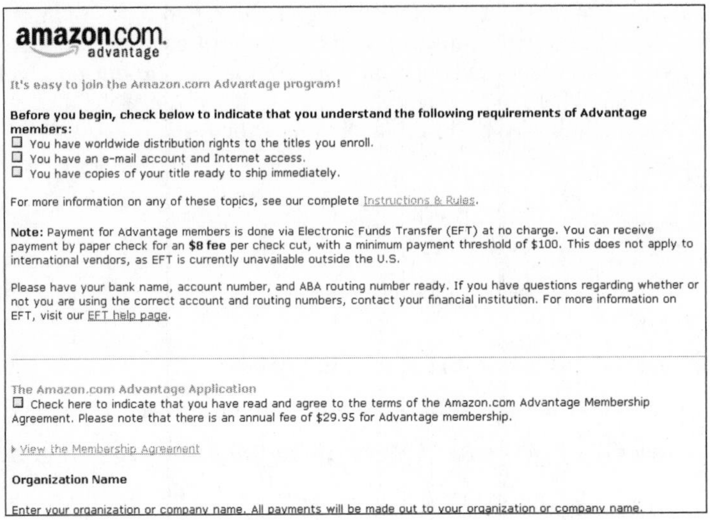

Figure 17-2:
Page one
of the
Advantage
applica-
tion — read
it carefully!

10. **Click Continue.**

    Now it's time to fill out your account info (as in Figure 17-3).

11. **Enter the contact information for the inventory person in the fields provided.**

    This is the person responsible for keeping your titles stocked. Amazon asks for all the usual suspects — name, e-mail address, and mailing address. Notice that the drop-down menu for country includes the U.S., Canada, and Mexico — and only those. Remember, Advantage is for North America only (that Advantage for books in the U.K. is so far the only exception).

12. **On the Business and Payment Contact side of the page, either check the handy box or enter your business-and-payment contact information in the fields provided.**

    If the business-and-payment person is the same as the inventory person, just check the box. If not, enter the new person's contact information.

13. **Enter your taxpayer identification information in the fields provided.**

    For the first field, if you're an individual, use your Social Security number. If you have a tax ID number, use that. Use the drop-down menu to indicate your taxpayer status.

14. **Click the appropriate circle to select how you want to get paid, and then click Confirm.**

    You don't have to choose electronic funds-transfer, but it's easier and cheaper. You can choose to have Amazon cut a check, but they have to owe you at least $100 before they can do it, and then they charge you $8 per check. Anyone who doesn't have a U.S. bank account has to opt for the check.

New Account Information

When you are done entering your information, click "Confirm" at the end of this page.

Inventory Fulfillment Contact

Person responsible for fulfilling your Amazon.com Advantage orders and managing inventory returns. Order notifications will be sent to this person. Inventory being returned will be sent to the address below. Items that cannot be returned because of incorrect or outdated address information will be liquidated or destroyed.

Contact person's name:

E-mail address: (one only, please)

Phone number:

Address line 1:

Address line 2: (optional)

City:

State:

ZIP/postal code:

Country:
--- Select One --- ⬍

Business and Payment Contact

Person responsible for your Amazon.com Advantage membership. Payment notifications will be sent to this person. Note: For security reasons, you must email advantage@amazon.com to change the "Payee name" listed below; it cannot be changed on this form.

☐ Check to use the same contact information as on the left, or fill out all fields below.

Payee name: (click here to change payee name)

E-mail address: (one only, please)

Phone number:

Address line 1:

Address line 2: (optional)

City:

State:

ZIP/postal code:

Country:

Figure 17-3:
Here's where you enter your account information.

15. **If you chose electronic funds-transfer as your payment method, enter your bank account information in the fields provided (as in Figure 17-4) and click Confirm. If you chose to receive a check, move to the next step.**

    You're asked to enter your bank name, your routing number (if you need it, use the Help link for some guidance with this one), your account number, and the name of the primary account holder. Use the drop-down menus to indicate the type of account.

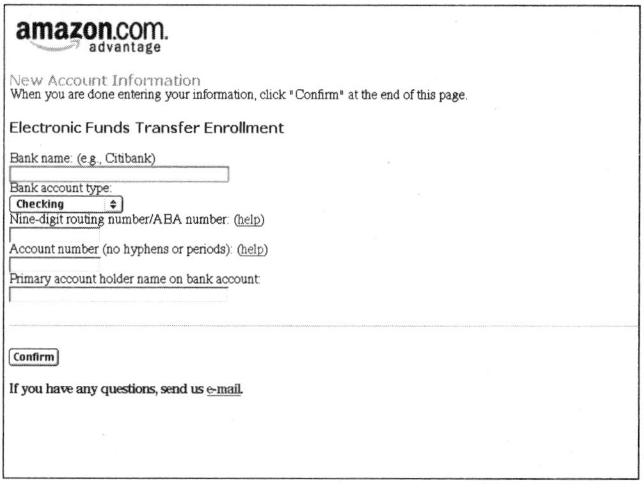

amazon.com.
    advantage

New Account Information
When you are done entering your information, click "Confirm" at the end of this page.

Electronic Funds Transfer Enrollment

Bank name: (e.g., Citibank)

Bank account type:
Checking ⬍
Nine-digit routing number/ABA number: (help)

Account number (no hyphens or periods): (help)

Primary account holder name on bank account:

[Confirm]

If you have any questions, send us e-mail.

Figure 17-4:
You enter your bank account info to get paid electronically.

16. Enter the ISBN or UPC for each of your titles in the fields provided, use the drop-down menus to indicate product type, and then click Continue.

Your titles have to have ISBN or UPC numbers in order to be accepted into the program. ISBNs are 10 digits long and UPCs are 12. Don't include any hyphens or spaces, and make sure the numbers you enter in the fields (as in Figure 17-5) match the numbers on your titles. If they don't, Amazon can't accept them when they arrive.

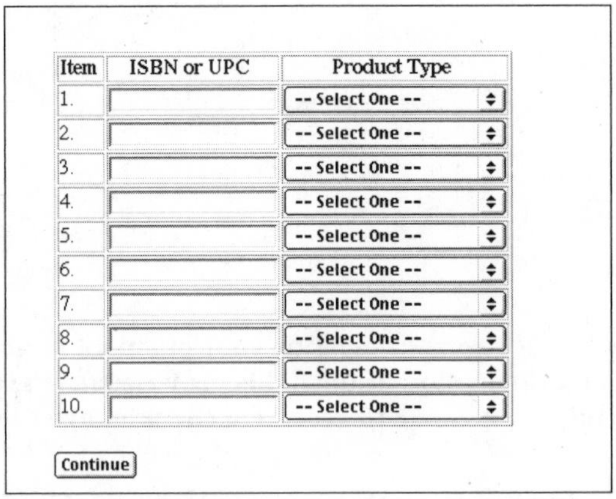

Item	ISBN or UPC	Product Type
1.		-- Select One --
2.		-- Select One --
3.		-- Select One --
4.		-- Select One --
5.		-- Select One --
6.		-- Select One --
7.		-- Select One --
8.		-- Select One --
9.		-- Select One --
10.		-- Select One --

Continue

Figure 17-5: Enter the UPC or ISBN for your titles here.

17. Enter your title's critical information in the fields provided.

You come to a page that looks like Figure 17-6. (This is a book page. CD and DVD/video pages differ as you might expect). You fill out a page like this for each title you are submitting. Note that you're asked for the item's suggested retail price. Keep in mind that Amazon has the ultimate say here.

18. Enter any optional information and click Continue.

You have the option to enter a description of the title, an author/artist bio, and any excerpts from reviews the title has gotten. Do it! The more information you give, the more likely someone is to buy.

Applicable copyright laws dictate that you can only use up to 20 words of a review from any given source. Also, make sure you indicate the source of the review in the designated field, *not* in the review field itself.

19. Confirm your application and then click the Yes, I Want To Add New Title(s) To My Advantage Account button.

Your application won't be complete until you click that button. When you do, you're taken to a confirmation page. Phew!

Applications take a couple of weeks to process, but you receive an e-mail almost immediately confirming that your application was received.

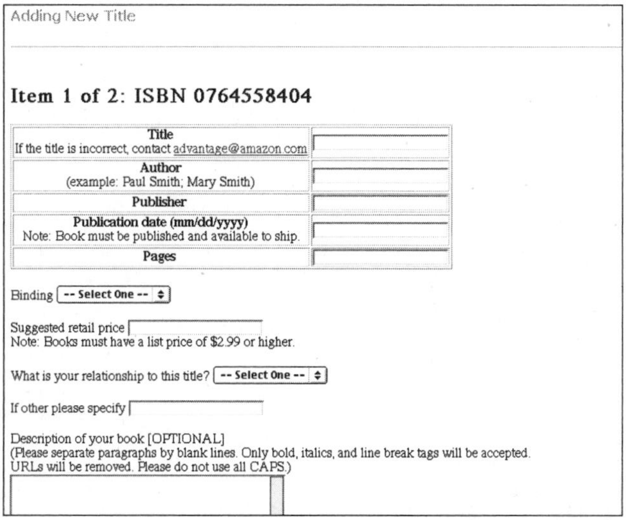

Adding New Title

Item 1 of 2: ISBN 0764558404

Title	
If the title is incorrect, contact advantage@amazon.com	
Author	
(example: Paul Smith; Mary Smith)	
Publisher	
Publication date (mm/dd/yyyy)	
Note: Book must be published and available to ship.	
Pages	

Binding [-- Select One --]

Suggested retail price [   ]
Note: Books must have a list price of $2.99 or higher.

What is your relationship to this title? [-- Select One --]

If other please specify [   ]

Description of your book [OPTIONAL]
(Please separate paragraphs by blank lines. Only bold, italics, and line break tags will be accepted. URLs will be removed. Please do not use all CAPS.)

Figure 17-6: Here is where you enter critical information on your title.

Members Only

After you're accepted into the program, you find a wealth of resources at your fingertips. I can't tell you how to use each one in this book. (That'd be a book on its own. Okay, maybe not a book, but a *large* pamphlet.) But I can give you a bird's-eye view of what's there and what you can do with it.

First things first. Here's how you log in:

1. **Click See More Stores.**

   You find this at the top of almost every page on the site, just to the right of the tabs.

2. **Click Advantage in the Make Money box.**

   This is on the right side of the store directory page.

3. **Click the Log-In button.**

   This takes you to the official login page. Bookmark it so you have easy access from now on.

4. **Enter your login name and password in the fields provided and click Log-In.**

   You have entered Advantage Valhalla (depicted in Figure 17-7).

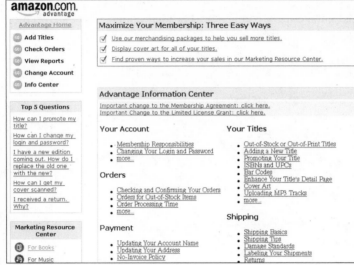

Figure 17-7:
The
Advantage
home
page for
members.

The magic box

On each page of the Advantage member site is a little box in the upper-left corner. Figure 17-8 gives you a close-up view.

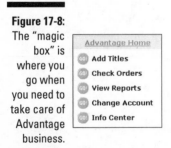

Figure 17-8:
The "magic
box" is
where you
go when
you need to
take care of
Advantage
business.

Here's what you can do from the magic box:

✔ **Add titles.** Just click the button and fill out a quick form to identify yourself. You're swooped back into the title-adding process (from the application, remember?).

✔ **Check your orders.** Your Check Orders page gives you a history of new orders, orders that have been confirmed but not received, and completed orders (as in Figure 17-9). Click any order to see its details and a shipping label to use when you send copies of it off to Amazon.

✔ **View your reports.** Find out how your titles are performing by viewing your reports. You get sales and inventory information for each title in the program.

✔ **Change your account info.** Here's where you change things like contact information, payment options, and so on.

✔ **Access the Information Center.** The Information Center is your good friend. Find everything from shipping info to payment help here. It's a humble little box — free of festoon — but it's the central nervous system of the program.

The Information Center

This page is essentially the same as the Advantage members home page. Click Info center in the magic box at the top left of the page and you see that the only change is the disappearance of the Maximize Your Membership box at the top. True to its name, this is where you can find out just about anything you might ever want to know about your account and the program. But remember, it's not called an *Action* Center; if you're ready to get stuff done, use the magic box. The *Information* Center is more of a resource.

Here's a quick overview of the areas in the Advantage Information Center:

✔ **Your Account.** Your Account is where you find info on your membership responsibilities, how to contact Amazon, how to edit your contact information and change your login and password, and how to close your account.

- ✔ **Your Titles.** This is the everything-you-ever-wanted-to-know-about-your-titles-but-were-afraid-to-ask" section. You can find info on everything from how to submit cover art to whom to contact if you need a new ISBN or UPC.

- ✔ **Orders.** Here's where you get the word on everything from order-processing times to Amazon's lost-orders policy.

- ✔ **Payment.** Ah, yes. The money. Go here for all payment-related information.

- ✔ **Shipping.** This refers to how you should ship your titles to Amazon, and it's the meatiest of all sections. You'll probably use this area often. Find out about everything from damage standards to how to ship entire pallets (and I hope you have a need for the latter, because that's a sign you're doing some wheeling and dealing).

The Matter of Marketing

When you're an Advantage member, your titles appear in Amazon's catalog. But you can make them perform better by marketing them. Some of the marketing opportunities available to you cost money and some are free. You should definitely take advantage of the free ones; if you're flush, consider the others as well.

You are responsible for the fate of your titles. Advantage offers a great selling forum (Amazon.com, of course) but *you* have to market your titles yourself!

Using the Marketing Resource Centers

The first thing you should do is check out the Marketing Resource Centers. There are three — books, music, and video (DVD) — and they're free. You can access them most easily from the box on the lower-left side of the Advantage member home page (shown in Figure 17-10). This box is also on most other main pages in the member site.

Figure 17-10:
Access the
resource
centers
from this
box.

These resource centers probably aren't going to change your life, but they do offer some good information. You find things like articles on how to market your titles, tips for "guerilla marketing," contact information for publications (so you can get your titles reviewed and get some free PR), and more.

Making your detail page sing

This is the key to selling well on Amazon.com. You can easily make your detail page a winner — and it's 100 percent free. Here's how you can make your detail page stand up and sing:

- ✔ **Include a good photo.** You can scan the cover art yourself and upload it to the site, or send Amazon a copy (don't send it to the distribution center, but to the Advantage department) and they'll scan it for you. Either way, make sure there's a picture on each of your titles' detail pages. For books, you can also include interior images (and you should).

- ✔ **Write a thorough description.** Give prospective buyers the info they want. The more they know about your title, the more likely they are to buy.

- ✔ **Include comments.** You have the option to include comments from the publisher, label, studio, author, or artist. Do it! It's fun for buyers to get a glimpse behind the scenes, and remember, more info is good.

- ✔ **Include a table of contents or track listing.** Tempt them with a peek at the goodies inside. (When you shop at Amazon, don't *you* like to see this stuff?)

- ✔ **Include reviews.** Including industry reviews is a good way to gain credibility. Just be sure you obey applicable copyright laws; reviews are usually somebody's copyrighted work.

- ✔ **Upload MP3s.** This is a relatively new feature for music Advantage members. You can now upload your tracks to your detail pages as a part of Amazon's digital downloads.

You can find out more about how to spruce up your detail pages using the Your Titles section of the Information Center.

Paid placements

You may not already know this (and you may not remember the scandal that flared up around it in the late '90s), but Amazon.com has a co-op program (co-op is short for cooperative here and a co-op program, at least in this case, means that publishers pay Amazon for specific placement on their site). That means many of the items you see featured on the site are *in* the high-visibility spots because someone paid for the placement. Does that mean Amazon gives good reviews for money? No. It just means that a manufacturer, publisher, label, or whoever, can buy placement for their products on the site (and in printed marketing materials). The review is unbiased — and typically companies don't choose to pay for high-visibility spots unless their items have good reviews associated with them. (For the record, this is standard practice in the retail world. How about those display tables at the front of big chain bookstores? Co-op dollars put those books there.)

Paid Placements is a co-op program available to small Amazon vendors — including, but not exclusive to Advantage members — whose annual sales with Amazon are less than $1,000,000. It's a chance for smaller companies to get their products noticed, not just by more people, but by the *right* people to help them succeed.

There are two paid-placement programs:

- ✔ **Single New Product e-mails.** These e-mails feature new releases and go to a very targeted audience. Remember, Amazon has tons of info on the people who buy from them and they put that info to use when sending out marketing e-mails. They find people who have bought similar items (or items from similar artists) and mail only to them. You choose which titles are featured in a Single New Product e-mail.

- ✔ **Buy X, Get Y.** This is a promotion that lets you give shoppers a deal for buying two titles together. The "deal" is featured on both titles' detail pages for one month (sometimes listed under the Best Value heading). This is a great way to get lesser-known titles in front of your audience.

Here's how to get more info on the Paid Placements program:

1. **Click See More Stores.**

   You find this at the top of almost every page on the site, just to the right of the tabs.

2. **Click Paid Placements in the Make Money box.**

   Notice that Paid Placements has its own button in the Make Money box — it's not a part of the Advantage section. That's because there are several small publishers, labels, and studios that sell at Amazon but aren't in the Advantage program.

3. **Click the Sign Up button.**

   You can also click Click Here at the top of the page. Both take you to a page that looks like Figure 17-11. You are not actually signing up here, just filling out a form to get more information.

4. **Enter your name and your business name in the fields provided.**

   Notice that they want your last name first.

5. **Use the drop-down menu to choose your product line.**

   Notice that Paid Placements are only available for books, music, video, and DVD.

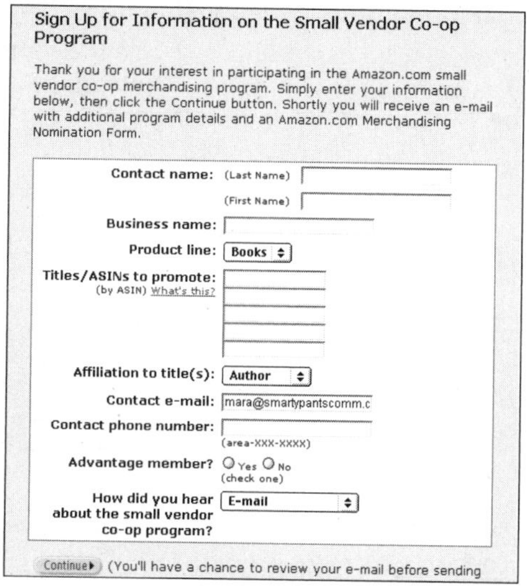

Figure 17-11: This is not a sign-up page — just an information request form.

The form shown reads:

Sign Up for Information on the Small Vendor Co-op Program

Thank you for your interest in participating in the Amazon.com small vendor co-op merchandising program. Simply enter your information below, then click the Continue button. Shortly you will receive an e-mail with additional program details and an Amazon.com Merchandising Nomination Form.

Contact name: (Last Name)
(First Name)
Business name:
Product line: Books
Titles/ASINs to promote: (by ASIN) What's this?
Affiliation to title(s): Author
Contact e-mail: mara@smartypantscomm.c
Contact phone number: (area-XXX-XXXX)
Advantage member? ○ Yes ○ No (check one)
How did you hear about the small vendor co-op program? E-mail

Continue▶ (You'll have a chance to review your e-mail before sending

6. Enter your ASINs or ISBNs in the fields provided.

To enroll in Paid Placements you have to already have a title or titles in Amazon's catalog. Every title in the catalog has a number that identifies it — an ISBN for books and an ASIN for everything else. You'll find these numbers in the product information section on the detail page.

7. Use the drop-down menu to describe your relationship to the title.

The choices are Author, Artist, Publisher, Studio, Label, and Other. Anyone is eligible here as this is only a request for information.

8. Enter your e-mail address and phone number in the fields provided.

If you already have an Amazon account, your contact e-mail address is filled in automatically. You can change it if you want to.

9. Click the appropriate circle to indicate whether you're an Advantage member.

10. Use the drop-down menu to tell them how you heard about the program, and then click Continue.

You're asked to review your information before submitting it. Use the Edit button to make any needed changes.

11. Click Submit.

You come to a confirmation page assuring you that info is on the way. You should get that info via e-mail almost immediately. In that e-mail you find the program costs, nomination form, and instructions on how to proceed. All communication for the program is done via e-mail, so fill out the form and send it back to the address included in the body of the e-mail.

"What about costs?" you may be asking. Single New Product e-mails cost $500 per new title, per e-mail; Buy X, Get Y costs $1,500 per one-month promotion. You can pay Amazon yearly, quarterly, or title by title, but you have to send them a check before they let you participate in the program.

The Matter of Money

Unlike other selling programs at Amazon.com, Advantage takes a serious cut of the cash — 55 percent of list price, to be exact (and they determine the list price to boot). So you may ask yourself, "What's to stop me from getting myself a zShop, selling my titles there, and paying only 5 percent?" Technically nothing, but don't do it.

If you asked most Advantage salespeople why you should join, they'd tell you that Advantage is great because it helps get products out there. They'd tell you that it takes the burden of fulfillment off the little guy and lets you focus on producing. They'd probably tell you about the ease of keeping your inventory up-to-date and the joy of getting paid on time. All that is true, but the real reason to join Advantage is *exposure.*

With Advantage, your titles are in there with the big guys. Your books are in the bookstore. Your CDs are in the music store. And your videos and DVDs are in the video and DVD stores. When shoppers are browsing in those stores, they find your titles just as they would those of the big publishers, studios, and labels. Advantage puts you in the game in a way that zShops can't.

Payment terms

Amazon automatically pays you at the end of every month for the items sold the previous month. They pay 45 percent of the list price and they deposit it automatically in your checking account. If you don't have a U.S. checking account, they write you a check (but they'll charge you eight bucks for it!). So, if in March (for example) you sell 17 copies of a $10 book, you'll find about $76 in your checking account at the end of April.

Annual fee

The Advantage program has a $29.95 annual membership fee. Amazon deducts it from your Advantage account each May.

The fee is nonrefundable — even if they terminate your agreement.

Chapter 18

Cash by Association: Amazon Associates

1 have a Web site for my company. My business partner spent weeks putting it together — painstakingly designing it so that it would look and be just right. When we first started our business, that Web site was our baby. In the beginning, it was a source of pride — "Look . . . isn't it nice!" But now, three years later, it's just a Web site, and I find myself thinking, *What has that Web site done for us lately?*

You don't have to have a lazy Web site. You can put your Web site to work. With just a little bit of effort up front, you can make your Web site earn money (and if you've got the right Web site, a lot of money). How? Become an Amazon Associate, and instead of *selling* with Amazon.com, you can *partner* with Amazon to earn some extra cash.

Associates is Amazon's referral program — and with more than 1,000,000 members, it's the Web's largest. The concept is simple: You link from your site to Amazon's, and if one of your visitors uses your links to go to Amazon and buy something, you get a referral fee. It's an easy way to use your existing Web site to earn money.

In this chapter, I'll explain the ins and outs of Associates. I'll show you how to join and I'll explain how to take advantage of the spoils in Associates Central — Amazon's resource center for the Associates program. I'll help you get that lazy Web site of yours off its keister and on its way to the bank.

Associates Basics

Associates is a referral program — but with a high-tech spin. You sign up on the site, you communicate via e-mail, you get paid via electronic funds-transfer (or Amazon gift certificate), and all your referring happens on the Web. So do you have to be web savvy to be an Associate? Yes. You don't need to know how to write HTML freehand, but you need to have a Web site that you can add links to, and you need to know enough about HTML that you can figure out where to paste the code that Amazon supplies.

Who can join?

You do have to have a Web site to be an Associate, but having a Web site doesn't automatically make you eligible. This is Amazon we're talking about. They have a reputation to uphold. So here are the restrictions:

- **Nothing XXX.** Erotica, yes. Hard-core porn, no. Rough-and-ready rule with Amazon is *Keep it artsy and you're usually good to go.*

- **No sites that promote violence.** Because that's just creepy. Besides, what would you refer people to? *Fight Club*?

- **No sites that encourage discrimination based on race, sex, religion, nationality, disability, sexual orientation, or age.** Sorry, white supremacists, but Amazon is raining on your little hooded parade.

- **Nothing illegal.** If you've got a Web site that teaches people how to manufacture crystal meth in their basements, you can forget about being an Associate.

- **No sites that have faux-Amazon names.** This is a strange one, but it has to do with Amazon protecting their intellectual property. Basically, they don't want you if your URL is an Amazon knockoff. The examples they give are `amazon.mydomain.com`, `amaozn.com`, and `amazonauctions.net`. (None of which exist, by the way.)

- **No sites that violate intellectual property rights.** So no "come here and download a bunch of pirated software" sites, or anything like that.

These are the things that will definitely keep you from being an Associate. Amazon also reserves the right to refuse anyone admission into the program for any reason. That said, if you're none of the above, you'll likely be accepted.

How it works

On the simplest level, it works like this:

✔ You sign up and are accepted into the program.

✔ You use Associates Central to get tagged links and graphics to add to your site.

✔ Your visitors click the links and go to Amazon.

✔ They buy qualifying products during their sessions. (More on this later.)

✔ Amazon keeps track of their purchases (thus, your referral fees).

✔ You get paid quarterly in the total amount of your referral fees.

Good news! You get a referral fee any time a user goes from your site to Amazon and makes a qualified purchase — even if you linked them to a specific product and they bought something totally different.

What you get

How much do you get paid? The short answer is from 2.5 percent to 15percent on the purchase price of all qualifying products. But it's actually much more complicated than that.

There are four things you need to consider when figuring out what your Associates booty might be:

✔ **Qualifying products.** Not all products sold at Amazon earn referral fees. *The following are exempt:* products sold through Auctions or zShops, products sold by the Gap, Old Navy, or Nordstrom, products sold by partners like drugstore.com^tm, and most of the wireless service plans sold on the site.

✔ **The session.** *When* your buyer buys also determines whether a purchase earns a referral fee. The span of time during which referral fees can be earned is called the *session*. It starts when a potential buyer clicks from your site to Amazon, and ends when 24 hours goes by, or they order the product, or they click another Associate's link.

✔ **Varying referral fees.** Different products earn different fees:

- "Individually linked books" earn the magic 15 percent. This is a special category — and the only one that earns such a high referral rate. To get this rate, you have to link directly to a book from your site and a user has to go there and buy it immediately, without going anywhere else on the site first. Also, the book must be listed at 10 percent to 30 percent of the publisher's listed price.

- ToysRUs.com, BabiesRUs.com, and Imaginarium.com products earn 5 percent.

- Third-party-seller products (this includes anything in the apparel store and all used products) earn 2.5 percent.

- All other products earn 5 percent unless you used Easy links on your site (more on this later), in which case they earn 6 percent.

✔ **The fee structure you choose.** There are two fee structures within the Associates program: the Classic fee structure and the Tiered fee structure. The Classic fee structure calculates your referral fees on an item-by-item basis according to the amounts described above. Until fairly recently, this was the only fee structure. The Tiered fee structure also uses the amounts described above, but offers an additional bonus. The catch is that you have to meet certain criteria to be eligible for the bonus.

- **You have to make at least 121 referrals a month that result in a qualified sale.** If you make fewer than 121 but more than 40, you get no bonus. If you make fewer than 41, you pay Amazon. Yes, that's right. *You* pay *them* 20 percent of the referral fees you earned that quarter.

- **At least 5 of those 121 must be nonmedia items.** That means anything *but* books, music, videos, or DVDs.

So the Tiered program is really for "bigger" Associates. In fact, it's great for bigger Associates. The more you refer and sell, the bigger your bonus gets. Figure 18-1 is the Tiered fee schedule for the fourth quarter of 2003.

Figure 18-1:
The Tiered fee structure can earn you big bucks for big referrals.

Total Items Shipped	Tier Earnings Bonus %	Effective Referral Rate	Minimum Non-Media Items Shipped
1-40	-20%	4.00%	0
41-120	0%	5.00%	1
121-300	5%	5.25%	5
301-700	10%	5.50%	15
701-1800	15%	5.75%	50
1801-4000	20%	6.00%	150
4001-8500	25%	6.25%	400
8501+	30%	6.50%	1000

There are a few other things you should know about the Tiered fee structure:

✔ **To be eligible, you have to use the new Easy Links on the home page of your site.** These links are updated dynamically by Amazon.com — very cool!

✔ **You have to opt in to the program.** If you don't, you continue to earn according to the Classic plan.

✔ **The payment structure is not permanent.** The Tiered fee structure is still in the development phase and Amazon is trying to find the happy zone. So they reserve (and exercise) the right to change the payment structure.

Surprise, Surprise . . .

Darrell Benatar's wife, Lisa, was the gift giver in the family. She was always looking for good ideas and asking friends for gift-giving suggestions. Darrell thought, *What if there were a place on the Web where you could solicit and offer good gift-giving advice?* And Surprise.com was born. (See the figure included here.)

They wanted the site to have both depth and breadth, so they knew they couldn't carry all the gifts they were suggesting as inventory. They also wanted Surprise.com to be totally credible. By simply referring people to good products, they could hold on to that credibility — they'd never have to unload inventory or kowtow to advertisers. But the question then became,

"How do we make money if we're not selling anything and we want to remain credible?" The answer was referral fees — and Amazon.com was a natural choice. They had an established referral program in Associates, the broadest selection, and great customer service.

So can you make any money doing this? In non-holiday months, Surprise.com brings in $5,000 to $10,000 per month from Amazon.com alone. In the fourth quarter, those numbers triple. And consider this, Surprise.com started doing business before the dot-com crash. Not only have they survived, but they also have remained profitable through it all.

You're One in a Million: Joining Associates

There are more than 1,000,000 Associates out there making money. What about you? Signing up for Associates is a snap. It's fast and it's free, and the only commitment you make by signing up is agreeing to their rules. Here's how to do it:

1. **Click See More Stores.**

   It's at the top of almost any page on the site.

2. **Click Associates in the Make Money box.**

   You'll find this on the right side of the store-directory page.

3. **Click the Join Now button.**

   This is on the left side of the page. It takes you to a page that looks like Figure 18-2. You don't have to have an Amazon account to be an Associate, but make sure you click the appropriate circle.

4. **Enter your e-mail address and password in the fields provided and click Submit.**

   Be sure to enter the e-mail address you want them to use when communicating with you about the program. You can use your Amazon password (if you have one) or create a new password. Just be sure it's easy for you to remember and hard for someone else to guess.

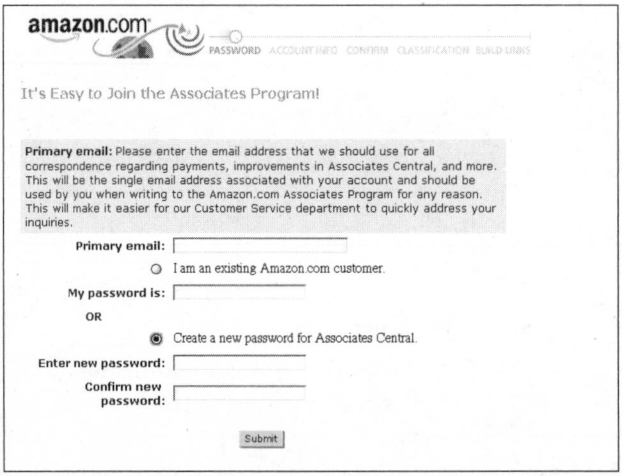

Figure 18-2: Enter your e-mail address and password here.

5. **In the new page that appears, check the box to indicate that you've read and agree to the terms and conditions in the Operating Agreement.**

   Make sure you read that agreement. Nobody wants churlish lawyers snapping at their heels.

6. **Enter the payee information in the fields provided.**

If you're applying as an individual, enter your name. If you're applying for your company, enter its name. This info tells your buyers who to write the checks to, so to speak.

7. **Enter your taxpayer information in the field provided and use the drop-down menu to indicate your status.**

   Individuals can enter Social Security number; companies enter a tax ID number.

8. **Enter your contact information in the fields provided or check the box if your contact information is the same as your payee information.**

9. **Click the appropriate circle to choose how you want to get paid.**

   You have three choices. You can be paid by electronic funds-transfer (but only if you have a U.S. bank account), Amazon gift certificate, or check.

   They charge you an $8 fee per check.

10. **Enter the name and URL for your Web site in the fields provided.**

11. **Describe your Web site and what you plan to list in the fields provided and then click Submit.**

    You can also use the drop-down menu to tell them how you found out about the program. If you've chosen to be paid by electronic funds-transfer, you'll come to a screen that looks like Figure 18-3 and asks for your bank account information. If you chose one of the other two options, you'll skip the next step.

12. **Enter your bank account information in the fields provided and click Submit.**

    They ask you to enter the bank name, account type, routing number (if you need help on this one, click the Help link), account number, and account holder name. Don't fret. This information is perfectly safe.

13. **Confirm your information and click Submit.**

    This confirmation page shows you the information you just entered. Check through your application and use the Edit button if you need to make changes.

14. **Click the appropriate boxes to indicate which products you may be referring and use the drop-down menus to further describe your company or organization.**

    You come to a page that looks like Figure 18-4. This is what I call the "getting to know you" page. Don't worry. You're not committing to anything here — just giving them a little info. For that second drop-down, they're really asking, "What kind of site are you?"

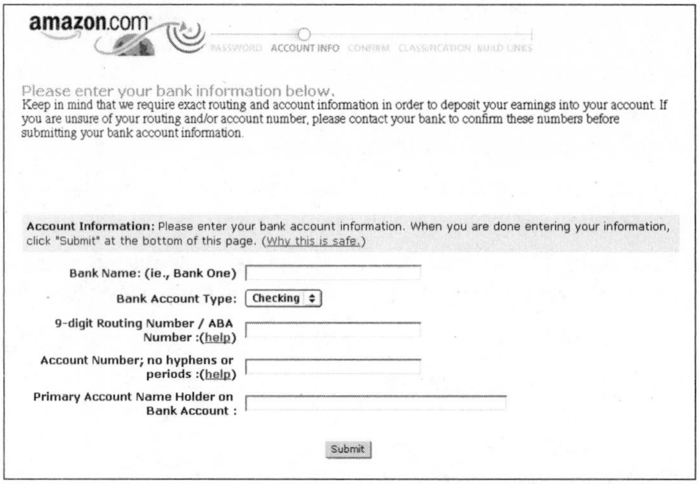

Figure 18-3: Enter your bank account information to enable electronic funds-transfer.

You're finished. Your application is reviewed quickly — figure on no more than a couple of days — and you receive an e-mail welcoming you to the program (as in Figure 18-5). Because most people are approved, Amazon gives you immediate access to Associates Central so you can get started on building your links right away.

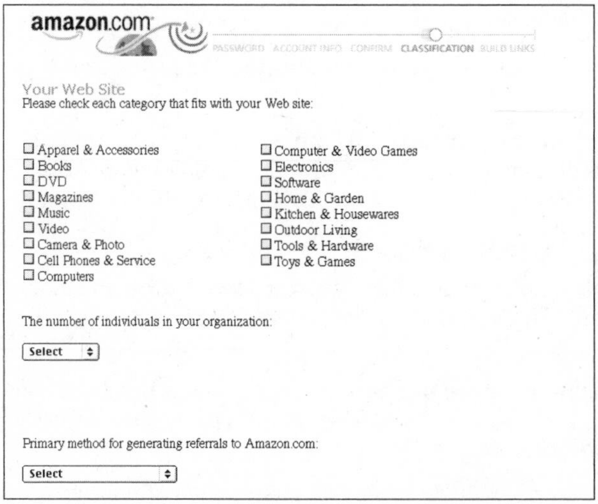

Figure 18-4: Describing your Web site.

Figure 18-5:
Your
acceptance
e-mail
includes a
link to the
Associates
login page
and
instructions
on how to
"Build-A-
Link."

Associates Central

Associates Central is your information resource for all things related to the
Associates program. It is the hub of the program and you'll use it regularly to

- ✔ Build links to your site
- ✔ Look at your online earnings reports
- ✔ Get graphics for your site from the graphics library
- ✔ Update your account information
- ✔ Get news about Associates offers and program changes
- ✔ Find out how to better use the program

Before you can use Associates Central, however, you have to know how to get
there. Here's how to access it from Amazon.com:

1. **Click See More Stores.**

   It's at the top of just about every page on the site.

2. **Click Associates in the Make Money box.**

   You'll find this on the right side of the store-directory page.

3. **Click the Log-In button.**

   This is on the left side of the page in the Member Sign-In box. You'll come to the Log In screen, which looks like Figure 18-6. Bookmark this page so you can access it quickly in the future.

Figure 18-6: Bookmark the Associates Log In screen for easy access.

amazon.com.

Associates Central

Log In to Associates Central

My e-mail address: [   ]

My password: [   ]
Have you forgotten your password?

[Log In]

If you are not already an Associate, click here to learn more about the Associates Program. If you have already signed up to be an Associate, you will receive login instructions with your approval e-mail.

If you are having trouble logging in, please contact us.

4. **Enter your Associates e-mail address and password in the fields provided and click Log-In.**

   There are two things to remember here. First, this is the e-mail address and password associated with your Associates account, not necessarily your Amazon customer account. Second, your Associates e-mail and password are case-sensitive (unlike your Amazon customer account).

Home

Figure 18-7 is the Associates Central home page; if you're looking at it, you're logged in. The home page is a good place to get your Associates news. Make sure you scroll down because sometimes there are goodies hiding below the fold.

You can always get back to the Associates Central home page by clicking either the Associates Central Home graphic above the nav on the right side of the page, or by clicking the Associates Central Home link in the nav.

Figure 18-7:
The
Associates
Central
home page.

To get back to the Amazon.com Welcome page, click the Amazon.com logo at the top left of the page above the nav. You can move in and out of your Associates account without having to log back in.

Clicking the Amazon logo takes you out of Associates Central, but it doesn't log you out. Notice the Logout button in the box in the upper-left corner of the page below the nav. If you're logged in and idle for long enough — that means no clicking around or activity — Amazon logs you out automatically, but the length of time before they do that is significantly longer than it is with your customer account. If you're using a public terminal, it's important that you log out when you're done using Associates Central or you risk giving strangers access to your Associates account.

Leaving Home: A quick lay of the land

The choices in the Associates Central nav are completely different from those in the usual Amazon.com nav. There are no tabs here and no subnav. Just to be clear, you are no longer in the store.

Here's a quick look at the different parts of Associates Central:

- ✔ **Browse Associates Web sites.** This is a relatively new feature. You can use it to see how other Associates are using the program.

- ✔ **Build-A-Link.** You'll be using this area a lot. This is where you'll find instructions and HTML for the different kinds of links that you can add to your site. These links fall into two categories: Amazon Recommends links (which are dynamic) and Static links. The former links — which are especially cool — allow you to do everything from adding promotional links that get updated automatically to creating dynamic links based on specific keywords (also known as keyword links).

✔ **Logos & Graphics.** This is the kissing cousin of Build-A-Link. Associates has a huge library of buttons, banners, and logos you can download and add to your site. You'll find them here.

✔ **Best Practices.** Best Practices is essentially a guide to getting the most from the program. You'll find tips, ideas, case studies, and more.

✔ **View Reports.** Here's where you find your performance results, including your earnings to date.

✔ **Update Account.** Use this area to do everything from editing your e-mail address to changing your site classification.

✔ **Payment Options.** This is not related to your referral-fee structure, but to the way in which Amazon compensates you. You can edit your current payment option information or change your chosen method of payment.

✔ **FAQ.** The FAQ in Associates Central is really more of a Help department. You'll find tons of answers to questions you may have, plus a glossary of terms, and a link to the operating agreement.

✔ **Discussion Boards.** Associates is a community. The discussion boards are a great way to participate in that community. You'll also find a read-only announcement board in this section; look there for Associates program news.

Adding to your site: Build-A-Link versus Logos & Graphics

There are two places to go within Associates Central to get graphics to add to your site: Logos & Graphics and Build-A-Link. Here's a brief description of each:

✔ **Logos & Graphics.** This is what Associates started out as: a library of prebuilt buttons and banners that lead to the stores and to many top-level category pages. There are literally hundreds of static and animated buttons and banners to choose from in this section. You'll also find Amazon.com logos here; you can use those to link to the Welcome page.

When you use these buttons and banners, you have to *host* them yourself. That means that, after you download them, you are responsible for putting them (and keeping them) up on your site. You copy the images from the Associates site and then upload them to your site's directory.

✔ **Build-A-Link.** Build-A-Link, for the most part, doesn't offer prebuilt images. Instead, it gives you a variety of ways to create customized and/or dynamic links for your site. They're easy to create, but (unlike the images in Logos & Graphics) they do require some setup work.

Whether you're using images from the image library in Logos & Graphics, or creating your own keyword link (a dynamic link based on specific keywords) in Build-A-Link, Amazon.com makes adding to your site as simple as is possible. Here are a few things you should know about how the process works:

- ✔ **Amazon generates the HTML.** All you have to do is cut and paste it into your site's code.

- ✔ **Your code is automatically tagged.** When you log in, Associates knows to tag any HTML they create for you with your specific information. That's how they recognize the shoppers you refer.

- ✔ **Amazon can serve some of your links.** For many of the links available, you can choose to have Amazon.com serve them. What this means is that you paste the HTML they provide into your site's code and you're done. You don't have to upload graphics. Amazon will take care of that dynamically through the code they give you.

- ✔ **You upload the graphics if you're hosting your own links.** If you choose not to use the dynamic links they offer, you'll need to copy the graphics for your link from Associates Central and then upload it to the image directory you're using for your Web site.

More on Build-A-Link

There are several different kinds of links you can create in Build-A-Link. They fall into two categories: Amazon Recommends links and Static links.

Amazon Recommends links

These are dynamic links that Amazon serves and updates regularly. You enter the code and (in some cases) choose the subject matter; Amazon refreshes the content of the link accordingly. In other words, you don't have to upload any graphics to your site. The idea is to keep your content fresh without having to do any additional work. Here are the different types of Amazon Recommends links:

- ✔ **Easy Links:** Easy Links promote special offers at Amazon.com. They are essentially advertising and Amazon will update them with whatever hot offers they have at moment. See Figure 18-8 for an example of an Easy Link.

- ✔ **Amazon.com Platinum Visa® Card Links:** When you add one of the banners or buttons to your site, you receive a $20 referral fee for each applicant who gets approved. This is actually a special promotion that Associates is offering its members; it may end at any time, depending on the success of the program. In the meantime, it's a great deal. The good news is that if it does end, you don't have to worry about updating your site. Because this is a dynamically served link, Amazon just refreshes the content with other promotional offers — your Visa promo link becomes (in effect) an Easy Link.

✔ **Keyword Links:** These are very cool. You choose a product category and then enter keywords and Amazon serves up a variety of relevant graphics to your site. So, for example, if you have a Louisiana travel site, you might choose "books" in the drop-down menu and then enter "food" and "New Orleans" in the keyword field. If you did, you'd get something that looks like Figure 18-9.

✔ **General Bestsellers Links:** These links allow you to grab the current top sellers in a particular category. They change as the top sellers in that category change. Figure 18-10 is an example of a General Bestseller Link for cooking, food, and wine books.

✔ **Browse-based Bestsellers Links:** These links allow you to be more specific with your top seller lists. While General Bestseller Links access top-level categories within each store, browse-based bestseller links allow you to drill down until you're just above the detail page. And, like General Bestseller Links, these are updated as they change on the site.

Figure 18-8:
An Easy Link
promoting
the Gold
Box.

Figure 18-9:
Here's an
example of
a keyword
link for
"food" and
"New
Orleans."

Figure 18-10:
A General
Bestseller
Link for
cooking,
food, and
wine books.

Static links

Static links don't refresh as Amazon Recommends links do, but they allow you to be more specific with the content you offer. Here are the different types of Static links that you'll find at Associates Central:

✔ **Individual Item Links:** These are exactly what they sound like: links that go directly to a specific item's detail page. You pick the item and you can either have Amazon *serve* — deliver via the Web — the graphic to your Web site or *host* it yourself (for example, keep it on your own server and deliver it yourself). I recommend the former, though, because the served graphics include the item's price and a Buy from Amazon.com button. Figure 18-11 is the preview for a served individual item link for *eBay For Dummies,* including the HTML on the box on the left.

✔ **Quick-Click Links:** These allow your customers to buy individual items without having to go to Amazon.com. Your graphic includes a button that says `buy from Amazon.com`. When users click the button, a window pops up with a Ready to Buy? box. (See Figure 18-12 for an example.) All Ready to Buy? boxes have the Add To Shopping Cart button, but if that person is a recognized Amazon customer, they'll also have the option to buy with 1-Click.

Figure 18-11:
The served
individual
item links
include
each item's
price.

✔ **Amazon.com Home Page Links:** According to Associates, these are the most effective Static links. They're also incredibly simple — in effect, they're plug-and-play.

✔ **Search Box Links:** There are two types of Search Box Links: with a drop-down menu and without. Either way, your visitors will use these just as they do the Search box on Amazon's site. They'll enter keywords and be taken to search results. If you choose to have a drop-down menu included, you can customize the contents of the menu by using the Customized Search Box feature. Figure 18-13 is my electronics Customized Search Box Link. You can choose to have the contents in a drop-down menu or listed out.

✔ **Search Results Links:** If you know what content you want your user to see, create the search results yourself. With these links, you choose the subject matter and your visitors are taken to those search results.

✔ **Subject and Genre Browse Menus:** These take your visitors to specific browse pages. There are 17 different choices for Browse Menu Links and each one has a drop-down menu.

✔ **Favorite Destination Links:** These are prebuilt links to Amazon hot spots.

✔ **Links to Any Page:** This is the catch-all. If you can't find what you need anywhere else, try this, but note that you can't use it to link to search results. You have to use the Search Results Link for that. Also, if you're thinking of linking to a seasonal page, keep in mind that the page goes away after the season.

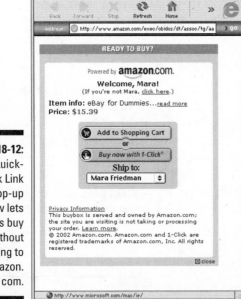

Figure 18-12:
The Quick-Click Link pop-up window lets users buy without going to Amazon. com.

Figure 18-13:
A custom-
ized Search
Box Link.

More on Best Practices

Best Practices is basically a free Web marketing tutorial from the best in the
business. So it's worth your while to take advantage of it. You'll find it by
clicking on it in the Associates subnav. Here's an overview of what you'll find
in that section of Associates Central:

- ✔ **Cross-promotion tips:** There's a big push in the Associates program to
  promote nonmedia products — anything other than books, music,
  videos, and DVDs (those are, of course, the first four products Amazon
  offered, and they get plenty of attention). This section helps you promote nonmedia products on your site. It includes things like how to pick
  the right products to promote, and how to use your reports to help
  determine what products your visitors want to buy.

- ✔ **Get more traffic:** As they state in the introduction to this section, traffic
  is the key to success when it comes to the Associates program. It doesn't
  matter how well you pick products or how many great links you add if
  nobody comes to your site. This is a rich section of Best Practices. (See
  Figure 18-14 for the Get More Traffic category page.) You'll find good
  advice on how to work with search engines, plus case studies on what
  other Associates have done to generate traffic.

- ✔ **Promote smarter:** This section is a good complement to the cross-
  promotion section. It includes tips on how to select items and tips on
  how to best use the links Associates offers.

- ✔ **Learn from other associates:** This takes you to a box at the bottom of
  the Best Practices page where you'll find a collection of case studies in
  the Best Practices section.

- ✔ **Power Users:** This section is for Associates who want to use Amazon
  Web Services as a part of their participation in the program. (See
  Chapter 16 for more on Web services.)

- ✔ **Other helpful tips:** This resource section offers links to other sites.
  You'll find links to HTML how-to sites, links to online marketing sites,
  and so on.

Figure 18-14:
The Get
More Traffic
section
of Best
Practices is
full of good
advice.

More on View Reports

Build-A-Link, Logos & Graphics, and Best Practices are definitely where you need to start when you join the Associates program. But the View Reports section of Associates Central may be the most important place in terms of determining your future success.

Your reports are pieces of a puzzle and it's your job to put them together. If read carefully and extrapolated from effectively, they can help you figure out what it is that your visitors want to buy, and how you should get them to those products from your site. You may think the answer is obvious — "I have a site about dogs so I'm going to sell dog books to my visitors by linking directly to them." But your reports may tell a totally different story. You may find that though your visitors are dog enthusiasts, they are clicking from your site to the dog books you recommend, leaving those detail pages, and buying CDs.

All this gallivanting on the part of your visitors is no reason for dismay! That's good information. Remember, no matter what product you recommend, if a visitor goes from your site to Amazon and buys a qualified product within 24 hours, you get a referral fee. So if you discover that visitors from your site want to buy CDs instead of dog books, put that knowledge to work for you. Send them to the Music store or send them to the Welcome page. Test out both options and then review your reports again to see what worked.

The Snapshot

Figure 18-15 is the Snapshot page of the View Reports section for an Associates account. (This is actually a test account and so doesn't have a lot of action associated with it.) This is the first page you come to when you visit View Reports. You'll notice that there are two kinds of reports that you can look at: earnings reports and traffic reports. You'll also notice that there's an overview of your link performance. This tells you whether or not specific link types are actually generating sales for you.

Figure 18-15: The Snapshot page of View Reports gives you a quick overview of your Associates account.

Earnings reports

If you click the See Report button next to the Your Earnings heading on the Snapshot page, you'll come to the Earnings Reports page. You can view your earnings reports by total or by per-item earnings. You can also tailor your report by date.

Figure 18-16 is a per-item earnings report. It's essential that you look not only at your total earnings, but also at your per-item earnings. The latter can help you figure out how to better identify what your visitors want to buy.

Traffic reports

Traffic reports are equally as important as earnings reports. You can access your traffic reports by clicking the See Report button next to the Traffic Summary heading on the Snapshot page. You can view traffic by day, by item purchased, by click through, and by linking method. Figure 18-17 shows a traffic report by click through. You can see that of all the items this Associate linked to, the Lord of the Rings item had the highest click through rate — that is, more people clicked on that link than any of the others.

KEY:	(HB)=Hardcover Book (PB)=Paperback Book (Ab)=Audio Book (CD)=Compact Disc (DVD)=Digital Video Disc (VHS)=Video Tape (TOY)=Toy

Earnings by Item Report For amazonpatrol2

January 1, 2003 - October 14, 2003   Glossary of Reporting Terms

Item Name	Price	Referral Fee %	Items Shipped	Shipped Items Revenue (Amazon)	Shipped Items Revenue (Marketplace)	Referral Fee Earnings
Music						
Speakerboxxx/ The Love Below(CD) - Amazon.com	$13.49 (39% off)	5.0%	1	$13.49		$0.67
DVD						
Dr. No (Special Edition)(DVD) - Marketplace	$10.98 (0% off)	2.5%	1		$10.98	$0.27
TOTAL SHIPPED			2	$13.49	$10.98	$0.94
TOTAL RETURNED**			0	$0.00	$0.00	$0.00
TOTAL REFUNDED				$0.00	$0.00	$0.00
TOTAL EARNINGS						$0.94

Figure 18-16: The per-item earnings report gives you a sense of what your visitors want to buy.

Traffic by Item - Click Throughs Report For amazonpatrol2

July 1, 2003-September 30, 2003   Glossary of Reporting Terms

Item Name	Clicks
The Lord of the Rings - The Fellowship of the Ring (Widescreen Edition)	2
Betty Crocker's New Cookbook: Everything You Need to Know to Cook (8th Ed)	1
Greece from the Air	1
Beauty Fashion	1
Logitech USB KEYBOARD FOR PS2 (967199-0100:)	1
Cavaliers Reebok Men's NBA Player Replica Home Jersey (sz. XL, White : James, LeBron : Cavaliers)	1
Mow the Lawn	1
Spurs Reebok Men's 2003 NBA Locker Room Champion Tee (sz. XL, Spurs)	1
Panasonic DVD-S35K Ultra-Slim Progressive-Scan DVD Player (Black)	1
Fun With Milk & Cheese	1
Hitachi NV65AH Siding Coil Nailer	1
TOTAL	12

Figure 18-17: The click through traffic report tells you which items get people to the store.

Some Good Examples

There are more than 1,000,000 Associates out there and some of them are really making the most of the program. Here are a few good Associate sites to check out:

✔ **Surprise.com.** This great-gift-ideas site uses several different types of links. It also runs the gamut in terms of what types of products it features. Go to www.surprise.com.

✔ **Musicchoice.com.** This is a music lovers' site that has news, audio streams, and recommendations for CDs that users can purchase at Amazon. You'll find it at www.musicchoice.com.

✔ **Boxofficemojo.com.** This is a movie lovers' site. They're making good use of the Easy Links on their home page. Guess where it is? That's right: www.boxofficemojo.com.

Part V
The Part of Tens

In this part . . .

It wouldn't be a *For Dummies* book without The Part of Tens. In this particular Part of Tens, I show you ten e-mails you might get from Amazon — everything from your Order Confirmation to a Special Occasion Reminder to a notice that your Marketplace item has sold.

I also point out ten ways to get good deals on Amazon. com — good news for the bargain hunters out there. Some of them show up in other chapters in the book and some only show up here. But all are good for helping you save a little cash.

Finally, a little bit of fun: The last chapter features the ten weirdest things on Amazon.com — compliments of some of my former coworkers. And you thought they just sold books!

Chapter 19

Ten E-Mails You Might Get from Amazon.com

For the first year or so that I worked at Amazon, I was responsible for crafting the e-mails that we sent to customers. Even back then, we were very conscious of people's aversion to spam — so we took painstaking measures to make sure those e-mails were as un-spamlike as possible. My assignment was to make each e-mail brief but informative, friendly but professional, relevant, engaging, intelligent, and if possible, witty. I developed an appreciation for e-mail.

When you circulate in the Amazon community — as both a buyer and a seller — you find that your inbox quickly fills up with Amazon-related e-mail. There's a lot of communicating to do, and it all happens electronically.

In this chapter, I identify ten of the e-mails you might get from Amazon.com. I show you the e-mails you automatically get as a buyer, the e-mail you automatically get when you sell something at Amazon, and a few of the e-mails you might get if you choose to take advantage of some of Amazon's fun features.

Order Confirmation

The Order Confirmation e-mail (see Figure 19-1) is the cornerstone of Amazon's e-mail communication. You get one every time you order and it contains all the info you might need regarding that order: links to Your Account, purchasing information, and an order summary.

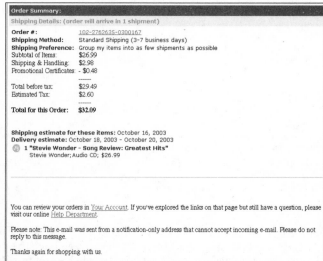

Figure 19-1:
The order-
confirmation
e-mail.

Your Item Has Shipped

You receive this e-mail as soon as your order leaves the distribution center. It includes a link to Your Account, a summary of what was shipped and where they shipped it, and a tracking number (Figure 19-2 shows what to look for.)

You Are a Winner!

Of course you already knew that, but still, it's nice to get some validation from Amazon.com. There's nothing out there that satisfies the competitive shop-a-holic quite like the Amazon Auctions You Are A Winner! e-mail. (Check out Figure 19-3.) It means that not only are you going to get something you wanted, but you also beat someone else out in the process. Hooray!

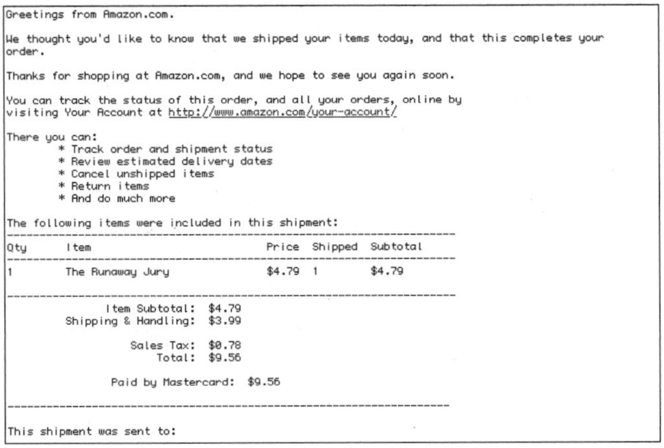

```
Greetings from Amazon.com.

We thought you'd like to know that we shipped your items today, and that this completes your
order.

Thanks for shopping at Amazon.com, and we hope to see you again soon.

You can track the status of this order, and all your orders, online by
visiting Your Account at http://www.amazon.com/your-account/

There you can:
        * Track order and shipment status
        * Review estimated delivery dates
        * Cancel unshipped items
        * Return items
        * And do much more

The following items were included in this shipment:
-----------------------------------------------------------------
Qty     Item                          Price  Shipped  Subtotal
-----------------------------------------------------------------
1       The Runaway Jury              $4.79   1       $4.79
-----------------------------------------------------------------
            Item Subtotal:  $4.79
        Shipping & Handling:  $3.99

               Sales Tax:  $0.78
                   Total:  $9.56

        Paid by Mastercard:  $9.56
-----------------------------------------------------------------

This shipment was sent to:
```

Figure 19-2: Your item has been shipped!

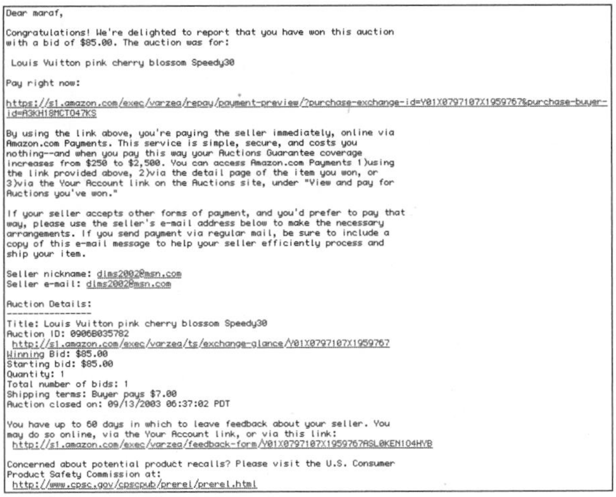

```
Dear maraf,

Congratulations! We're delighted to report that you have won this auction
with a bid of $85.00. The auction was for:

 Louis Vuitton pink cherry blossom Speedy30

Pay right now:

https://s1.amazon.com/exec/varzea/repay/payment-preview/?purchase-exchange-id=V01X0797107X1959767&purchase-buyer-
id=A3KH18MCT047KS

By using the link above, you're paying the seller immediately, online via
Amazon.com Payments. This service is simple, secure, and costs you
nothing—and when you pay this way your Auctions Guarantee coverage
increases from $250 to $2,500. You can access Amazon.com Payments 1)using
the link provided above, 2)via the detail page of the item you won, or
3)via the Your Account link on the Auctions site, under "View and pay for
Auctions you've won."

If your seller accepts other forms of payment, and you'd prefer to pay that
way, please use the seller's e-mail address below to make the necessary
arrangements. If you send payment via regular mail, be sure to include a
copy of this e-mail message to help your seller efficiently process and
ship your item.

Seller nickname: dims2002@msn.com
Seller e-mail: dims2002@msn.com

Auction Details:

Title: Louis Vuitton pink cherry blossom Speedy30
Auction ID: 0906B035782
http://s1.amazon.com/exec/varzea/ts/exchange-glance/V01X0797107X1959767
Winning Bid: $85.00
Starting bid: $85.00
Quantity: 1
Total number of bids: 1
Shipping terms: Buyer pays $7.00
Auction closed on: 09/13/2003 06:37:02 PDT

You have up to 60 days in which to leave feedback about your seller. You
may do so online, via the Your Account link, or via this link:
http://s1.amazon.com/exec/varzea/feedback-form/V01X0797107X1959767ASL0KEN104HVB

Concerned about potential product recalls? Please visit the U.S. Consumer
Product Safety Commission at:
http://www.cpsc.gov/cpscpub/prerel/prerel.html
```

Figure 19-3: I'm a winner! Woo-hoo!

Sold — Ship Now!

Almost as thrilling as the thought of winning is the thought of selling your stuff. The very first time I posted something on Amazon.com using Marketplace, I was doubtful. I did it as an experiment more than anything else. When I got the e-mail announcing that my item had sold, it was a shock. For some reason, I didn't believe it would work. But it did, just like that, and I was suddenly a few bucks richer.

The Sold e-mail is a bit more complicated than other e-mails you might get from Amazon.com because it contains the information you need to complete your transaction. Figure 19-4 is a standard "sold" e-mail for Marketplace. It includes the sale details, the buyer's shipping address, a packing slip to include when you ship, and other important information.

Figure 19-4: The Sold — ship now! e-mail has all the info you need to complete your sale.

```
Dear marg@smartypantscomm.com,

Your Amazon Marketplace sale is official! We've deposited your
earnings from the sale of this item into your Amazon Payments
account.

Please ship item immediately via media mail.

1 of eBay for Dummies

You have agreed to ship no later than two business days after the
buyer's purchase on 05-Oct-2003.
**********************************************************************
Important--Prepare Your Packages With Care.  See our guidelines:
http://www.amazon.com/exec/obidos/tg/browse/-/1161254
**********************************************************************
Here is your buyer's shipping address (use your own address as the
return address, and enclose the packing slip in this e-mail for
your buyer's reference):

Shipping Label
- - - - - - - - - - - - - - - - - - - - - - - - - - - - - - - - - -
Kenneth C Bonnem
4028 40th ave. sw
Seattle, WA 98116

- - - - - - - - - - - - - - - - - - - - - - - - - - - - - - - - - -
PACKING SLIP:
Amazon Marketplace item: eBay for Dummies
Listing ID: 1005B712058
SKU:
Quantity: 1

Purchased on: 05-Oct-2003
Shipped by: marg@smartypantscomm.com
Shipping address:

Ship to: Kenneth C Bonnem
Address Line 1:
Address Line 2:
City: Seattle
State/Province/Region: WA
Zip/Postal Code:
Country: United States
```

Shared Wish List

Do you have a Wish List yet? Have you read Chapter 12? If you answered "no" to either question, you need to get a-crackin'. There are occasions to be celebrated and gifts to be purchased . . . for you, of course.

When you create a Wish List (and any time after you create a Wish List), you can elect to share it with loved ones. This may seem a little brutish, but I'm telling you, it makes life easier for the people who buy you gifts.

When you share your Wish List, your loved ones get an e-mail from Amazon.com (next best thing to a little bird telling them). You can use the default message that Amazon supplies, or you can fill in your own — as I've opted to do in Figure 19-5.

Figure 19-5:
Amazon's
version of a
little bird —
the Wish
List e-mail.

Cancellation E-Mail

When you cancel an item that you've ordered (before it's hit the shipping process, of course) Amazon will send you an e-mail confirming your cancellation, as shown in Figure 19-6. Notice that the e-mail is very brief (don't take it personally). It tells you the status of the order — cancelled — and lists the item that was in the order.

```
Dear Amazon.com Customer,

Your order has been successfully cancelled. For your reference, here is a
summary of your order:

You just canceled order #102-5287500-8304956 placed on October 26, 2003.

Status: CANCELLED


  1 of Autobiography of a Fat Bride: True Tales of a Pretend Adulthood
    By: Laurie Notaro
    $0.00


Because you only pay for items when we ship them to you, you won't be
charged for any items that you cancel.

Thank you for visiting Amazon.com!

Amazon.com
Earth's Biggest Selection
http://www.amazon.com
```

Figure 19-6:
My order
was
successfully
cancelled!

New for You

This is another e-mail notification that you can sign up for (in Your Store). New for You e-mails (see Figure 19-7) include new releases, recommendations, and articles or interviews. But it's not just a random selection of stuff. The content is chosen for you, based on your purchase history. So it's stuff you're likely to be interested in.

Figure 19-7:
New for You
e-mails
whip up fun
content that
reflects your
buying
history.

Share the Love

Will Share the Love unite the world in its shopping embrace? Probably not, but it is a good way to help your pals while helping yourself. Share the Love is Amazon's program that lets shoppers give their friends discounts on certain items they've bought. If those friends then buy the items, the original shopper gets a credit to apply to some other purchase down the line. (If you need a refresher, read Chapter 12.)

You don't have to do a thing to receive a Share the Love e-mail (except be someone who's loved). When you receive one, it looks something like Figure 19-8. (Okay. I admit it. I sent this one to myself.)

Special Occasion Reminders

You set up these reminders in the Friends & Favorites area of your store. You choose the occasion, when and how often to be reminded, and then enter the date. Amazon sends you an e-mail reminding you. (See Figure 19-9.) If you give them the giftee's e-mail address, they hunt to see whether there's a Wish List associated with it — and surface that for you. If gift giving is the meat and potatoes of your relationships, these e-mails can really save your rump roast (and maybe your marriage).

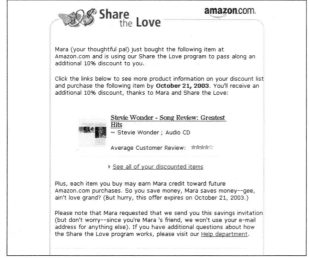

Figure 19-8: When you Share the Love, this is what you're sending.

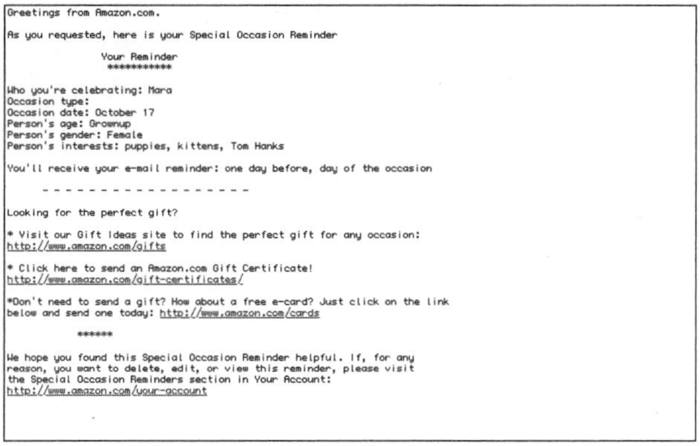

Greetings from Amazon.com.

As you requested, here is your Special Occasion Reminder

Your Reminder
****

Who you're celebrating: Mara
Occasion type:
Occasion date: October 17
Person's age: Grownup
Person's gender: Female
Person's interests: puppies, kittens, Tom Hanks

You'll receive your e-mail reminder: one day before, day of the occasion

- - - - - - - - - - - - - - - - - -

Looking for the perfect gift?

* Visit our Gift Ideas site to find the perfect gift for any occasion:
http://www.amazon.com/gifts

* Click here to send an Amazon.com Gift Certificate!
http://www.amazon.com/gift-certificates/

*Don't need to send a gift? How about a free e-card? Just click on the link below and send one today: http://www.amazon.com/cards

******

We hope you found this Special Occasion Reminder helpful. If, for any reason, you want to delete, edit, or view this reminder, please visit the Special Occasion Reminders section in Your Account:
http://www.amazon.com/your-account

Figure 19-9: A special occasion reminder for me from me.

Weekly Movie Showtimes

This is a nifty feature that you'll find in Amazon's Video and DVD stores and in the Store Directory under the Services heading. You enter your zip code, and Amazon will send you an e-mail every Friday (sometimes late Thursday night) with showtimes in your area for the week to come. Figure 19-10 is one of the Weekly Movie Showtimes e-mails that I've gotten. I've scrolled down a bit here to get to the actual showtimes, but these e-mails also feature reviews of current movies — very cool!

Figure 19-10:
Weekly
Movie
Showtimes
are very
handy.

Chapter 20

Ten Ways to Get Great Deals

1 love a bargain. I love the hunt. I love the moment of finding that amazing deal — and even more, I love the moment of telling someone about it. Even when I don't need a bargain, I want a bargain. It's the malcontent in me. I like the sensation of pulling a fast one. I want to feel that I'm outsmarting the man.

Amazon.com is a great place to hunt for bargains. Truth be told, you don't actually have to look that hard. There are bargains everywhere — ripe for the picking. Recently, I got a pair of red leather Kaeppa tennis shoes for $9.95 (plus shipping). I saw them two days later on the site for $49.95. That was a small victory for me.

In this chapter, I show you ten ways to get good deals at Amazon.com. Some of them I've already covered in the book, and some are new material. Some offer really good deals, and some will just save you a few bucks. But if you're anything like me, they all tickle your fancy and tempt the bargain-hunter in you.

The Outlet

Did you know that Amazon has an outlet? It's true, and you don't have to drive to the middle of nowhere to get there. (And they don't have racks and racks of weird colors and size zeroes.)

The easiest way to access the Outlet is from the Bargains section of the Store Directory. (Click the <u>See More Stores</u> link at the top of the page to get to the Store Directory.) The Outlet is the most obvious place to go for deals. It's a collection of everything in the store that's on clearance — plus you can link to the refurbished items and the Friday sale from the Outlet subnav. (More on the Outlet in Chapter 7.)

My particular favorite is the Kitchen and Housewares outlet. I have my eye on the Ronco compact rotisserie — and look at that price (see Figure 20-1)! Can you beat it? (If you can, please e-mail me.)

Figure 20-1:
The Outlet is square one for great deals.

Striking Gold in Your Gold Box

Have you ever noticed the sparkly golden goodness in the upper-right corner of every page? If you've got an Amazon account, that box even bears your name. That's *your* Gold Box, and if you've never looked at it, you're a stronger person than I am.

Your Gold Box is like your own personal bargain stash. It's filled with ten good deals on items chosen according to your shopping history. But here's the thing: it changes every day, the offers are good for only 60 minutes from when you open the box, and you only get one chance to buy — if you pass, you pass forever.

Figure 20-2 is the first screen you see after you open your Gold Box. Fellow shoppers, we are being taunted by Amazon.com — dared into passing up a good deal. Them's fightin' words! (Please note: if you're a bargain-hunter and an indecisive person, Gold Box will be your undoing.)

Figure 20-2:
Ten goodies a day in your Gold Box.

At the Bottom of the Page

I mention this briefly in Chapter 9, and I'm mentioning it here again: There are good deals to be found at the bottom of the page — *every* page. Fittingly enough, they're called "Bottom of the Page Deals" and they change every day.

One thing I've noticed about these deals is that they're decidedly unglamorous. If you're looking for a cute sweater at a steal, you're not going to find it at the bottom of the page. That said, you *can* find great savings on stuff you might actually need.

Figure 20-3 is a look at one day's worth of bottom of the page deals. Is there anything there that's going to give me bragging rights with my girlfriends? No. Would I be glad to save $30 on beef jerky? Yes. (And I'm the person who might buy the massive bag of beef jerky online.)

Often you find mundane, household-type items at the bottom of the page. But don't knock it. If you're going to buy the gigant-o-pack of beef jerky, wouldn't you rather get it for 30 bucks less and then spend that $30 on something more fun? (If you saved it, then it's free money!)

	Our Price	You Save	
Ultrasonex SB300U Rechargeable Toothbrush with 3 Replacement Brushes The best value for your money--professionally clean teeth at a bargain price.	$19.99	$30.00 (60%)	☐
SOLD OUT FOR TODAY Altoids, Peppermint (24 Tins) The tin is in. Save on Altoids, the curiously strong breath mint.	$29.99		
Starbucks Decaffeinated House Blend Whole Bean Coffee, 6 12-Ounce FlavorLock Bags (72 ounces total) Enjoy the smooth, rich roasted flavor you love, without the caffeine.	$42.99	$6.00 (12%)	☐
Wüsthof Cutting Board A great gift for your favorite cook--an essential tool with the elegance of maple.	$14.99		☐
Ray-O-Vac AAA Alkaline Battery (72 Batteries) Get 50% off top-quality Ray-O-Vac batteries--stock up and always be prepared!	$35.97	$35.62 (50%)	☐
Oh Boy! Oberto Original Beef Jerky (6-9 Ounce Bags) All the original flavor and protein power of Oberto jerky, at over 40% off.	$48.12	$32.76 (41%)	☐
Metabolife Ephedra Free Formula to Enhance Energy (400 Tablets) All the energy boosting, without the ephedra, for just 20 cents a tablet.	$82.76	$41.64 (33%)	☐
Accu-Chek Softclix Sterile Lancets (600 Lancets) More than 40% savings on the precise, gentle way to test glucose levels.	$43.23	$37.71 (47%)	☐
Kodak 1976463 Premium Picture Paper, High Gloss, 8.5"x11", 100 Sheets Enjoy sharp, high-quality photos with Kodak's resin-coated photographic paper.	$28.99	$8.00 (22%)	☐

🛒 **FREE Super Saver Shipping** on orders over $25. See details.   ▶ Add selected items to cart   ▶ Buy selected items with 1-Click®

Figure 20-3:
Bottom of the page deals — humble, but worthy of a daily look.

Super Saver Shipping

If you've got time, and you're spending more than $25, you can save money with Super Saver Shipping. Super Saver Shipping is Amazon's way of helping you save money and giving themselves a little extra time to ship your stuff. Here's how it works:

1. **Find more than $25 worth of *eligible* stuff that you want to buy.**

   This can be one item or several, but make sure all items are eligible for Super Saver Shipping. You'll know because they're marked with the little shopping-cart icon.

2. **Put the products you want in your Shopping Cart by clicking the Add To Shopping Cart button on their detail pages.**

   This is important. You don't get Super Saver Shipping automatically — you select it during the checkout process. There is a way to get it with 1-Click, but it's actually more complicated than just buying with the shopping cart.

3. **After you've added your last item, click Proceed To Checkout.**

   You come to a Sign In screen.

4. **Enter your e-mail address and password in the fields provided and click that secure server button.**

   You come to your Order Review page. Notice that you have several choices for shipping (as shown in Figure 20-4). To get Super Saver Shipping, you must ship your items to a single U.S. address.

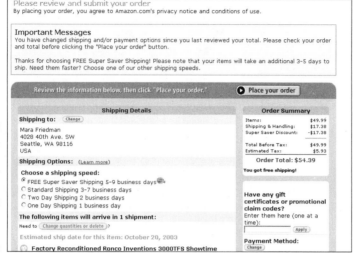

Please review and submit your order
By placing your order, you agree to Amazon.com's privacy notice and conditions of use.

Important Messages
You have changed shipping and/or payment options since you last reviewed your total. Please check your order and total before clicking the "Place your order" button.

Thanks for choosing FREE Super Saver Shipping! Please note that your items will take an additional 3-5 days to ship. Need them faster? Choose one of our other shipping speeds.

Review the information below, then click "Place your order."   ▶ Place your order

Shipping Details   **Order Summary**

Shipping to: (Change)   Items: $49.99
                                Shipping & Handling: $17.38
Mara Friedman   Super Saver Discount: -$17.38
4028 40th Ave. SW
Seattle, WA 98116   Total Before Tax: $49.99
USA   Estimated Tax: $5.93

Shipping Options: (Learn more)   Order Total: $54.39

Choose a shipping speed: You got free shipping!
◉ FREE Super Saver Shipping 5-9 business days
○ Standard Shipping 3-7 business days
○ Two Day Shipping 2 business days   Have any gift
○ One Day Shipping 1 business day   certificates or promotional
                                            claim codes?
The following items will arrive in 1 shipment: Enter them here (one at a
                                                 time):
Need to (Change quantities or delete)?   (Apply)

Estimated ship date for this item: October 20, 2003   Payment Method:
                                                       (Change)
○ Factory Reconditioned Ronco Inventions 3000TFS Showtime

Figure 20-4:
Click the
Super Saver
Shipping
option for
free
shipping.

5. **Click the Super Saver Shipping circle to select that as your shipping speed.**

   Your order will take, on average, about 3 to 5 days longer to ship. So if you're in a hurry, Super Saver Shipping is not for you. (Hey, either it's time or it's money.)

6. **Click Place Your Order.**

You can save a lot of money. A lot! Check out Figure 20-4. Before I selected Super Saver Shipping, I was going to pay almost $15 in shipping fees.

Amazon.com Trivia

This isn't really a great deal, but it is kind of fun. On the Welcome page, below the fold, is a trivia question (see Figure 20-5). If you answer it correctly, Amazon puts a nickel in your account. If you click the Try for Another Nickel button, they give you another question. If you answer that correctly, you get another nickel. You can do this until you get bored, or until your boss catches you.

I know. A nickel won't buy you much. But you can answer the questions several times a day, for several days in a row, and stockpile them. I have a friend who's saved up $1.35.

Figure 20-5:
Amazon
trivia is fun,
even if it
won't get
you that
rotisserie
you've been
dreaming of.

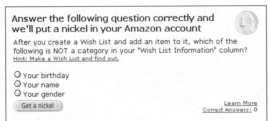

Answer the following question correctly and
we'll put a nickel in your Amazon account

After you create a Wish List and add an item to it, which of the
following is NOT a category in your "Wish List Information" column?
Hint: Make a Wish List and find out.

○ Your birthday
○ Your name
○ Your gender

Get a nickel ›

Learn More
Correct Answers: 0

Trivia isn't always there. Depending on what else is going on in the store, that
Welcome page real estate may be devoted to something with a higher profile.
Check back, though, and you'll find it eventually.

You can use your trivia money toward a purchase on the site for up to 10 percent of the purchase price — not on any product; some restrictions apply. To
find out what those restrictions are, click the Learn More link below and to
the right of the trivia question.

Amazon.com Credit Card

The Amazon.com Platinum Visa is like a frequent flyer miles card, but for
shopping. It's an awesome thing that I'm not allowed to get because I've been
barred (by my husband, not the law) from applying for any more credit cards.
You, however, are free to apply. Here's the deal:

✔ You get 3 points for every dollar spent at Amazon.com, and 1 point for
  every dollar spent anywhere else.

✔ For every 2,500 points you get, you get $25 to spend at Amazon.com.

Plus, there's no annual fee. If you want to apply, just go to the Store Directory
(by clicking See More Stores) and click on the Amazon.com Visa Card link
under Services heading. Like all things Amazon, you apply online.

Better Together

This is sort of like twofers on the Web. Maybe you've noticed it on the detail
pages of certain items. (If not, check out Figure 20-6.) Amazon will offer up
another recommended item and you can buy them both at a discount.
Sometimes the discount isn't much, but sometimes you luck out. Also, I've
noticed that sometimes this feature is called Best Value.

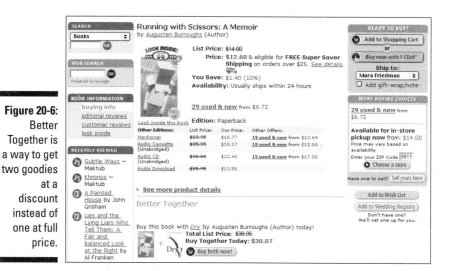

Today's Deals

Today's Deals mean that every day at Amazon.com is a sale day. (Music to the ears of us bargain hunters.) There's a general Today's Deals area, and then most individual stores have their own daily deals.

You can access the general area most easily by clicking on Today's Deals in the subnav of the Welcome page. You'll find deals for most of the different product lines that Amazon sells, plus you can access all of the goodies they advertise in the Sunday circular (of the newspaper, that is). To find daily bargains within a specific store — DVD, Kitchen & Housewares, etc. — simply click on Today's Deals in that store's subnav.

A word of caution: when you go to Today's Deals, be prepared to buy. Just this week I was browsing Today's Deals in Kitchen & Housewares and I ended up buying myself a $210 mandolin. BUT, I got it for the low, low price of $65 . . . *and* it came with a fancy baking sheet as a free gift . . . *and* I qualified for free Super Saver Shipping. Did I say the deals are good? I mean reeeeeeeeeally goooooooood.

In Your Box

This isn't necessarily a way to save money *at* Amazon, but a way to save money *compliments* of Amazon. If you've ever ordered from Amazon — not a Marketplace order, but a regular Amazon order — you probably found a bunch of marketing material in your box when it arrived.

In that marketing material, you find discounts at other pal-of-Amazon stores. I myself am a big fan of Bluefly.com — and there are always Bluefly discounts in my Amazon shipments. I've saved a bundle, compliments of my former employer — and you can, too. But don't throw the marketing material away! You need the promotional codes in there when you make your purchase.

Friday Sale

Every Friday, Amazon has a special sale with extra special discounts. But only on Friday. You can access the Friday Sale from the subnav in the Outlet (and you can access the Outlet from the store directory). Figure 20-7 gives you an idea of what you can find there.

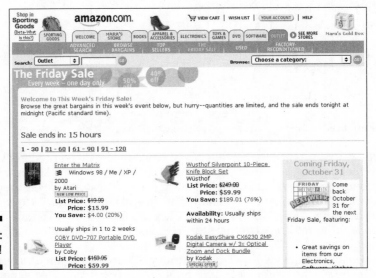

Figure 20-7:
TGIF!

Chapter 21

The Ten Strangest Items for Sale

*H*ave I told you the story of the Turducken? It's the chicken, stuffed in a duck, stuffed in a turkey. The year zShops launched, it was the talk of the office. People loved the Turducken and they were actually buying it for the holidays. It was fascinating, in a train-wreck-meets-Renaissance-fair kind of way. Who would think to do this? (Paul Prudhomme, it turns out.) And who would think to sell it online? (Not Paul Prudhomme.) I've since discovered that in any traditional Turducken (*traditional*? who knew?), the birds are boneless. So the notion of finding just the right-size fowl and then cramming one into the other and then the other has been debunked. But still . . . how strange!

I admit that "strange" is a relative term — subjective and open to interpretation. And there is certainly no governing body at Amazon to identify universal criteria for "strangeness." But disclaimers aside, there are some wonderfully odd items being sold on Amazon.com (and I say that with love in my heart).

In this chapter, I show you ten of them. Maybe they're not the strangest — it's a big catalog, after all — but they're definitely up there.

CyberPounce

Forget about balls of yarn and little rubber mice. If you are a pet owner of the new millennium, you must buy your cat CyberPounce — the computer game for cats. (See Figure 21-1.) It has two modes — one where your cat "plays" alone, and one where the two of you can play together. This is a good way to stimulate your cat's imagination — and besides, it helps them master their multiplication tables.

I don't know. My cat's not smart enough to play computer games. He'd much rather sit on my stomach and claw me when I'm trying to read. I think CyberPounce is what happens when you allow software developers and animal behaviorists to fraternize.

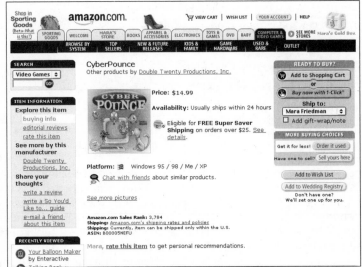

Figure 21-1:
Cyber
Pounce —
a computer
game for
cats.

Pyramat PM300 Sound Lounger

This subwoofer-meets-gym-mat is a gamer's delight. I'm teasing, but I have to tell you that I think the people at Pyramat are sitting (or lounging) on a gold mine here. It's a portable lounger/mat with a surround-sound speaker system built into the headrest. (Check it out in Figure 21-2.) This thing has 25 perfect reviews from people all across the country, including one that deems it the "butt-kicking chair of the future." I'm going to give this to my mother-in-law for Christmas along with a PS2.

Ducane ChuckWagon Gas Grill

This is a tailgater's dream. It has a grill, a fridge, a sink with running water, an umbrella — and tail lights, for crying out loud. (See Figure 21-3.)

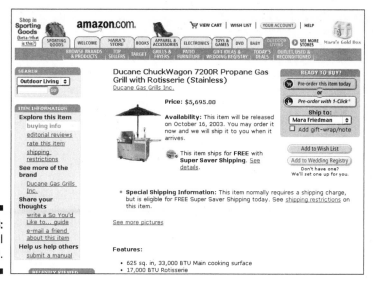

Trailer Park Tycoon

What I love most about Amazon.com is that they not only sell this, they have six used copies available, as you can see in Figure 21-4.

Figure 21-4: It's like the Sims in a double-wide.

SkyBox by Maytag Personal Beverage Vendor

I want this. Only I want mine to take quarters. Then every third time I go to get a drink, I want it to eat my quarters so I can simulate my work environment. (Uh-huh. I would also like to be charged for parking in my driveway.) Figure 21-5 gives you all the details.

Figure 21-5:
Your very
own mini
vending
machine.

Ronco ROES Electric Egg Scrambler

I love Ronco and I'm going to buy the chicken rotisserie because it makes delicious chicken. I have to say, I'm tempted to buy the little contraption shown in Figure 21-6 as well — just to see what a scrambled hard-boiled egg looks like.

Figure 21-6:
Throw out
your
whisks!

Ronco FD5 Food Dehydrator, Yogurt Maker, and Beef Jerky Machine

This one makes the list just because of the yogurt/jerky combo. I love a good jerky as much as the next girl, and, again, I'm tempted to buy myself something like this. But I hesitate when I see "yogurt" as part of the mix. That said, people generally like this machine. It's affordable. It makes good jerky and fruit rolls. I gather from the reviews that it's more of a "starter" dehydrator. That's okay with me. I'm not looking for a fancy dehydrator, just one that sucks the moisture out of meat. And, as Figure 21-7 clearly shows, the Ronco folks have space-age design down pat.

Figure 21-7:
Make your own beef jerky at home.

Monthly Doos: The 2004 Dog Poop Calendar

I appreciate that Amazon runs the gamut from lofty literary to potty humor. The very best thing about this detail page is the Customers Who Shopped for This Item . . . section. Check out the lisitngs in Figure 21-8.

Dr. Billinghurst's BARF DIET Freeze-Dried Patties

This is not the next generation of the Zone diet. In fact, this is not for us humans at all. BARF is an acronym for Biologically Appropriate Raw Food, and this is the *diet du jour* for dogs. I'm okay with all that, but why, why, why?! Why did they have to call it that? (Maybe it means something different in dogspeak?). You won't find the answer in Figure 21-9.

Segway Human Transporter

It wouldn't be a complete list without the Segway. Everything about the Segway is strange and wonderful. I'm hoping that by mentioning the Segway so many times, I'll get one as a gift, although secretly I'd rather have the Ducane Chuck Wagon. You can see it in all its glory in Figure 21-10.

Figure 21-10: Please give me a Segway.

Appendix

The Esoteric Amazon: Honor System and Amazon Anywhere

● ●

*T*here have always been two factions duking it out at Amazon.com: the people who think it's a high-tech company and the people who think it's a retail company. (Ask Jeff Bezos and he'll probably tell you that it's both.)

This is actually good for us customers. It's because of these two factions that Amazon is both technologically smart and a really good store. But every so often, the technology side wins out. This isn't bad for customers. It just means that, occasionally, Amazon develops a feature that's a little bit ahead of its time. Honor System and Amazon Anywhere are two of those features.

On Your Honor (System)

Honor System is Amazon's program that allows people who have Web sites to charge for their digital content or take voluntary donations. In other words, if you have a Web site, you can put a graphic on it that allows people to pay you via Amazon.com. Here's how it works:

- ✔ **You have a Web site.** And you want either to charge visitors for using it or you want to accept donations.

- ✔ **You create a PayPage at Amazon.com.** PayPages are essentially detail pages, but for your company or organization. Your PayPage lives on Amazon.com, and on it you explain what your company or organization is all about — and why you're asking for money. This is also where you list any minimum donation information and other things like that. (See Figure A-1.)

- ✔ **You create a PayBox to put on your Web site.** The PayBox is the graphic that Amazon supplies (and you customize) to call visitors to action! (See Figure A-2.)

✔ **Visitors click on your PayBox.** They're taken to your PayPage where they can enter the amount they want to give (for donations) or are paying (for content).

✔ **Visitors pay you via Amazon.** Amazon requires a minimum payment of $1 per transaction.

✔ **Amazon sends them a Thank You e-mail.** You create the text for this e-mail when you set up your PayPage and PayBox.

✔ **Amazon pays you and takes a commission.** Amazon's fees are 5 percent of the total transaction plus a flat fee of $.19 per transaction.

Figure A-1 is the PayPage on Amazon for Lost and Found Sound — a program on National Public Radio. Figure A-2 is the PayBox I clicked to access their PayPage. It was very easy.

If you want to set up an Honor System for your organization, you can access it easily from the Welcome page. Just scroll way down, almost to the bottom, and on the left side of the page is a box labeled *Special Features*. Honor System is a link in that box.

Figure A-1:
An Honor System PayPage on Amazon.com.

Figure A-2:
An Honor System PayBox.

Honor System is a great idea. It's especially good for charitable organizations on a small budget, or anyone with a content-laden Web site that wants to get paid for their hard work. But it hasn't really caught on . . . yet.

Amazon Anywhere

Amazon Anywhere is Amazon's mobile shopping program. Okay, I know lots of you will be wondering why I'm listing this as a feature that's ahead of its time. After all, there are lots of people out there shopping online with their Internet-enabled cell phones and PDAs.

It's true. But the reason I list it is because Amazon Anywhere has actually been around for years — long before shopping with your cell phone was something people knew about.

Amazon Anywhere launched when I still worked at Amazon.com. That was almost four years ago — when cell phones were still the size of small babies. Hardly anybody was using a cell phone to shop online — at least, nobody in the U.S. (Mobile shopping? What a concept!) I didn't even own a cell phone when they launched Amazon Anywhere (or AA, as I like to call it), because — let's face it — if you have to shop so badly that you need to be able to do it no matter where you are, you've got a problem.

Today, people in Japan use Amazon Anywhere like crazy, and it's good for more than just shopping. You can also use it to access Amazon content like customer reviews — handy when you're at the video store battling with your spouse over what to rent. So if you're inspired, and you've got a Web-enabled mobile phone, PDA, or pocket PC, try Amazon Anywhere. For instructions on how to get set up, go to the Amazon Anywhere section of the site. You can access it in the Special Features box at the bottom left of the Welcome page — the same place you go for Honor System.

Index

• *B* •

● **D** ●

FOR DUMMIES®

The easy way to get more done and have more fun

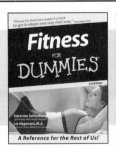
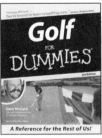

FOR DUMMIES®

A world of resources to help you grow

TRAVEL

0-7645-5453-0

0-7645-5438-7

0-7645-5444-1

EDUCATION & TEST PREPARATION

0-7645-5194-9

0-7645-5325-9

0-7645-5249-X

HEALTH, SELF-HELP & SPIRITUALITY

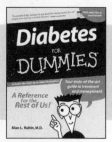

0-7645-5154-X

0-7645-5302-X

0-7645-5418-2

Available wherever books are sold. Go to www.dummies.com or call 1-877-762-2974 to order direct

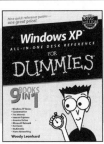

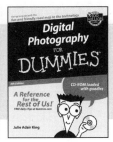